# Black Cop: The Real Deal

## The True Story of New York City's
## Most Decorated Cop

*Richard Lewis*

## Treasure House

An Imprint of
**Destiny Image® Publishers, Inc.**
**P.O. Box 310**
**Shippensburg, PA 17257-0310**

"For where your treasure is,
there will your heart be also." Matthew 6:21

ISBN 1-56043-583-6

For Worldwide Distribution
Printed in the U.S.A.

First Printing: 1996          Second Printing: 1996

This book and all other Destiny Image
and Treasure House books are available
at Christian bookstores and distributors worldwide.

For a U.S. bookstore nearest you, call **1-800-722-6774**.
For more information on foreign distributors,
call **717-532-3040**.
Or reach us on the Internet: **http://www.reapernet.com**

# Dedication

This book is dedicated to the memories of my father, James Edward Lewis, Sr.; Rev. John Cordes; Rev. Elisha Mashach; and all the police officers who have given their lives so that others might live.

# Endorsements

"Richard Lewis' life has been a crusade against crime. His street smarts and 20 years of experience on New York's police force has left him with a collection of commendations and citations that cover his uniform. He has patrolled the dark corridors of New York City's housing projects, arrested drug dealers, and helped re-build crime-polluted neighborhoods. Lewis was awarded the police department's Medal of Honor twice, and survived six shoot-outs.

"This retired detective's talents are still in demand. His contributions to media investigations helped free a man wrongfully convicted of torching a woman, and exposed a drug kingpin in one of the most dangerous criminal playgrounds in New York.

"While Lewis opposed godlessness in the streets, he witnessed the gospel. An ordained minister, Lewis served as a police chaplain and a pastor, and preaches the Word of God around the world as passionately as he battled crime around the corner.

"Richard Lewis is the brightest, bluest, and bravest of those who carry a badge."

Ben Farnsworth
WNBC News

\* \* \*

"This is a rare book.... Former Detective Richard Lewis has shared not only what his police duties obliged him to *do*, but what an active Christian faith enabled him to *be* as he did it—a caring person.

"As a counselor to police officers and their families, and after long-term service on a municipal police commission, I have seen what emotional strain does to many police officers and their families. After years of service on the streets of New York, Detective Lewis has emerged with a healthy spirit and a caring heart, largely the result of his active and steady faith in God. This story is more than a report, it is an essential witness that needs to be read."

James Earl Massey
Dean Emeritus
Anderson University School of Theology

\* \* \*

"Richard Lewis is an outstanding individual who has taken on many challenges in life from one end of the spectrum to the other.... I had the pleasure of being his flight instructor and was able to see a man with determination learn a skill that is not easily acquired. His enthusiasm was always strong and his love of life always shining. His stories of life as a police officer and minister show that his strong determination is found throughout all aspects of his life.

"Richard Lewis: a cop, a minister, a family man, and a pretty darn good pilot!"

Nick Gregory
Meteorologist
WNYW-TV Fox 5, New York City

\* \* \*

"You have never met a cop like Richard Lewis, the most decorated police officer in the history of the New York Police Department. In two decades as a detective patrolling one of the highest crime areas in the city, Lewis distinguished himself so much he was awarded the Medal of Honor twice, the highest honor a city can give to an officer.

"Now, in a story that only Lewis can tell, is his scathing indictment of a war he fought day in and day out throughout his illustrious career, a war against the very officers and their superiors he worked with and who regarded the color of his skin as a detriment even though he had become a hero in the war on crime.

"This is a story that brings you inside the police precincts and out onto the shadowy streets and the dark corridors of the sprawling housing projects, Lewis' beat. But it is also a story about the struggle against racism and against a police department where the color black was often more important than the color of NYPD Blue."

Dennis Duggan  
Reporter  
*New York Newsday*

# Contents

# Foreword

Very seldom in life does a true hero tell his own story in his words and in his way with such clarity and passion. Detective Richard Lewis is such a hero, and *Black Cop: The Real Deal* is his story.

The streets that nurtured Richie Lewis as a youngster growing up in the Red Hook Public Housing Project in Brooklyn, New York, were the same streets where, as a police officer with the New York City Housing Authority, he faced danger and even death. Those troubled streets where he learned early to run fast to avoid trouble were also where he developed the lightning speed as an accomplished track star that made it possible for Detective Lewis to catch criminals and bring them to justice.

Richard Lewis tells his story of personal growth, awareness, and "street smarts" as only a son of the ghetto could. He charts a course from the projects of Red Hook to his alma mater, Boys High School, where his track exploits became legend, to the far reaches of the globe as an enlisted man in the U.S. Air Force. He reveals what made him tick, who and what was the real Richie Lewis, and what destined him to one day become Detective Richard Lewis. His story demonstrates what police work in New York City is all about. It becomes clear that his family, especially his mother and father, were paramount and profound influences in his life. This is most graphically depicted when, eyeball-to-eyeball, he faced death in shoot-outs with violent felons, and lived to tell his story.

The career of Richard Lewis gives us insights into the causes of the problems facing inner city residents across this nation. Lewis shares his story from the perspective of an American hero, a cop who was more than courageous when it counted, and who was and still is black.

Senator Alton R. Waldon, Jr.
New York State Senator
Member 99th Congress

# Preface

*N*early 600,000 people make their home in New York City's 314 housing projects. These housing projects are protected by a "thin blue line" of 2,145 men and women in the New York City Housing Police Department. For 20 years, Detective Richard Lewis carried "Shield Numbers 3135 and 754" in the line of duty, first as a uniformed, foot patrolman, and later as a plainclothes detective. He was involved in nearly a dozen shoot-outs and was forced to kill two men in separate one-on-one gun battles in the line of duty. On each occasion, he was awarded the Medal of Honor "for action above and beyond the call of duty," making him the only police officer in New York City history to receive the city's highest award more than once.

Richard Lewis was one of the first cops in New York to warn of the impending danger of a new drug infiltrating the ghetto—crack cocaine. By 1986, it had become the street addict's drug of choice, and the drug trafficker's "pot of gold."

Richard Lewis quickly established himself as a rough, tough, no-nonsense cop on New York City's mean streets. He was both a career cop and an ordained minister who was dedicated to improving the quality of life for the city's troubled black communities. Drug dealers began to call Lewis the "Preacher Cop," the streetwise cop who even managed to gain the grudging respect of the criminals in his community. Lewis is the first black police officer from New York City to tell his story, and he tells it all—including both the good and the bad. His accomplishments and honors as New York City's most decorated cop make him an outstanding role model to a community crying out for someone to lead them—not by rhetoric, but by example.

Lewis became a star athlete and won a basket full of medals in high school and later competed in the United Athletic Association. His track accomplishments continued throughout his enlistment with the U.S. Air Force and later on in the Police Olympics. His running ability helped ruin the escape plans of countless criminals fleeing arrest, and he continues to run an average of six miles every morning today.

Lewis, the father of two grown daughters, retired from the Housing Police Department in 1988 with the rank of detective, 3rd grade (a rank he feels would have been higher had he been a white cop). He retired with letters of commendation from police commissioners, congressmen, New York City Mayor Edward Koch, and President Ronald Reagan. He left behind an imposing arrest record and conviction rate, setting a high standard for police officers and detectives to follow.

Somewhat in the tradition of *Serpico*, this book, *Black Cop: The Real Deal*, delves into the layers of corruption the author encountered as a Housing Police officer. This corruption went far beyond money to the shadowy and emotion-charged issues of color and racism. However, unlike Serpico's dark story of corruption and despair, this book offers solid hope and answers to those on both sides of the system who are frustrated with the status quo.

Finally, this is a book about a man who refused to settle for anything but being the best at what he tried to do. Whether he was on the streets or patrolling the dim hallways of the projects, he strove to excel. Preacher, college graduate, father, track star, private pilot, and highly decorated detective—in every way, the author was and is a positive role model. Richard Lewis' story is a testimony to readers of all colors and walks of life that the odds can be beaten. You can make it if you try.

# Introduction

I t is said, "Once a cop, always a cop." Police work is one of the most demanding, stressful, and hazardous professions in any society, yet it can also be one of the most rewarding vocations as well. Not many occupations provide such far-reaching authority or require the high levels of personal responsibility, skill, and knowledge demanded of a police officer. A law enforcement officer must balance the power to take a life with a sworn obligation to protect and preserve life. A single split-second decision by a police officer can carry lasting implications impacting entire communities.

Police officers are trained to act and react with intelligence, precaution, and sensitivity, while maintaining the utmost self-control. Black or non-white police officers, in particular, also face continual challenges related to ongoing racial tensions and prejudice on the job, sometimes even within the internal structures of their respective law enforcement agencies. The ideal is for any police officer who performs above and beyond the norm to be honored and rewarded for his or her dedication and superior service, regardless of skin color or ethnicity.

Unfortunately, racial discrimination against non-white police officers and civilians has caused a serious rift in many police departments and communities. It seems that each year brings new revelations of widespread acts of discrimination matching that of the widely publicized Rodney King case involving members of the

Los Angeles Police Department. While every police officer must accept the burdens and hazards that come with the vocation, no one should be harnessed with the restraints that prejudice and racial bias place on equal opportunity, respect, recognition, or admiration.

This book is the story of my life and career with the New York City Housing Police Department (now merged with the New York City Police Department). It details the dangers and hazards I encountered working thousands of "graveyard" shifts alone, patrolling the worst and most dangerous public housing projects in New York City. It describes the many dramatic criminal investigations I conducted to solve murder cases, capture drug lords, and close down countless drug operations in Harlem, Brooklyn, Manhattan, Queens, and the Bronx.

I want you to sense the gripping fear and numbing heartache I felt when I was forced to confront, and then kill, two armed suspects in separate incidents in face-to-face public shoot-outs in New York City, one of which occurred on the crowded sidewalks of New York's famous Fifth Avenue.

I also describe my sad discovery that racial prejudice was still alive and well in New York City's police departments (the city's three separate police departments were reorganized under the New York City Police Department in May 1995). Read how I battled for equal treatment in the headquarters office for more than a decade while also fighting crime in the streets.

This book will alarm the unaware, encourage the discouraged, and shock the complacent. Where there was prejudice, I tried to expose it. Where there was courage, I openly declared it. When corruption raised its ugly head, I did my best to expose and destroy it during my two decades of police work.

This is the honest story of a very human man with a very difficult job. In a way, it is also the story of every honest cop, regardless of color, who has dared to stand for right, when might seemed to line up with everything that was wrong.

As you walk with me through the dark streets and unlit stair-wells of America's deadliest high-rise residential projects, you will experience the agony of life lived under the dark shadow of drug traffickers, violent crime, and random murder on a whim. And you will see hope in the midst of despair.

More than anything else, I believe you will be encouraged to never give up—no matter how difficult your situation or problem may be. If a young black kid from one of New York City's worst housing projects can rise to become the city's most decorated cop in history, then you can rise from your ghetto too!

Richard Lewis
New York City
May 1996

# Chapter 1

# A Rookie From the Ghetto

It was a chilly day in March of 1971 when I looked through a doorway and noticed the young black male standing in front of 177 Sands Street. Only one hour before, I had left the Fort Greene police station near the infamous Fort Greene Housing Projects of downtown Brooklyn after being assigned to foot patrol at New York City's Farragut Housing Projects. I drew the four-to-midnight shift and had just finished walking the beat among the cluster of stark, high-rise apartment buildings—alone, as usual.

The man was about 5′ 3″ tall, and I estimated that he was about 22 years of age. He seemed uneasy and restless. His movements were too quick, and he had a habit of continuously scanning his surroundings that told me he was especially nervous (even for a resident of a New York City project). He was loitering in front of a high-rise located directly across from my police record office, a small police work station located in the basement of a multi-story project building.

After spending the last two-and-a-half years patrolling all of New York City's most dangerous projects, mostly at night and on foot, I had a habit of avoiding the front entrances of record offices. I preferred the clear view and privacy of rear or side basement doors. This particular side exit gave me a wide view of the complex, *and the front entrance of 177 Sands Street,* without being seen. I liked living, and I didn't particularly like the alternative, so I took the side door that day.

The man caught my attention for two reasons. First, I knew I hadn't seen him in the neighborhood before, and I made it my business to keep track of the faces I saw each day. The second red flag was his abnormal behavior. I sensed that something was going down, so I stood where he couldn't see me and watched him for a few more minutes before I decided to check him out.

I started to walk in his general direction, being careful not to look at him. He noticed my approach, and I tracked him from the corner of my eye as he scurried across Sands Street to the opposite corner. I acted like I was on a routine foot patrol. I didn't want him to know I was setting him up for a shakedown. He was watching me, and growing more nervous by the second, as I entered the project at 177 Sands Street. I stalled for a few minutes, and then exited the building.

The man was still standing at the corner across Sands Street, looking even more nervous and out of place than before. *It's time to turn up the heat,* I thought, as I stepped into the street again at the middle of the block and began to walk towards him. The man saw me coming his way and hurried across Sands Street again to the opposite side. When I called to him, he suddenly bolted away. I watched him closely, knowing that sudden changes of motion sometimes reveal what people want to conceal. As he ran, he suddenly grabbed the front of his coat with his right hand, as if to cradle or hold something underneath the lapel. *He's got a gun!* I thought, as I snatched my radio from its holder.

"I am in pursuit of a suspect, believed to be armed!" I told Central Command over my radio. I gave them an address, and then I began to pursue the man on foot, up Sands Street towards the Manhattan and Brooklyn Bridges. Prior experience told me that whatever this man was holding under his coat, it was *something he didn't want to get caught with.*

It was still winter in New York, and I was wearing a heavy uniform coat along with several pounds of standard (and bulky) police gear. (It was going to be a difficult foot race.) As I ran to the intersection of Sands Street and Gold Street, I noticed a city bus that had stopped to take on a passenger. *Hmm, the guy's got a good lead on me. I think I'll even out the odds a little.*

I put on an extra burst of speed and hopped on the bus through the rear entrance just as the doors were closing. The bus quickly caught up with the suspect, and I had to smile as I watched him from a side window. He was running and nervously looking back over his shoulder. He hadn't seen me board the bus, so I knew he was wondering where I was. I had already warned the bus operator that I wanted to catch up with the suspect and pointed him out as he ran up Sands Street.

As I watched the suspect through the side window, I suddenly felt the muscles of my face tighten up and a cold chill run down my back. I saw what appeared to be *the butt of a gun* protruding from the suspect's waistband as the front of his coat parted while he ran!

I signaled the bus operator who passed the runner, and he quickly stopped the bus. I timed my exit through the rear door of the bus perfectly and startled the young man. The moment he saw me get off the bus under the Brooklyn-Queens Expressway over-pass, he instantly changed directions and crossed the street to his left, behind the rear of the bus. He ran under the expressway over-pass, crossed the expressway on-ramp, and veered left onto a grassy area with hedges next to the expressway and a chain-link fence on the opposite end.

I felt my mouth go dry as I pulled my service revolver and en-tered the grassy area. The man was still running with his hand on the object under his coat. With gun in hand, I took cover behind some hedges and yelled, "Stop, police!" He suddenly turned in my direction and *pulled a shiny object from his waistband* under his coat. It was a nickel-plated revolver. I wasn't about to let him do some-thing stupid if I could help it. Suddenly I shouted with a voice of command, "*Drop it!*"

To my relief, the suspect looked down at the weapon and sud-denly threw it into the hedge. Then he started climbing the chain-link fence. I knew he hoped to cross the expressway on foot and lose me in the process. I jumped to my feet, holstered my revolver, and ran to the fence. Grabbing the suspect's coat, I pulled him down before he could get over the fence. He put up a brief struggle, so I had to use what the manual calls "necessary force" to subdue him.

By that time, a "backup" police unit had arrived, and two other police officers helped me complete the arrest and loaded the suspect into their cruiser. After searching the location where the suspect had tossed the gun, I recovered a classic "Saturday Night Special," a Clerke "first make." It was fully loaded with six live rounds. The suspect still had the holster in his waistband when I searched him. He was charged with possession of a dangerous weapon and resisting arrest. Meanwhile, I knew I would see that loaded "Special" in my dreams for a long time to come.

\* \* \*

Prior to their consolidation on April 28, 1995, the City of New York had *three* separate and distinct police departments. The largest of the three was the New York City Police Department (NYPD), followed by the New York City Transit Police Department (NYCTPD), and last but not least, the New York City Housing Authority Police Department (NYCHPD).

Each department had identical police enforcement powers under the New York State Penal Code. The New York City Police Department patrolled the city as a whole, while the New York City Transit Police concentrated on the preservation and protection of the city's transit system and the public it serves. The New York City Housing Authority Police protected the residents and property of the city's 300-plus housing projects.

All of the police officers in the City of New York had sworn to uphold the Constitution of the United States and the Penal Code of New York State, and to protect the life, limb, and property of the people of New York City. The majority of police officers working in New York's three police departments were white, and ironically, most of them lived *outside* the borders of New York City!

4

I was born in South Brooklyn on April 10, 1943, at Long Island College Hospital. My parents, James and Cornelia Lewis, lived at the Red Hook Housing Projects at that time. Most of the tenants at Red Hook were white back then, but that took a drastic turn in the late 1950's and early 1960's. For whatever reason, the tenant population became predominantly black and Hispanic in the mid-60's.

It was also around that time that we began to hear the word "ghetto" used in reference to the Red Hook Housing Project. More and more, we heard the media and city residents asking, "Can any good thing come out of the *ghetto?*" Before and during World War II, this disparaging term was applied to the undesirable areas of certain European cities where Jews were unjustly forced to live in isolation from other races.

Today, any reference to "ghetto" conjures up thoughts of poor, run-down neighborhoods where underprivileged black and Hispanic people live "at the expense of taxpayers." The truth is that the term was wrongly applied to public housing projects—even while they were still considered to be excellent family residences at the time—simply because minority races had become the majority of the resident population. Many, if not most, of the families living there were "middle-class" and hard-working. They simply were not white.

I am a "product" of a New York City "ghetto." I spent a total of 18 years growing up at the Red Hook project, but I didn't feel like a second-class citizen. I couldn't understand why we and our neighbors were the objects of a such a negative attitude, or why it seemed to be increasing throughout the city and the nation as a whole. I began to notice that people in so-called "ghetto communities" weren't given the same level of government services as people of other races and neighborhoods (such as police and fire protection, park and recreation development, and comparable public school facilities and staffing).

Like other normal children around the world, children in the projects of New York City have dreams and fantasies about becoming "somebody" one day. They are fascinated by the things and people they see paraded before their accepting young eyes. The things they come to admire can and will have a positive or negative impact on their lives.

Life and times were hard for people who lived in the "ghettos"—even in the 60's. I began to notice that the chances of a child in a "ghetto" fulfilling his or her hopes and dreams were far less than those of children growing up in other areas and under better circumstances. I didn't want to believe it, but I had to acknowledge that black or Hispanic children living in poor neighborhoods (like mine) would be confronted with more negative disadvantages than their white counterparts.

I discovered the hard way that citizens of the "ghetto" are considered the "have nots" of American society. They are often intentionally exploited by some of those who "have," and in most instances, this exploitation, along with general governmental neglect, contributes enormously to the eroding conditions that are prevalent everywhere in a "ghetto."

The high crime rates, escalating drug abuse, child abuse, the overt abuse and misuse of police authority, and other abuses too numerous to mention were allowed by elected officials to flourish for too long. They finally escalated into an uncontrollable epidemic. This would never have happened if there had been a genuine interest and concern for the residents of poorer neighborhoods on the part of government officials and community leaders.

These conditions began to have an extraordinarily destructive impact on the minds of New York City's housing project residents, both the young and old alike. The terrible living conditions took its toll on their lives and greatly influenced their thoughts and actions. The environment children are exposed to has a tremendous impact on their developing character and on their view of life.

Children bombarded with endless scenes of violence in their streets and playgrounds cannot help but be affected by their environment. When they are surrounded by constant incidents of depraved criminal activity, they will become accustomed to them.

Even worse, they may accept their presence as a normal, and even necessary way of life, unless they are taught differently.

I was blessed by a mother and father who refused to forget who they were. They drilled into each of their children the determination to succeed and excel. They defied every stereotype of the "typical ghetto dweller," sending us to music schools and encouraging us to get involved in numerous youth and sports organizations.

In September of 1962, I joined the U.S. Air Force for a four-year hitch. After my discharge from active duty in 1966, I joined the 904th Air Force Reserve Unit located at Steward Air Force Base in upstate New York. The 904th was activated and I was called back on active duty when North Korean naval forces captured the United States Navy intelligence ship, *Pueblo*. I saw active combat duty in the Vietnam "conflict" as well.

Just before I reentered the service, I took the "Unified Police Examination," a written test used by all three of New York City's Police Departments. Each department could draw new recruits from the list of those who passed. It was shown in later years that the New York City Police Department at that time had an unofficial "quota" limiting the number of black officers on its force (it wasn't on record, of course). The written test I took to qualify as a candidate wasn't as easy as the tests are today. My score on the test, which consisted of math, spelling, vocabulary, reading, comprehension, and other applicable subjects, was 87 percent of a possible 100 percent.

After I was discharged from the U.S. Air Force for the second time, I received a call from the New York City Police Department asking me to report for a candidate qualification physical. To my surprise, I was told that I had been disqualified because of my height! Somehow, the police department doctors had managed to measure my height at 5′ 7¾″, and the minimum height for NYPD candidates at that time was 5′ 8″. I wondered where the one-fourth inch had gone, since the U.S. Air Force doctors had always measured my

7

height at 5' 8". (Sources at police headquarters later told me that the New York Police Department routinely used the height requirement to omit blacks and other "undesirable" minorities from appointment to the police force whenever it was useful.)

I couldn't help but wonder why I was tall enough to fight for my country during the Vietnam War, but was turned down by the NYPD all because of a somewhat suspicious one-quarter of an inch! Some prospective police candidates literally went to chiropractors to be "stretched" so they could meet that ridiculous height requirement. Some candidates had themselves carried into the medical examination office while laying flat on their backs on a large plank of wood, hoping to somehow gain a few fractions of an inch. What puzzled me the most was that I was constantly seeing members of the New York City Police Department who were shorter than I was (without exception, they were white officers). I suppose the doctors used a different tape measure or did it in "bad light."

Even with the hassles, I was glad to receive notification that I had been appointed to the New York City Housing Authority Police Department on September 28, 1968, only two weeks after my second discharge from the U.S. Air Force. By the way, there were no women on the Housing police force at that time due to a physical strength test that required potential candidates to meet certain strength requirements as well as lift a certain amount of weight. One black woman was able to pass the physical strength test, and she became the first female ever to be appointed to the NYCHPD in the early 70's. It wasn't until the height requirement of the NYPD and the physical test standards of the NYCHPD were challenged in court that the two departments changed their requirements.

There I was, a brand new recruit assigned to the New York City Housing Police Department Academy. I had gotten over the hardship of being rejected by the NYPD, and at least, I had finally been given a chance to become a police officer in New York City. I thanked God for that. I was appointed to the largest police academy class in the history of the Housing Police Department, which numbered 235 recruits. At the graduation ceremony after six months of training, a number of things flashed through my mind as I was sworn in and given my commission as a police officer.

The police officials told us before we began academy training that background investigations of many of the new recruits hadn't been completed. We were given the option of accepting the appointment to the academy, knowing that if the investigation turned up some "discrepancy" in our history, we would be immediately terminated, even though we were already well into the academy training regimen.

When I heard that, I couldn't help but remember my arrest by the Transit Police at the age of 14. I was on my way to a "rumble" as a reluctant member of a neighborhood gang called "El Kovons." If I hadn't agreed to go with them to fight a rival gang, I would have been beaten up. It was on the way to this gang battle that our entire group jumped the turnstiles at a subway entrance to avoid paying for a transit token. We were caught in the act by a group of Transit Police Officers and hauled in to call our parents.

Since I was a juvenile, I was issued what was called at the time a "Juvenile Delinquent Card." This record was to be destroyed if you didn't get into any more trouble with the law, and it could not be held against you when you applied for a civil service job, which supposedly included a position on the police department. I never again got into trouble, but it still worried me that day. I accepted the appointment to the police academy and prayed for the best. I am happy to report nothing ever materialized, and I completed the police academy without incident.

The most haunting memory that flashed through my mind during the swearing-in ceremony was the time a Housing Authority Police officer brutally assaulted my younger brother, Stanley, at the Red Hook Housing Project. The incident with Stanley made a tremendous impact on me. It happened on a beautiful spring day in May of 1965 while I was home on leave from the U.S. Air Force.

At about 7:00 in the evening, there was a knock on my parents' apartment door. When I opened the door, I saw two young girls who were about 12 or 13 years old. They frantically told my mother and I that the Housing Police had taken my brother, Stanley, and another young man down to the basement of 37 Centre Mall, which was in the rear of the complex. They said they heard horrible screams coming from the basement, so they went to find a basement window and saw the police officers assaulting my brother and his friend!

I knew how brutal some of the Housing Police officers could be, so I took off for the basement location. When we arrived, two black police officers were coming out of the basement with my brother Stanley and his friend. When I saw my brother's disfigured face, I almost went berserk and had to be restrained by friends. Stanley's face was so badly disfigured that when my father and mother saw him for the first time as he stood before the judge in night court, they both wept openly. That had a devastating effect on me. I would never forget the painful sight of my parents weeping over the brutal beating of my brother by the Housing cops.

When the cops emerged from the basement, I noticed that one of the officers, named Meeks*, had blood flowing from his right hand. When I asked, "Hey, what happened to your hand?" he just looked at me and mumbled something to my brother, who was in handcuffs. I was dressed in my Air Force uniform at the time, and I continued to ask him, "Hey punk, what did you do to my brother? He never hurt anybody! What did you do?!" I called him a few other choice obscene names in my anger.

The family met at the night court to see what charges would be leveled against Stanley. When I heard the charges, it was like adding insult to injury! My brother was charged with "disorderly conduct" plus "resisting arrest and assault on a police officer." These are the two standard charges used by police officers who want to cover or somehow justify conduct unbecoming of a police officer. I was to learn through 20 years of police work that crooked police officers who overstep their authority invariably turn to these two sections of Penal Law dealing with disorderly conduct and assault to cover up their criminal misconduct.

I watched my parents comfort one another as my brother stood before the bench in pain, with his face torn, battered, and swollen, and thought, *The judge should at least make some sort of inquiry about the disfiguring injuries obviously suffered by Stanley! He surely couldn't have inflicted those kinds of wounds on himself, and a night stick surely wouldn't have made those kinds of wounds!*

The judge hardly looked up. He just concerned himself with the busy work of arraigning Stanley and his friend. In fact, the judge pointedly ignored the verbal efforts of Stanley's legal aid attorney to draw attention to how badly my brother was injured. It is safe to say that the city court system, as well as many police officers, were very corrupt in those days, and the police got away with a great deal—even murder. So it was not unusual for a judge to intentionally "overlook" the severe injuries suffered by black suspects who were brought before him.

Judges rarely concerned themselves with how such injuries came about, especially when the defendants were charged with the catch-all penal violation: "assault on a police officer and resisting arrest." These charges were used to cover countless numbers of brutal police attacks on so-called "undesirables" who were seriously and critically injured by illegal police actions. If a suspect died in police custody from injuries suffered at the hands of the arresting officers, then "assault on a police officer and resisting arrest" would be added to the original charges, no matter what they were, solely to cover the actions of the officer or officers.

Today, as a retired detective and a 20-year veteran of the New York Police Department, I can honestly say that if a research survey could be conducted on the validity of the charge of "resisting arrest and assault on a police officer" and if these charges are preferred against people to cover up the misconduct and criminal behavior of misfit police officers, *the results would be alarming.*

The night court judge posted a $1,000 bond each on Stanley and his friend, and remanded them back to the holding tank until their court date, or until their bail was raised. It wasn't easy, but my parents managed to raise the bond money for my brother several days later. Meanwhile, Stanley didn't receive medical treatment for the severe injuries he had suffered at the hands of Officer Meeks until after my parents posted his bond and took him to the hospital themselves.

When Stanley finally came home, he told us that he and some friends were singing on the steps of the Red Hook Community Center on Mill Street when four Housing cops walked up to them. (In the late 50's and early 60's, it was normal to see small groups of young boys, black and white, singing on the streets of New York City. This was a form of socializing and recreation, as well as a pastime for the youth. When I attended Boys High School in Brooklyn, I saw and heard many high school boys singing on the subway platforms or on street corners near the school. Many of the top rock and roll groups started singing that way. (I distinctly remember seeing Little Anthony and the Imperials, who also attended Boys High School, singing on a subway platform before they made it to the big time.)

Stanley said the cops accosted them right on the Center's steps and ordered all of the boys to accompany them to the Housing Police office because they were investigating a "pass" robbery (involving transit passes or long-term tickets). The boys left with the police and walked the equivalent of three city blocks. It was odd that the officers didn't take the boys to the police record office, but to the locker room where the officers change their clothes. It was located in the basement of 37 Centre Mall.

When they reached the basement location, two of the officers took two of the four boys to another location while Officer Meeks and an officer named Myron Penn* took my brother and his friend down into the basement. Stanley noticed that several doors were closed and appeared locked, and the lighting was poor. The cops directed the boys to a door with "Housing Police" painted across the front. Penn used a key on his belt to unlock the door, and when Stanley was led into the room, he saw about ten lockers lining the walls with benches in front of them. There was also a desk in the far corner with a chair behind it and other chairs grouped around it.

Stanley watched as Officer Meeks slowly unbuckled his gun belt, took off his weapon, and walked to the desk to place it into a bottom drawer. Then they handcuffed Stanley and his friend to a metal bar anchored to a wall on the opposite side of the room from the desk. Stanley and his friend remember smelling alcohol on the breath of both officers.

Then Meeks approached Stanley as Penn sat down on one of the chairs. "Where were you a few hours ago, kid?" Meeks asked. "I was at home eating dinner," Stanley said. (I could vouch for that because I was upstairs when he came in at about 4:30 p.m. He didn't leave the house until after 6:30 p.m.) Then Meeks sneered at both boys and said, "I heard you were seen near Centre Mall and Clinton Street at about 5:45 p.m." The boys shook their heads and told Meeks they weren't anywhere close to that area at that time.

Meeks then said, "I am going to get the truth out of you, even if I have to beat it out of you! An elderly lady was 'taken off' [robbed], and I want to know who did it, even if it wasn't you." (Stanley, who was 20 years old at the time, hadn't even been picked up by the police in the past, and he wasn't into any criminal activities.)

Stanley responded to Officer Meeks saying, "I'm not into ripping off people! I've got a job, and I work for my money." The words were barely out of his mouth before Meeks struck him without any justification or warning. The policeman struck viciously, hitting Stanley in the head with his nightstick, a heavy wooden club equivalent to a small baseball bat. Stanley was still handcuffed to the metal bar at the time and totally helpless to defend himself or avoid the blow. He said he saw stars and fell to the ground, and then Meeks moved in and kicked his helpless prisoner in the stomach with all of his force.

Stanley cried out in pain and agony, and his friend shouted, "Leave him alone!" That is when Officer Penn hit Stanley's friend and drew blood. Stanley said he could also feel the blood dripping from his head where he was struck by Meeks' nightstick. "That is when Meeks started acting like a mad man!" he told us. "He started to hit me in the head and all over my body with his fists. Then Meeks suddenly stopped beating on me, and he went over to a locker and pulled out a smaller gun [his off-duty revolver]. Then he went to the desk drawer and pulled his service revolver out of its holster! He came toward me with both guns in his hands, and offered one of the guns to me, butt first."

Stanley refused to take the gun, of course. "Meeks tried for several seconds to get me to accept one of the revolvers. He had the look of murder in his eyes the whole time." When Meeks realized my brother wasn't going to go along with his demands, he suddenly struck Stanley with the butt of each weapon simultaneously, one on each side of his face! The pain and destructive force of the blows from the heavy metal revolvers was incredible. Stanley said he thought he even blacked out for a couple of moments, which was confirmed by his friend. When he came out of the stupor, he was bleeding so profusely that his blood, and the blood from his friend's wounds, was all over the wall and floor.

In the course of his brutal and illegal attack on his handcuffed prisoner, Officer Meeks received a severe laceration on his right index finger. This was the wound I had noticed when I saw him emerge from the basement. When I asked him what had happened to his hand, Meeks' only response was to ask my dazed brother who I was. Once he discovered that I was his battered prisoner's brother, nothing more was said. The cops hurriedly put my brother and his friend into a police car and drove away. The officers made it a point *not* to get medical care for the prisoners because that would have required them to fill out injury reports, which meant they would have to explain how my brother and his friend had received such serious injuries. They weren't worried about the usual "arrest reports," because they could cover their crime with the classic and often misused phrase, "necessary force was used to effect the arrest." (How much "necessary force" is needed to arrest a person who is handcuffed to a stationary metal pipe?)

Today, anytime a person is injured while in police custody, the duty or "desk officer," who carries a rank of sergeant or higher, is required to make sure that individual is taken to the hospital and treated by a doctor. If this isn't done, the police department and the city are liable. At that time, an official medical record of the type of injury and how it was obtained must be established to see if the injuries were related to the incident that led to the person's arrest.

This procedure wasn't in effect at the time of my brother's arrest, so he had to suffer with his untreated wounds for a couple days and nights before he could be taken to the hospital by my parents. Stanley was blessed in that the injuries he received did not get infected. He received four stitches for his head wound and medication for his face.

The cops inadvertently left the basement door open when they hurried to the cruiser with their prisoners, so I conducted a little investigation of my own. I went down into the basement and entered the bathroom where I saw blood in the sink and on the walls. There were a large number of bloody paper towels in the wastepaper basket and on the floor. I picked up the paper towels on the floor, along with those that were in the wastepaper basket and placed them in a paper bag I found in the bathroom. I carried them out of the basement after trying without success to enter the locker room where the attack occurred.

I was probably in violation the entire time I was in the basement, but I didn't care. When I saw the condition my brother was in, I became determined to find some evidence of the severe beating he had suffered at the hands of the police. I turned over the brown paper bag to my father, who turned the evidence over to my brother's attorney.

My military leave expired shortly after that, and I left New York City for Charleston, South Carolina, where I boarded a plane for the long trip to my post in North Africa. The Housing Authority's case against my brother and his friend was eventually thrown out of court, and all charges against my brother were dismissed— but only after a long period of legal shuffling by the court, the Housing Authority police department, and the city. My parents tried to bring suit against the police officers, the police department, and the New York City Housing Authority, but their suit failed because of legal loopholes in the matter, even though the police officers involved were found negligent in the incident!

When I took the Unified Police Examination after my first tour of military duty, I was determined to make a difference somehow. I knew something, somehow, had to change in the way laws were enforced in New York City. Maybe I was only one black man, and maybe I was "just a product of the ghetto," but I knew I had to at least try.

After I had finally been sworn in as a police officer, I realized that despite my disappointment and anger over the poor image presented by certain Housing Authority officers in the past, I still looked up to New York City police officers as symbols of safety, protection, and guardians of the public welfare. Now it appeared that it was my turn at bat...

---

*The names of these individuals have been changed or altered for reasons of safety, anonymity, and privacy, and bear no actual relationship to persons alive or dead. The situations and incidents, however, occurred exactly as described in this book, and in official court records.

# Chapter 2

# New Cop on the Beat

*M*y first official police assignment was to report to the headquarters of Police Service Area #3 (P.S.A. 3), located in the Fort Green Housing Project in downtown Brooklyn, New York. P.S.A. 3 provided police services to five city housing projects: Fort Greene, Farragut, Gowanus, Wyckoff, and Red Hook.

At that time, the Housing Police Department was seriously undermanned, and the city government was in the process of slowly building it up. The growing drug problem, among other things, was causing all kinds of related criminal activity and felony crimes to rapidly escalate, which had finally lit a fire under many indifferent government bureaucrats.

At the time of my appointment to the Housing Police in 1968, there were approximately 300 or more major housing projects in the City of New York (the numbers have increased over the years). They housed more than 600,000 people, with another 300,000 or more visitors flowing in and out of the residential buildings every day (and night). This "small city" of nearly a million residents and visitors was protected by a "thin blue line" of approximately 1,200 Housing Police officers, nearly 67 percent of whom were black. Our job was to patrol and protect all of the city's housing dwellings and the people who lived in them, along with their visitors, 24 hours a day. It was an awesome task.

Ninety-five percent of all patrolling by the Housing Police was done *on foot*, because most of the city's housing developments

17

didn't have streets going through them. The housing projects covered an enormous area of real estate, yet they had been designed so that no vehicle traffic would pass through them.

One of the first things I learned was that the making of a good cop doesn't begin with what a new recruit learns in police academy. It starts with the qualities the individual person has developed over his or her lifetime. The moment I first stepped onto a sidewalk as a commissioned police officer, I brought all my memories, experiences, and dreams with me. The things my father and mother had said to me over the last 25 years, the positive pressures I'd faced from coaches, drill instructors, teachers, and peers in competition—they all stepped onto that sidewalk with me. Even my experiences as a child growing up in the Red Hook Housing Project, the habitual caution and awareness, and the street-smart knowledge of human behavior and weaknesses were all there, just waiting to be tapped in times of stress and danger, or conflict.

Everything new cops are exposed to before their appointment plays a significant role in determining whether or not they will turn out to be a good cop or a bad cop (and there are both kinds in nearly every police force). My experiences growing up in a poor environment, but under the guidance of exceptional parents, were crucial to my character development. They saw to it that I went to church every Sunday, and I got involved in young people's activities at the church. My mother kept up with our schoolwork and activities, and we were all given private piano lessons by my father's sister. We even attended the New York School of Music. All of these positive and negative things combined to help make me the kind of cop I became.

No, I wasn't a perfect kid, but I knew where to draw the line. My parents raised me with dignity, and I knew the consequences I would have to face for misbehaving. My biggest challenge, and the greatest challenge faced by youth today, was overcoming the wrong influences of friends. I recall the time I went with a few friends to buy some clothes and stole a ring from a jewelry store.

The proprietor of the store was showing one of the boys some jewelry, and I noticed that he had forgotten to close the sliding door to the counter display where I was standing.

I was about 13 or 14 years old, and I had never stolen anything before, though some of my friends had committed petty theft on a number of occasions. I guess I was hoping to "prove" myself to my friends, so I nervously reached over and behind the counter to remove a ring from its place and pretended to look at it. When I was sure that no one had seen me remove the ring, I put the ring in my pocket.

I can't explain why I did it or express how horrified I was after I stole the ring. I was so troubled in my mind after I left the store that I didn't even tell my friends what I had done. I finally threw the ring down a sewer. I wanted to return it, and knew I should have, but I was too frightened to follow through. Many of the things I did and got involved with while growing up in the ghetto might be conceived as bad or mischievous.

In my early teen years, there were a number of programs and organizations that helped keep a lot of kids off the streets and out of trouble. Most of the city housing projects had community centers where boys and girls could go after school and participate in various educational and sports activities. There was also the Police Athletic League, the Boy and Girl Scouts, and a number of Military Scout Organizations, such as the Blue Jacket Guards, to which my older brother and I belonged.

There was a great deal of gang activity in New York City, even in the 60's. I was "drafted" against my will by the "El Kovons," a predominately black gang that was based in the Red Hook Housing projects. My involvement with the gang was very minor because I was deeply involved with my church youth program, the Sea Scouts, and the Boys High School track team.

I did "go down" with the "Kovans" on two occasions ("going down" meant a gang was going to fight another rival gang); because I knew that if I didn't, I would have been beaten up by the members. I describe those incidents in a later chapter comparing gang activities then and now. The second incident was the time we were busted for jumping the turnstiles of the subway station at Smith and 9th Streets, and I was given a Juvenile Delinquent Card. That was the incident I was worried about while in the police academy.

After that brief brush with the law, I devoted all of my time to sports and other activities. Track competition became a passion for me at Boys High School in Brooklyn, where I clocked a 9.7-second 100-yard dash and was placed in the sports hall of fame. After my high school graduation in June of 1960, I joined a track club called the United Athletic Association and was an active member of the Amateur Athletic Union (A.A.U.). A coach named Jimmy Borden helped me become a much better sprinter than I had been in high school, and I saw my times in the 100- 220- and 440-yard dashes improve immensely.

I competed successfully for two years with United Athletic Association track club, and entered the United States Air Force on September 11, 1962, when I was sent to Lacklin Air Force Base in San Antonio, Texas, for basic training. Due to continuous track training, my physical condition was at a competition level, and my running ability proved to be a great asset during basic training. When the physical training instructors (PT's) discovered that I could run so fast and long, they made life a little more difficult for me by calling me "front and center" to lead the rest of the airmen recruits in endurance runs.

Nothing in my previous training had taught me how to lay back or slow down. I couldn't help but overtake the field and lap my fellow recruits several times. Once the PT's discovered that, their devious minds came up with a great plan to make all of us unhappy. They sarcastically announced to all of the troops, "Everyone who gets lapped by Lewis gets to do *an extra lap!*" Despite my efforts to slow down, the entire training group always had to do an extra lap every time we had physical training. (This didn't win me the "Most Popular Man" award with some of the other airmen in basic training, of course.)

The increased training and practice, along with competition when and where I could schedule it, improved my running ability even more during my four-year hitch with the United States Air Force. When I was discharged from the Air Force in September 1968, I was still training and running almost every day. This was when I took the "Unified Police Examination." My training continued even through my reenlistment with the Air Force Active Reserves. As I was to discover, my love for running and other key physical activities helped prepare me for my career as a New York City policeman.

During the first few months after my graduation from the police academy, I experienced many of the pros and cons of police work. I quickly learned that many of the things I had learned in the academy were only meant to enhance my ability to make the best decision in given situations, not spell out my decisions for me. No two situations are the same when you are dealing with people. No one knows exactly how a person or persons will react in a given situation, so we have to rely on individual judgment and instinct.

At times, a police officer is required to make split-second decisions that could mean the difference between life and death. Police officers are literally given the power, the authority, and the responsibility to preserve life or take it in certain situations.

Drugs were becoming a big problem (which gradually began to affect the entire City of New York) when I was first appointed to the police department. I began functioning as an "active" or aggressive cop from the first day I was assigned to a field training officer while in the academy. On my very first day out in the field, I saw a robbery go down before my field training officer noticed it. I alerted him and immediately took off after the suspect on foot, apprehending him just a few blocks away. He had knocked a woman to the ground while trying to snatch her pocketbook, which I also recovered after I caught up with the suspect.

My track background continued to play a prominent role in those early years of my new career. I was on foot patrol at the Fort Greene Housing Projects one time when I saw a young man who was about 20 years old selling drugs in a playground area at the project. When he spotted me coming towards him, he took off like a jackrabbit! I took off behind him as he ran off the project site and crossed Myrtle Avenue into Fort Greene Park.

As the drug pusher ran, he kept looking back as I continued to gain on him. He had a big lead, and he was a good runner, but I managed to shorten the distance between us in the pursuit. He must have looked over his shoulder about a dozen times to see if I was still behind him. I could only guess what he was thinking when he realized that I was steadily gaining on him. By the time the pusher had run at maximum speed for a couple of minutes, he was completely exhausted. When he realized he could not shake me, he stopped and sat down on a park bench, just shaking his head and breathing heavily. Had he not stopped, I would have overtaken him in a matter of seconds anyway.

When I approached him, he was desperately trying to get rid of and disguise the controlled substance he was selling. With my revolver in hand, I warned him to move slowly and ordered him to slide off the park bench and lay facedown on the ground with his hands behind his head. After I cuffed his hands behind his back, I searched him for weapons and contraband. The search uncovered a gun and several glassine envelopes (made of a thin but dense semi-transparent paper) that were under and in his clothing. There were also several glassine envelopes under the bench where I had seen him throw them. Each of the glassine envelopes contained a white powder that I was sure was heroin. The suspect was later charged with possession of a deadly weapon, sale of a controlled substance, and possession of a controlled substance with intent to sell.

Most of the thousands of arrests I made in my career were made while patrolling alone, and I became proficient at collecting, tagging, bagging, and verifying the things I confiscated from prisoners, such as weapons, drugs, money, and personal effects. For I knew that minor technicalities such as misplaced or misidentified pieces of evidence, could make the difference between the conviction of a guilty suspect, and his release to plague the public again. The furor over the apparent mishandling of the O.J. Simpson case by investigating officers gathering evidence at the murder scene highlights the importance of these crucial details.

From that first arrest as a trainee onward, my career as a police officer in New York City unfolded and developed in the shadow of its high-rise housing projects. Although I already knew what it was like to grow up in the projects, I discovered just how hazardous it was for police officers on patrol, especially on the night watch tour. Because of the lack of manpower at the time I joined the police force, I worked many of my scheduled midnight-to-eight a.m. tours *alone.* My only source of police backup was the New York City Police Department.

My first few years on the job were filled with all kinds of exciting and dangerous experiences. When I first worked the Gowanus Housing Projects in Brooklyn, I walked the eight-to-four daytime beat. While I was on patrol the first day, a group of preteen kids realized that I was a new cop on their beat. They started to test my patience by repeatedly making verbal insults and running away. This went on for several minutes, and it was basically annoying but harmless until one of the youth decided to throw a small piece of broken plastic at me before running away again. That was when my tolerance of their behavior ended.

I went into the police record room in the basement of one of the Gowanus Housing Project buildings and quickly changed from my police uniform to civilian clothes. Then I hit the streets again using a side entrance. By taking an alternate route, I managed to walk right up on the kids without being noticed. I suddenly grabbed the boy who had thrown the plastic object, along with one of the more vocal kids, catching them completely off guard!

I took the frightened boys to the police record room and notified their parents. I released them directly to their mothers after making an elaborate point of recording their names in the record book. I admonished them about the seriousness of their behavior and bluntly told them I wasn't going to tolerate such behavior in the future. I never had any trouble with that group of boys again.

Again, my years as a project resident helped me understand how to deal with these young boys in a way they and their parents would understand and respect. As my career with the police department progressed, I learned that black police officers, particularly those who had grown up in the projects, were generally more tolerant than white police officers in their dealings with residents and members of the black community.

\* \* \*

The 1960's and 1970's were difficult and disturbing decades of change for the nation, as African-Americans rose in unity to claim equal rights under the Constitution, and as unrest continued to grow concerning the Vietnam War, a new influx of drugs, and the changing moral values sweeping the nation. No one was exempt from the changes, not even the law enforcement community. Every prejudice, bias, fear, or character flaw that appeared in society as a whole was reproduced in the mind-set and actions of the overall police population as well.

During my early years with the police force, there was a great deal of friction and animosity between the New York City Police Department and the New York City Housing Authority Police Department. I believe this was mainly due to a high percentage of Housing Police officers who were African-American, as opposed to the majority of white officers in the larger city force. Incidents of racism and unprofessional rivalry between white officers of the NYPD and black officers in the NYCHPD became so frequent and obvious that the NYPD's Patrolman Benevolent Association employed a research firm to review and analyze the productivity of each department in the early 70's. Early results of the survey showed that man-for-man, the productivity of NYPD police officers didn't compare with that of NYCHPD police officers in terms of arrests made, cases closed, and ratios of officers to population served. In embarrassment, the P.B.A. president allegedly ordered the survey stopped.

Understanding has always been the most important bridge between cultures, attitudes, and differences among races. Unfortunately, there was very little understanding shared among New York City's three police departments at that time. I believe the main reason was because very few police officers in New York City actually *lived there*. They didn't share the lifestyles, concerns, or difficulties of the people they were sworn to serve and protect.

The City of New York consists of five boroughs—Manhattan, Queens, Brooklyn, Bronx, and Staten Island. Men and women who lived in adjoining cities and counties were allowed to join the police departments in New York City. In fact, historically, *the majority* of all police officer candidates are white males who live outside the boundaries of New York City. Many live in upstate New York, as far away as Newberg, and far out on Long Island. A good number of NYPD officers don't even live in the state but commute from New Jersey.

Ironically, anyone who lives in one of the five boroughs of New York City is automatically disqualified and denied the privilege of serving on the police departments of any of the aforementioned cities and counties. Each of these governmental units has adopted strict residency laws requiring *all civil service workers* (which includes police officers, of course) to reside within their city and/or county limits. This is an especially effective way to disqualify people of color, who comprise a large percentage of New York City's population.

Over the decades, this inequity has caused serious problems by skewing the hiring patterns of the NYPD away from minorities who dwell in New York City proper, particularly black and Hispanic applicants. When I joined the force, there were only a handful of ranking black police officials. Most of the upper level positions were dominated by several generations of white, non-resident police officers who sometimes provided preferential treatment to applicants from their own families, residential areas, or race. It was commonly known on the street that white candidates who had or at one point did have relatives on the NYPD were almost certain to be appointed to the academy over black and Hispanic applicants from within the New York City limits, even if the black and Hispanic applicants had higher test scores. This bias, although unofficial and strictly "off the record," tended to follow through in many promotion and disciplinary actions as well.

One of the most surprising personal encounters I had with white NYPD officers happened in my early years on the Housing Department police force. It all started with two white officers from the NYPD 88th Precinct who began crossing their precinct lines into the 3rd Housing Police Precinct on the midnight tour. They thought it was fun to illegally put parking summonses on the private vehicles belonging to NYCHPD officers who were on patrol in the projects. This was just a typical example of the outright harassment and racism that went on.

These antics continued for a while until early one spring morning, I caught the two NYPD officers in the very act of writing the illegal parking summonses before they could slip away! When I confronted them in a not-so-friendly manner, one of the officers actually called for backup on his radio, as if he was being accosted by an armed criminal!

I had no choice but to call for assistance on my radio as well. Four police cars from the 88th Precinct showed up, and every one of the ten NYPD officers confronting me was white. Meanwhile, a group of seven other NYCHPD officers had joined me—all were African-American. Things were tense enough, but evidently one of the white officers felt the NYPD had the upper hand in the situation, so he made a smart remark and pushed me.

Now I have to admit that I had a temper in those days, and I would fight at the drop of a hat. The NYPD cop who pushed me had his nightstick in his hand, and he stood right in front of me taking up the same combat stance we had all been taught in the police academy. As far as I was concerned, "the hat had been dropped." I grabbed the white officer's nightstick with my left hand and suddenly jerked him toward me. At the same time, I hit him square in the face with a single punch from my right hand, knocking him to the ground, and pandemonium broke out.

All you could see were black and white uniformed New York police officers *fighting one another*! To make matters worse, the fight occurred at 7:30 in the morning, in plain view of all the people who were on their way to work and all the children who were walking by on their way to school. On top of that, the Housing precinct was located near a busy hospital! (I hope the patients and medical staff enjoyed the show.)

When I knocked down the white officer who had hit me, one of his fellow officers came up behind me and put a choke hold on me using his nightstick. I had studied the martial arts for nearly a decade, and I managed to free myself by flipping the officer over my back. By that time, I had lost it. I fought with both of the white officers at one time, and when a sergeant from the 88th Precinct tried to step in and restrain my arms, in my rage, I somehow broke free of him and struck him to the ground. Fortunately, a black Housing Police officer named Seldon took hold of me and told me to cool it. I backed off and let him take me to the Housing precinct headquarters.

I found out later that several more patrol cars from the 88th Precinct responded to the backup call, along with a NYPD supervisor, who happened to be the sergeant who tried to grab me. I also learned that our melee wasn't just one isolated incident of racially motivated violence. Several others had also occurred between police officers around the city! No one got into any trouble from the incident in Fort Greene, but it *could* have been much worse. I learned that while the fight was going on, a black Housing cop used his service revolver to hold at bay all of the reinforcements that had arrived from the NYPD's 88th Precinct.

When it became so apparent that there was bad blood brewing between the two New York City police agencies, police officers from both departments through the city were ordered to get together to talk out their differences. Each police officer was scheduled to go to assigned police precinct locations while on duty to meet other officers from both the NYPD and NYCHPD. These meetings and dialogues were devoted to breaking down walls of indifference and to establish a line of communication and new understanding. We all knew it was serious business, because if things were allowed to continue on their current course, the situation could end up being fatal.

Those meetings helped police officers on both sides of the "race fence" to realize that they needed each other. Most of the NYPD officers gained a new professional respect for their fellow officers in the NYCHPD. The dialogues helped them realize that a police officer's job in the housing projects was just as hazardous as any other policeman's duty.

Most important of all, those meetings reminded all of us that on numerous occasions, personnel from both departments had worked side-by-side in critical situations where the safety of all depended on the professionalism of each officer involved. It was at least a start, and though many inequities and problems remain to this day, I am glad to report that relationships between the two agencies continued to generally improve over the years.

# Chapter 3

# Streetwise

One of the most important attributes separating exceptional police officers from average police officers is their "knowledge of the streets," and this is especially important in New York City. A law enforcement officer's ability to function and effectively serve a community is directly related to how well he or she knows the streets or activity patterns of the community.

A cop's knowledge of the street language, the lifestyle, and body language of black and Latino neighborhoods can and will make the difference in his success in New York City. A cop doesn't become "streetwise" just by patrolling a given community, although that certainly plays a part. The most successful streetwise cops are usually brought up in the same types of neighborhoods they are assigned to patrol. That is why it is generally easier for black or Latino cops to function in their respective communities. It takes a streetwise cop to blend into a neighborhood in a high crime area, identify with the people who live there, and establish ongoing relationships. This is the only way to earn the confidence and cooperation of the residents of these neighborhoods.

Since I grew up in the Red Hook Housing Projects of South Brooklyn, I was a natural candidate for foot patrol in black and Latino high crime areas. Due to the limited manpower of the Housing Police Department, almost every probationary police officer worked vacation relief, even though each had been assigned to a specific Police Service Area. There were advantages

29

and disadvantages toworking vacation relief, but the disadvantages outweighed the advantages by far.

Anytime one of the more than 315 housing projects in New York City needed additional police coverage on a given tour, the respective borough commanding officers routinely redistributed any two-man teams working at their projects, and reassigned one of the two to another project to fill the shortage. This was known as "flying," or going from one area of the city to another. For a number of reasons, "flying" was unpopular with police officers, especially junior cops.

When a cop was reassigned to another project, that always meant he would have to patrol an area *alone.* If he was unfortunate enough to be assigned to a housing project he wasn't familiar with, then he not only had to patrol his new beat alone, but he had to walk the beat "blind," not knowing what areas to watch for or what types of conditions he would encounter. These problems made "flying" much more frustrating and hazardous, especially during the four-to-midnight tour. Most, if not all, of the foot patrol officers assigned to patrol the city's housing projects populated largely by black and Latino residents were themselves black and Latino officers.

I was used to working these tours alone in my assigned location, although that was dangerous enough. But then I was well acquainted with the area, the people, and the conditions of my assigned projects. Despite my background in the projects, it was still extra hazardous for me to "fly" to unfamiliar areas for the "graveyard patrol."

I knew from my experiences growing up in the projects that if I was to survive my solo patrol assignments during the high-risk, four-to-midnight and midnight-to-eight shifts, I would have to learn how to function in a way that preserved my own personal safety. You can't help but be more "street conscious" when at any given time your life depends on reacting quickly and correctly to a life-threatening situation. Night patrol on foot in some of America's most dangerous (and most poorly lit) high-rise buildings, frequented by thousands of armed night predators, can make you live with a whole new level of awareness.

Just imagine for a moment that you are walking around at midnight in an unfamiliar area of New York City. You are entering dark buildings and walking lonely streets that are known to be drug prone, in the heart of a "high crime area." You would certainly become more sensitive to your surroundings than usual. Unless you had a death wish, you would take all the necessary precautions to make your personal security sure.

My overall sensitivity to the rhythm and moods of the street was greatly enhanced because I and my fellow Housing Police officers had to adapt to incredibly hazardous working conditions that constantly reminded me of active war zones in Vietnam. I learned that whenever white officers were sent into such areas on midnight tours, they were literally told to *stay in the police record room* for their own safety and not to patrol the streets alone! If and when an emergency call came in requiring the response of a police officer, and no black or Latino officers were available, the standard procedure was to notify the local NYPD precinct of the call, which would dispatch one or two patrol cars depending on the nature of the emergency. Those patrol cars would often rendezvous with the white Housing Police officer in front of the police record room, and then arrange to meet at the emergency location with a black police officer when possible.

On any given day of the week, no matter what time of the day or night, somewhere in the majority of New York City's 315 housing developments there is a violation, misdemeanor, or felony being committed, even as I write this book.

I worked most of my critical tours during the "graveyard shift" alone. Many times, I had to respond to dangerous situations of all kinds without backup ever showing up, even when I asked for it by radio. As a New York City Housing Police officer, my job was, among other things, to patrol *inside* the residential dwellings as well as outside. Any cop was at great risk patrolling inside those high-rise buildings alone during the day. Can you imagine how much greater the danger cops face when trying to patrol those dark buildings *alone* on a midnight tour?

A high percentage of the crime in any city housing project takes place *inside* the project buildings. The conditions that exist inside the majority of the city's housing tenements are alarming at best. Most of the stairwells are enclosed, so they provide a great haven for criminals and their illegal activity. Many times the light-bulbs or fixtures in those stairwells were either broken or missing, making them totally dark. In some cases, they were even dark in daylight hours.

Would-be assailants often lie in wait either in a dark stairwell for victims to stumble into their path or watch through a stairwell door to pounce on victims coming off the elevator. A person stepping off of an elevator on his or her way to an apartment usually isn't aware that a mugger or rapist may be lurking in the dimly lit or dark stairwell, just waiting for the right opportunity to attack and rob an unsuspecting victim.

The victims are often young teenage girls or women who pass by a stairwell door without looking. The door suddenly opens without warning and out steps a perpetrator with a knife or gun in his hands, forcing the victim into the poorly lit or totally dark stairwell. If the assailant just wants to rob the victim, they will normally do so at that location. All too often, these predators will take female victims up to the roof landing or out on the roof itself to assault their victims.

"Push-in robberies" are another common crime in public housing buildings that especially target the more vulnerable elderly and physically handicapped residents. Assailants often follow their elderly victims into the building and actually join their unsuspecting victims in the elevator. The perpetrators usually exit the elevator on the same floor as their targeted victims, but some will go on to the next floor, or get off one floor below the floor selected by their victims to allay any suspicion. Then they will rush back to the floor where their victims reside and wait out of sight, while their intended victims open the door to their apartments. Before the victims know what is happening, the assailants suddenly appear behind their weaker victims, push them into the apartment and quickly close the door. These assailants sometimes assault their victims before robbing them of any money or valuables they can find, hoping they will be too afraid to cooperate with police.

After spending 20 years patrolling project buildings and investigating the kinds of crimes common to them, I firmly believe that if people, young and old alike, would simply pay attention to what's going on around them, they could, in many instances, avoid becoming a crime victim. In fact, it is wise to always be aware of any area you are in, whether it is a parking lot, a traffic intersection, or the interior of a public housing project. Constantly look over your shoulder and scrutinize the entire area. Look for suspicious persons and avoid them as much as possible to help decrease your vulnerability.

Many people don't realize that elevators are almost as popular with criminals as stairwells and hallways. They provide ideal shelter for their vicious behavior. Elevator bandits or rapists make good use of the seclusion offered by the project elevator cars. These criminals usually work alone. Almost every elevator car has a trap door on top of the car. Would-be perpetrators sometimes climb up through the trap door at the top of the car and hide until a potential victim enters the car. The attackers wait until their intended victim selects his or her floor and the elevator car begins its climb. Then the perpetrator will reenter the car through the trap door and surprise his victim.

Other elevator attackers wait on the ground floor looking for victims, and enter the elevator behind them. Depending on their victim's ability to fight back, the perpetrators will usually try to block the front of the elevator door so their victim can't exit the elevator. In most instances, both the "walk-on" and "drop-in" elevator assailants will stop the elevator car between floors and carry out their crimes. Once they have completed their crime, they might release the elevator to move upward again and quickly exit on the next available floor and flee. I advise people who find themselves stuck on an elevator car when a suspicious person or persons suddenly enter the car to start screaming the moment they feel threatened or in jeopardy. This will usually cause would-be perpetrators to flee the car, the building, and the area.

One of the oddest survival facts I give people is to *use their nose!* Areas in city housing projects that are frequented by criminals for criminal activity invariably exhibit obnoxious odors, especially the odor of urine. Undesirable individuals tend to use their favorite stairwells and elevators as a bathroom, simply because they spend so much time there waiting for victims. When entering these enclosed areas, be on guard if you are met with an unbearably offensive odor.

Drug addicts (junkies) use housing dwellings to "shoot-up" or take intravenous drugs. They especially favor roof landings in certain buildings. Most of the drug addicts on the street are called "junkies" because they are addicted to illegal substances that are known to be mixed with other foreign chemicals and substances (or "junk"). Heroin and cocaine addicts are especially easy to locate because when they inject their drugs intravenously, the chemical rush is said to be so powerful that they have an uncontrollable urge to defecate. Again, a cop's sense of smell comes into play because you will always find human excrement on the roof landings. I also found additional evidence at these locations as well, including numerous objects connected to specific addictions.

I always looked for signs of fire and any kind of container that had water in it. These two items were used to liquefy controlled substances before they were drawn into syringes and injected into the veins of the drug abusers. Another sure sign of intravenous drug abuse was the presence of blood spots on the floor, or paper or bags with blood on them.

Statistics collected from various law enforcement reports suggest that many drug abusers actually live in the dwellings where they are apprehended in the act of "shooting up." These same drug addicts are invariably responsible for a great number of burglaries committed in their own buildings. Their knowledge of their fellow tenants' work and travel patterns makes it easy for them to perform daytime burglaries in an apartment building. These criminals might live next door to you, on the next floor, or in an adjacent building. They simply watch from their window or from a vantage point outside. After you leave, they quickly enter your apartment by knocking the cylinder out of the lock (if there aren't more than two locks on the door), or through a window. Some of these drug addicts and burglars have tried to enter apartments by tying a rope around a solid stationary object on the roof lowering themselves down to an apartment window, which is extremely dangerous. Some of the New York housing projects are over 20 stories high. Some of these burglars have plunged to their death when their ropes broke or became untied.

The people who live in New York City's housing projects have been subjected to every kind of crime and criminal activity you could think of (and some that you could *never* dream up). The consistently aggressive, violent, and dangerous environment endured on a concentrated basis day and night by Housing Police officers has made them exceptionally knowledgeable and streetwise cops. Any cop, virtually anywhere, faces danger in the line of duty. However, any police officer assigned exclusively to walk the dark path of interior and exterior foot patrol in the nation's most crowded, poorly lit, and high-crime housing projects, knows what it is to face potential (and even probable) death every day of his career.

The ongoing manpower shortage plunged most Housing cops into this tense environment in total isolation. When I first joined the Housing Police force, it was so undermanned that even if you were assigned to work a given ghetto area with another cop, each cop was literally assigned to *different posts* and patrolled different areas due to the large area of real estate the housing projects covered.

You had to quickly learn the "ins and outs" of patrolling those dangerous buildings and streets, knowing full well that what you did and the way you carried yourself could make the difference between life and death on any tour, let alone affect your effectiveness in the streets. Although the typical Housing cop is equipped with standard police gear, including a handgun, a baton, handcuffs, a flashlight, etc., that equipment in and of itself does not "make a cop." Only the image presented by the individual behind the shield can determine whether or not they are a good or exceptional cop.

Any police officer must be ready to react quickly, even under the most hideous and outrageous of conditions, in a way that preserves his own safety and that of others.

I always tried to stay in tune with what was going on around me. I learned to increase my powers of observation far beyond the norm, just as a matter of survival. I became especially sensitive to the movement and sounds of individuals on my beat. I made it my business to know everyone in my area. I studied their patterns, personalities, and peculiarities. Along the way, I discovered that once a cop goes to the trouble to become familiar with the people and daily activities on his beat, then he will be somewhat accepted as part of the community. This put me in a unique position to distinguish the norm from abnormal occurrences.

This is an easy task for a black cop who was raised in the ghetto. To a certain extent, I can understand why police officers from "outside" are so fearful and shocked by the hostile environment of the projects. Many people claim they can "feel" the difference when they drive into an area, but I can personally vouch for the fact that when you enter a building in a ghetto, it is an altogether different setting from anywhere else in the world. You feel like you have entered another world. The scene and atmosphere change drastically from that of the streets (and most people think the *streets* are bad).

I found that all of my senses, and especially my sight and hearing, were automatically heightened. Every time a cop, whether black or white, enters a housing project building, he finds himself in an isolated and hostile environment. You are secluded from the eyes of the public, and suddenly you sense that your personal safety and well-being have become your first priority! Any cop who walks alone in a project building does so at great personal risk, because the odds are extremely high that at any given time, day or night, he will encounter a dangerous crime *in progress* involving one or more *armed* perpetrators.

One cold night in February of 1974, I was working a midnight tour alone at the Farragut Housing Project in downtown Brooklyn. I had learned that the roof landing of a 17-story project building at 111 Bridge Street was being used as a "shooting gallery," a place used by junkies to "shoot up." Several robberies had been reported at that location.

I had a gut instinct about the place. I had spent too many years on the street to ignore the signs and the street talk. I knew that drug abusers, especially those who use needles, have a certain time and place where they like to "get off" or shoot up. Many times, I set up a one-man stakeout on the roof landings of project buildings to lay in wait for junkies coming up the stairs to shoot up.

It was a dangerous thing to do. Any law enforcement officer who has ever had to deal with junkies can tell you horror stories about trying to arrest junkies who were feeling extra high and keyed up because they needed a hit or a fix of the drug they were abusing. These addicts are often unnaturally immune to pain, and they are irrational and unpredictable. In their drug-induced paranoia and compulsion, they will fight violently and desperately to get away. You always have to be ready for a physical struggle.

On this particular midnight tour, I decided to go hunting. I made my way to Bridge Street and entered the dark project building alone, 45 minutes after midnight. This particular building had two elevators. One elevator only stopped on even floors, and the other only served odd floors. Since this building had 17 stories, I entered the "odd" elevator and took it up to the fifteenth floor.

I never went directly to my target floor, because it was dangerous, and it was a dead giveaway to any suspects in the area. Instead, I would always take the elevator to a floor at least two floors below the roof landing. Some city housing developments have two or three large buildings attached together, so they have three separate stairwells leading to the roof. In these buildings, I liked to use the stairs to gain access to the roof or to reach the other buildings and roof landings.

As I climbed the stairs of the final two stories, I stepped carefully to avoid making any sound in the stairwell. All of my powers of concentration were focused on my senses of hearing and sight. Suddenly, I heard sounds coming from the roof landing. I had already turned off my radio so some blaring announcement or radio call would not reveal my presence in the stairwell. When I reached the top floor of the stairwell, I noticed that no lights were working. The roof landing was totally dark.

I could still hear movement on the roof landing. I had no idea what I was going to be confronted with this time. I knew that roof landings like this one were not only used by junkies to "get off," but they were also favored by the homeless as places to bed down for a night, and by couples wanting to engage in sexual activities unnoticed. Many times, they were the favorite hiding locations for criminals with guns.

I knew I had to take every precaution that I had learned to take. If I wanted to live a long life, then I had to do everything I knew to do to keep the odds in my favor. *A project cop has to expect the unexpected.* I silently pulled my service revolver, checked the rounds, and held it in my right hand, and kept my oversized flashlight in my left hand.

After taking a shielded position behind the stairwell wall to keep my body from being exposed, I peeked from behind the wall and turned on my flashlight. When the light beam shined on the roof landing, I saw a black male who was about 23 years old, holding a bottle of water in one hand and some matches in the other.

As soon as the light hit him, the suspect started to go through the door leading out to the roof itself. Just before he was about to vanish through the opening, I shouted, "Police! Freeze!"

Reluctantly, the suspect complied with my command and stopped. "*Slowly* place your hands on the back of your head. Right, now walk backwards down the steps. Easy!"

When the man reached the landing where I was, I had some difficult choices to make (although by this time, I made them automatically, without conscious thought). I could put my revolver back in my holster, or lay down my flashlight to handcuff the prisoner, or juggle both somehow. This is where a police officer finds out what he or she is made of. When police officers work as a team, one officer keeps his firearm leveled at the suspect while the other officer conducts the "handcuff and personal search" procedure for maximum safety. However, an officer on "solo patrol" has to fend for himself.

"Now, put both hands on the wall, step out and lean on the wall, and spread both feet apart. Wider!" As soon as I was satisfied, I glanced around again to make sure no one else was nearby to attack me from a blind side. Then I moved in close to the suspect while quietly holstering my weapon, clamped my handcuffs on one hand first, pulled the arm behind his back quickly, and in one movement moved the other arm behind his back to cuff the other wrist.

Once I had the suspect handcuffed, I asked, "Do you have any syringes on you?" (I didn't want to get pricked by a stray needle in the dark. This was long before we were required to wear surgical gloves during an arrest or search, and caution is an officer's only protection against needles anyway). When the man nervously muttered that he didn't have anything on him, I searched him and recovered two glassine envelopes containing a white powder (later confirmed to be heroin).

"Upstairs—you go first. I want to see if you 'accidentally' dropped anything when I dropped in on you."

Sure enough, I saw a shiny gleam on the floor of the roof landing in the beam of my flashlight. When I moved my prisoner closer to the shiny object, my suspicions were confirmed. My flashlight revealed a used syringe, along with a bottle top that had a hairpin attached to it, and a little ball of cotton stuck inside it. This was my suspect's "cooker."

Before I surprised him, he had planned to put some heroin into the bottle cap with a little water, and heat it over a small fire to liquefy the substance. Then he planned to draw the poisonous fluid from the bottle cap with the syringe through the ball of cotton to filter out anything other than the liquefied heroin.

I gathered all the evidence and tagged it with my badge number, and then called Central, "I have a suspect under arrest for criminal trespass, loitering for the purpose of drug use, and criminal possession of a controlled substance." Then I gave my location and headed for the elevator with my prisoner. A cruiser from the local NYPD precinct met me as I was walking my prisoner to the police record room and took the suspect off my hands. I learned later that the suspect was a tenant of the building at 111 Bridge Street and that a number of other drug addicts were using the same location to shoot up.

Many times cops from the various NYPD precincts would tell me, "Lewis, I wouldn't have your job for all the money in the world! I'd never go into a project building alone. You're crazy, Lewis! How can you patrol those buildings alone?" When I look back at all of the incidents and predicaments I've experienced in two decades of police work—*when I was alone at midnight and inside a dark, highrise housing project*—I can still feel a chill run up my spine! I have literally made thousands of arrests on all kinds of charges, and many of these arrests required necessary force (physical force up to but not including the use of a firearm), and even deadly physical force (meaning a firearm was used).

I would be lying if I said I was never afraid when I entered a building alone, at midnight, to check it out. I can't tell you how many times fear came over me. The important thing was that when the time came to act, I always seemed to overcome my fears and do what I had to do to get the job done and come out on top.

Many times, I came across more than one person on those lonely roof landings or on the roof. In some cases, I found several junkies together involved in violations or even in the commission of a felony. I have made numerous arrests where fully loaded guns were recovered from the people I had to arrest alone. I even made a couple of "rape-in-progress" arrests, to the great relief of the victims involved. In one of those arrests, I was forced to give the perpetrator a good "working over" before he would allow me to get my cuffs on him.

Basically, I was just one of more than 2,000 Housing cops who was out there doing the job. As with any cop, my arrest record spoke for itself. Because of my aggressiveness, I was gaining a great deal of respect in the streets. This is always an asset for an active cop who clearly cares about the well-being of a neighborhood and its people, because it encourages the "good people" of the neighborhood (the majority in every case) to kind of watch out behind a cop's back.

Cops who commit themselves to the job for which they were hired, trained, and sworn to do, will be highly visible in the community. As in my case, word will quickly get out around the community about their views and positive actions, and he or she will become a welcomed and valued figure in a community that is sadly short of positive role models.

# Chapter 4

# Where Terror Reigns Supreme

*N*ew York City is famous for her enormous structures and for being the home of the Statue of Liberty, the New York Yankees, live Broadway shows, Wall Street, the Empire State Building, United Nations Headquarters, and the glamorous Fifth Avenue shops. The "Big Apple" is the city of lights, the city that never sleeps; it is the cosmopolitan mecca that has hosted the world's largest and most famous New Year's Eve Party for decades.

In spite of the countless positive attributes enjoyed and earned by the City of New York, this massive city is now being overshadowed by the plague of high crime. It is the consensus of people throughout this country and in most nations of the world that New York City is a city under siege by criminals! Many people are too afraid of the risks involved to even visit this beautiful city in broad daylight!

Although this perception is grossly inaccurate and untrue overall, there are certain neighborhoods located in the five boroughs of New York City *where terror reigns supreme.*

One of the greatest tragedies our society has to contend with is the great number of crimes that go unreported each year. No one really knows how many serious and even violent crimes go unreported each year, but the sad truth is that an unreported crime is usually a crime that will be *quickly repeated.* There are undisputed facts that are often ignored in any discussion of crime conducted by political leaders, media representatives, and public forums:

1.  It is absolutely impossible for any police agency or collection of agencies to enforce every code and law of the Penal Code of New York State, and

2.  The biggest deterrent to crime has always been cooperative support and vigilance of law-abiding citizens themselves.

The New York City Housing Authority tried for years to suppress the alarming news of the high growth of crime in the city's hundreds of public housing projects. From the time I was appointed to the force, I noticed that crime seemed to be growing and escalating at an incredible rate. Even more alarming to me was the fact that the age of the perpetrators was getting younger and younger, and the level of violence was getting worse!

For several decades, any serious crime committed in a poor or low-income black neighborhood seemed to get minimal or no news coverage at all. The average New York City resident had no idea that the epidemic of serious crimes being committed against innocent residents in the city's housing projects was virtually out of control. Sadly, it seemed that anything that took place in the so-called "ghetto" was of little or no concern to most New Yorkers, perhaps because "those people" were so far removed from their daily lives.

As time passed, the efforts of a few cops who, like myself, faced death in well-publicized confrontations involving deadly force and equally deadly criminals, began to provide clues to the general public that a growing terror was loose in the projects and heading their way.

The media gradually began to publish stories about some of the *good people* who lived in the city's housing projects, and the terrible crime and terror they had to contend with. As the abuse of drugs increased, so did heinous crimes; and the media and the public finally began to take notice.

I suspect that if the heinous crimes that were occurring in poor communities would have received proper press, then an early public outcry might have forced city officials to do more than was done to arrest the new crime epidemic. Unfortunately, the city did not act until the entire city was being affected physically and economically by a nearly uncontrollable crime epidemic.

When the city finally launched an "all-out effort" to curtail the crime crisis, inner-city citizens were already the unwilling targets of more than *three out of every four* serious crimes committed in New York City! To this day, most people in the United States don't realize that *more than nine out of every ten crime victims* in any poor or low-income community are black and Latino! Once the local and state governments finally realized that the "terror in the ghettos" was beginning to engulf the entire city, the cry went out for more police officers to patrol the streets of New York, with a high police presence in the ghetto.

As a black police officer assigned to work in the ghetto, I could almost feel myself becoming a "product" of, or at least an emotional and sometimes physical "victim" of, the reigning terror in the projects. Yet, I couldn't help but be an extremely active cop. I grew up in those high-rise neighborhoods, and I could feel the pain, fear, and desperation of the people who were trapped there by circumstance and poverty. My duty and conscience demanded that I continually expose myself to the hazards of every neighborhood I patrolled. Duty led me into all kinds of dangerous conditions and situations where I was forced to confront countless individual suspects who lived among, visited, and preyed upon the people residing in New York City's housing projects.

The things a police officer sees and gets involved with eventually begin to take their mental and physical toll. However, the combination of my aggressive law enforcement pace, my desire to provide safe living conditions for the families living in the projects, and the overabundance of felony crimes taking place right on my police beat, allowed me to effect a greater number of arrests in my first three years on the job than most New York police officers handle in six full years of service anywhere else.

This prolific enforcement action against so many offenders, in itself, helped enhance my expertise on local drug trafficking patterns. I quickly added valuable knowledge to what I had already learned as a project resident about how to know when drug activity was going down on my post. It required an intimate knowledge of the habits and actions of local street pushers and drug abusers.

Since growing drug abuse and trafficking were quickly spawning new levels of felony crime and violence, I had to be bold and stay alert all the time. I had to stay on guard from the moment I left my house until the moment I sank down into the easy chair in my living room at the end of a long tour. One reason I survived and succeeded as a cop in the housing projects was because I had acquired a keen ability to sense when drug activity was getting ready to take place or was in progress at a given location.

For one thing, I had learned that drug addicts, in their drive to get a fix, will often give themselves away unknowingly and without concern, along with the identification of their local pushers! I can still remember the hot Monday night on July 13, 1970, when I was again assigned to the four-to-midnight shift at the Farragut Housing Project in downtown Brooklyn. As usual, it was a pretty active night.

I had just teamed up with another officer to settle a domestic dispute and made a status call to Central at about 11:00 p.m. I had one hour left before my shift was over. I remembered that several days before, I had seen a large group of men with a few women assembled in front of 177 Sands Street. When I approached the group that day, they had dispersed quickly, and one man had ducked into the building and disappeared. By their actions, I had every reason to believe there had been some drug activity in progress.

I knew there was a growing drug problem at the Farragut Housing Projects, and I even knew some of the people who were involved. Since we were already at the same location, I told the other police officer (who was actually assigned to the adjoining post in that project), "I've got a growing drug problem on my post. I think I've got a line on the pusher behind a lot of the action. How would you like to help me put this guy out of business tonight? I think we can probably nail him before our shift is up."

After we mapped out a little strategy, we positioned ourselves in separate locations in a secluded area favored for drug activity. Once again, my "shy" group of men and women started to collect in front of 177 Sands Street at around 11:30 p.m. I maintained visual and radio contact with the other officer, although we had already agreed to wait until we saw several drug transactions go down before we would move in on the pusher. The pusher emerged from the building and started peddling his poison to the 15 or more junkies who had encircled him. He was so involved in selling his goods that he didn't notice me and my partner rapidly approaching his position.

When he finally saw us, it was too late. He tried to get away, and at the same time, he tossed a small brown object over a fence near the building. I was closest to him and was able to subdue him after a brief struggle. With the help of the other officer, I cuffed the pusher whom I identified as Swanson*. Then I jumped over the fence and recovered the brown paper bag Swanson had tried to throw away. While my prisoner watched, I carefully counted out 23 glassine envelopes, each of which contained a small amount of white powder that was later confirmed by lab tests to be heroin. These envelopes of heroin were selling for about $10 each at that time.

While the other officer provided backup, I searched Swanson's clothing and recovered a fully loaded .32-caliber pistol and about $150 in cash. I was pretty sure my suspect was a resident of Farragut, since it was normal for drug pushers (and their junkies) to prey on the same communities where they lived and purchased drugs. The people who were directly involved in the sale of drugs (such as my suspect), usually packed weapons to protect themselves from being ripped off (robbed) by other criminals. (You know times are rough when a "decent criminal" can't conduct a crime without protecting himself from other criminals!)

Swanson was convicted of the sale and possession of a controlled substance and was sentenced to a grand total of only 18 months in jail. (I saw this happen all too often.) The Farragut community, like many other drug-plagued communities across New

York City, had finally started to come together and speak out about the crimes and violence in their community. They knew that much of the crime in their area was directly linked to the increased sale and abuse of drugs in their streets, residential buildings, and playgrounds.

Drug abusers who do not work are almost certain to rob and steal from their neighbors (or their own families and relatives) to support their compulsive drug habits. Drug abusers and feuding drug dealers literally launched a relentless assault on poor communities in cities across America in the 70's that continues to this day. These thugs have kept innocent residents in these areas imprisoned in their own neighborhoods and in a constant state of fear.

People who live in public housing projects leave their apartments or homes and worry all day that their homes may be burglarized, their valuables stolen, and their living quarters ransacked in their absence. In some projects, it wasn't a question of "if" your apartment would be hit, it was a question of "when" and of "how bad" would it be hit? Many residents tried to take reasonable precautions by securing their residences with bars on the windows and extra locks on their doors. Project residents also knew they had to be extra careful on payday, which is usually on a Friday. Nearly every project neighborhood had its share of robbers who would lay in wait to rob residents of their hard-earned wages on every payday. A great number of these victims were also assaulted, and some of these attacks, I'm sad to say, were fatal.

Drug abusers in the City of New York come in all colors. They are not only black, white, or Latino, but they also include virtually every ethnic group and social stratum in America's greatest "melting pot" city. However, the greatest concentration of crime is committed in the poorer black and Latino neighborhoods *by predominantly black and Latino perpetrators!* A small number of white residents can be found in some of the ghetto communities around New York City, especially senior citizens. Senior citizens are one of the most vulnerable groups of people living in the ghetto. They have suffered immensely at the hands of violent, low-life criminals.

48

Since I was a compulsively aggressive neighborhood cop, I learned to know *who was doing what* in the criminal element of the communities I was assigned to patrol. All human beings have distinctive ways and patterns of doing things. Criminals are no different, despite their claims to the contrary. That is why there is such things as "repeat felons."

Every day of my career, I saw the grief caused by criminals who preyed on innocent victims and families living in the projects. It only made me more determined to bring to justice those who were committing heinous crimes in my assigned communities. I knew my only hope of success and personal safety lay in my ability to learn and recognize the behavior patterns of the small number of repeat felons who were constantly committing crimes in the communities under my jurisdiction.

After years of fighting crime and tracking criminal activity in so many housing project neighborhoods in New York City, I began to develop a good idea of who was behind certain types of felonies when they occurred in my assigned communities, whether they were burglaries, drug-dealing activities, muggings, or purse-snatching incidents. I knew who had committed such acts in the past, so I would first focus my attention on these past offenders before looking for new suspects. I learned quickly that whenever certain crimes were committed, went down, I would also see certain individuals "disappear" from the area until they thought things had cooled off. This "insider" knowledge helped me solve a great number of crimes because I knew the behavior patterns of many of the repeat felons in my patrol areas.

It is impossible to "overstate" the importance of the confidence I won with the people in communities around the city through fairness and consistent dedication to their personal well-being. Their cooperation and willing assistance were my greatest assets and law enforcement tools. These ongoing positive relationships were the key to my effectiveness as a career police officer serving residents in the nation's most difficult and dangerous neighborhoods.

The deplorable crime conditions in the Fort Greene and Farragut Housing Projects typified the conditions plaguing more than 85 percent of New York City's public housing projects and the other poorer communities it contained. Entire families were involved in drug trafficking and drug pushing in the street and even from their apartments. All a cop had to do was lay in wait in the stairwell or on the floor of the apartment where drugs were being sold, and he would collar or apprehend drug abusers in possession of controlled substances all day and night.

It definitely wasn't hard for an aggressive police officer to enhance his monthly productivity in the presence of so much blatant criminal activity. All he had to do was be observant and keep a mental or written record of all the abnormal behavior he observed on his post. Many times, I decided to go "incognito" (with my identity concealed) so I could gather some firsthand information about problems on my post. If the people of one of my neighborhoods became outraged with a given condition, I would get anonymous phone calls at the precinct telling me what was going on, what went down, and who was involved. I was able to solve quite a few top felony crimes due to a phone call or being tipped off by someone who knew me from the area.

One incident really struck close to home on August 15, 1974. I'll never forget it as long as I live. I was working the four-to-midnight tour again. When I reported to precinct headquarters before going to my assignment, someone said, "Hey, Lewis, there was another homicide at the Farragut houses. They don't know who did it yet." I put on my uniform and impatiently stood for roll call before hurrying out to my post at the Farragut Housing Projects to assist in the investigation. When I reached the crime scene, the police officers told me, "The victim was, uh, Shelly Breeland*. Let's see, she was a black female, about 28 years of age..."

I didn't hear the rest of the answer because my mind was flooded with pleasant memories of better times and fresh emotions of bitter loss. Shelly and I grew up together in the Red Hook Houses, and at one time, we had even dated. I had lost contact with her for a number of years. After taking a moment to regain my thoughts, I took a deep breath and started the serious business of conducting an investigation with the assistance of another police officer named Robert Moron, one of the best officers in the projects.

One of the Housing Police officers from the day tour told me the murder took place around 3:00 in the afternoon. He also said, "By the way, several units from the NYPD's anti crime task force arrived at the scene too. As usual, they were very uncooperative." We had learned the hard way that that was "standard operating procedure" for some members of NYPD. They never dared to step foot in the housing projects alone, so whenever they had to respond to any emergency in a New York City housing project, they always responded in vehicles and in groups of three or more when possible. With the investigation I was faced with that night, I didn't give the NYPD officers on the case one thought. I would need to draw on every insider source I could find for this case.

I began by contacting everyone I believed could give me some information about the homicide that day. It didn't take me long to hit pay dirt this time. I located a female contact who lived in Farragut Houses who knew exactly who the assailant was and where I could find her. She even gave me the names of two people who had witnessed the incident.

The suspect was Jean Morton*, and she was thought to be hiding in apartment 6F of the project at 191 Sands Street. Officer Moron and I were walking to that location when a black man intercepted us and said, "I'm Marcell Green*. My aunt is Jean Morton. She wants to talk to you. She's in apartment 6F. I'll take you there if you want to meet her."

We accompanied Green to apartment 6F where he used a key to open the door to the apartment. We followed him into the apartment, and he asked us to wait in the living room while he went into the back to get his aunt. Given the nature of the crime we were investigating, I knew my partner and I had to carefully monitor our actions and anticipate every possible move of the suspect. I was especially sensitive to the possibly volatile frame of mind she might exhibit.

An unusual silence and stillness seemed to come over the apartment for a few seconds (they don't tell you about these things in the police academy), then the suspense was broken by the sound of footsteps coming from the rear of the apartment. It was about 5:00 in the evening, and it was still hot. In the harsh light of bare lightbulbs, I couldn't help but notice that the apartment was poorly kept. The sofa and two chairs in the living room were in poor condition, and there was debris all over the floor.

All of a sudden, Marcell Green appeared, followed by a terribly frightened-looking woman. She was small in stature, standing maybe five feet high. She must have weighed every bit of 95 to 100 pounds, and her black hair was very short. She stopped about ten feet away from Officer Moron and I and just stared at us quietly.

"Ms. Morton?" I asked, and waited until she nodded. "Your nephew, Mr. Green, told us you would like to talk to us. Is that true?" When she said "Yes" in a low voice, I continued, "I am Officer Richard Lewis, and this is Officer Robert Moron. Why don't we all sit down?"

When Ms. Morton nervously sat on the edge of the sofa, I looked into her eyes and said, "Ms. Morton, some sort of altercation took place in Farragut today. Somehow a young woman named Shelly Breeland was stabbed to death, and her assailant ran away. We have learned that you might have some important information about this case. Is that right?" She nodded again." In fact, we have reason to believe that you were the other person in the confrontation. Can you tell us what happened this afternoon?"

When Ms. Morton nodded and looked down, I advised her that I would have to read her her rights before speaking to her, and she said it was all right. Taking a small, well-worn, laminated card from my memo book, I began to read the Miranda rights, memorialized by so many cop shows over the last two decades:

"You have the right to remain silent and refuse to answer any question. Anything you do say may be used against you in a court of law. You have the right to consult an attorney before speaking to the police and to have an attorney present during any questioning now or in the future. If you cannot afford an attorney, one will be provided for you without cost. If you do not have an attorney available, you have the right to remain silent until you have had an opportunity to consult with one. Now that I have advised you of your rights, are you willing to answer questions without an attorney present?"

I asked Jean Morton six statements in the Miranda rights to acknowledge that she understood each of the questions and she confirmed that she did, and that she was willing to talk. (I was determined to "walk the line" on this arrest. I didn't want anything in this investigation to be lost or voided by some illegality or legal loophole later on.) Then I said, "Tell me what transpired between you and Shelly Breeland, the deceased," and Jean began speaking in a low, trembling voice.

"It was about 2:30 p.m., and I was walking around the project area looking for my 12-year-old niece, Lisa. When I walked by Shelly, who was seated on a bench with another woman at the rear of the building at 224 York Street, Shelly said, 'There goes that b—h.'

"Then Shelly jumped up and pulled off the wig I was wearing. Before I could do anything, she grabbed my hair and started pulling it. Then we started fighting, and it went on for a while until a man came over and parted us. After we had been separated, Shelly continued to shout obscenities at me. Then she pulled off her shoe and came at me, striking me in my face and head with the heel."

Jean paused for a moment and looked down. Then she took a deep breath and, in what appeared to be a remorseful tone, she said, "I pulled a knife from my pocketbook because she was hurting me real bad with the shoe, and I hit at her with the knife," while using her right hand to demonstrate the stabbing motion she had used. Again Jean paused briefly and tears started to flow from her eyes down her face as she said, "I felt the knife blade go into her chest, and she screamed out, 'Oh Lord!' and turned to walk away. Then she fell to the ground, and I got real scared and ran, dropping the knife at the same time. I didn't mean to kill her! I didn't mean it!" Jean muttered, moving her head from side to side. "God knows I didn't mean to do it."

I paused a few seconds and then said, "Jean, do you know why Shelly attacked you?" Morton nodded and said, "She said it was over her man. Shelly accused me of messing with her boyfriend. And this wasn't the first time we had words, but it...but I never thought it would come to what happened today." Then I asked, "Were you and Shelly involved with the same man?" She answered, "At first I was, but after I found out he was seeing her, I stopped; but she kept on accusing me of messing with him."

"Is there anything else you want to tell me before we go to the police station?" I asked, and she replied no. "Ms. Morton, police procedure requires me to put handcuffs on you for the ride downtown, but it won't hurt." After I put the handcuffs on her, I called Central on my radio and asked for a patrol car to meet me in front of 191 Sands Street to pick up a homicide suspect.

Any time I made an arrest, I had to shuffle a small mountain of paperwork, but a homicide arrest called for much more. I had to send notifications to Housing Police Headquarters and the Brooklyn District Attorney's office. When we arrived at Brooklyn Central Booking, which at the time was located in the 84th Precinct, Jean Morton was booked, searched, and placed in a cell, or holding pen, until I had completed the required paperwork.

The suspect agreed to be interviewed by the assistant district attorney on videotape, so I was also asked to sit in on the interview as the arresting officer in the homicide. After the interview, I placed Jean back into the holding pen to await arraignment on the charge of murder. Two witnesses to the incident came forward, and they too were interviewed by the assistant D.A. I had to testify before the Brooklyn Grand Jury along with the two witnesses, and the jury later indicted Jean for murder. She pleaded guilty to first degree manslaughter and was sentenced to three to five years in the New York State House of Correction for Women.

Crime was escalating all over the city, along with my arrest record and fatigue level. My life and the lives of the people I was sworn to protect were placed in jeopardy on a number of occasions involving necessary and deadly force in the line of duty. Just in my work with the Fort Greene and Farragut Housing Projects alone, I was involved in every kind of arrest on the books, including homicides, felony assaults, and countless robberies. It was getting so bad that people were afraid to walk the streets, even in broad daylight, but especially at night.

Ironically, my involvement with Jean Morton's family wasn't over yet. Nearly two years after the arrest of Morton, in the midst of the growing crime spree, I received information that Marcell Green was pushing drugs on the streets of the Farragut Housing Project. On June 17, 1976, I was working the four-to-midnight beat as usual, when I saw Marcell Green from a distance. He was standing at the side of a project building at 190 York Street with several men around him. It was about 6:45 in the evening, and it was still nice and bright outside.

I knew by the looks of things that Marcell was dealing drugs at that location, so I moved closer and took a position out of his sight where I could observe his every move and action. As I was watched Marcell conduct his criminal drug sales that beautiful summer evening, I couldn't help but recall the time I first met him almost two years before, when I arrested his aunt for murder.

I watched Marcell conduct several drug transactions before I called by two-way radio to ask another patrolman to meet me on the side of 190 York Street to assist in an arrest for the sale of a controlled substance. After I briefed the other police officer, who was also assigned to patrol the Farragut Houses that tour, we approached Green from opposite directions to cut off his chances of escape.

Marcell was too involved in peddling his poison to the men around him to notice either one of us approaching him. When he finally saw us, we were on either side of him. All of his would-be customers suddenly walked way from him, but the cop who was working with me grabbed Marcell's last buyer while I focused my attention on Marcell himself.

By that point, a third Housing Police officer had arrived at the location. Marcell started to put his right hand into his right pocket, but I quickly said, "Uh-unh, Marcell. Keep your hands where I can see them. You are under arrest!" That was when he tried to bolt away from us. I had to knock him to the ground and use necessary force to subdue him. I remember that he was dressed in some pretty flashy clothes, because when he resisted arrest, his nice jacket and pants were ripped and his shoes were scuffed up badly in the struggle.

During my search, I discovered some interesting things in Green's pockets. I found a quantity of glassine envelopes containing a white powder (which was later confirmed to be heroin), along with $387 in small bills and some change. Marcell was booked for the sale and possession of a controlled substance and resisting arrest. When I looked at his rap sheet (a record of his past arrests), I discovered that Marcell Green had an extensive arrest history. He had been arrested 15 or more times, dating all the way back to 1962, in Altanta, Georgia, where he had served more than five years in jail!

Green's police record indicated that he had been arrested for grand larceny auto, burglary, possession of a loaded firearm, robbery, and criminal possession of a controlled substance, just to mention a few. At the time that I arrested him, Green was out on bail pending a Class-A felony trial on charges of committing murder while in the commission of a felony. At Green's arraignment hearing, the judge placed a very high bail on Marcell at the request of the ADA, due to his past arrest record and the fact that he had the murder and robbery cases pending.

About two months after the arrest, while waiting to go to trial for his pending cases, Marcell Green, along with another inmate, escaped from the Riker's Island Correctional Facility. This maximum security prison is located in the middle of the East River and surrounded by the Bronx, Queens, and Manhattan. The only way anyone can get on or off the island is by crossing a well-secured and closely guarded bridge, or by boat.

Evidently, Marcell and his accomplice chose to swim across the East River to one of the three boroughs surrounding the prison. It is believed that they swam to the shore somewhere near La Guardia Airport in Queens, since that was the closest point to Riker's Island, and the water isn't as rugged in that area. Once the fugitives reached the shore, they robbed a woman in her home near the location where authorities believe they came ashore. The victim later told police that the two men told her they were with the government, and they wanted to use her phone to contact their office. They convinced her by using their prison identification cards as a means of identifying themselves. Once she let them into her house, they robbed her of about $200 in cash.

The woman, who happened to be white, said she feared for her life the whole time the fugitives were in her house. She had been alone when she invited what she thought to be two city employees into her home to use her phone. They quickly overpowered her and threatened to kill her if she didn't cooperate with them. After taking what cash she had and some of her husband's clothes, the two escaped prisoners tied her up and left the house. When the woman's husband came home from work that evening, he found his wife tied up, but unharmed. He untied her and immediately called the police after she told him about her traumatic experience with the two escaped prisoners from Riker's Island. By that time, state authorities already knew the two prisoners were missing from prison. A massive search was launched since both escapees were considered extremely dangerous.

I first learned about Marcell's daring escape while watching a television news program. Then Police Headquarters sent a notification to all commands, informing of the escape of Marcell Green and another prisoner. That same day, my commanding officer called me into his office to personally ask me to be on the lookout for Marcell since I was the last officer to arrest him. He thought Green might try to go back into the Farragut Houses area he had frequented before his arrest.

I took the captain's words very seriously because I was *positive* that is what would happen. I went to the Farragut Housing Projects and contacted a number of tenants I knew I could count on to contact me or the desk officer if Marcell Green came into the Farragut projects. Just as I suspected, Marcell Green did return to the housing project on a cool rainy day in October. When I saw him, he had a white raincoat draped over his shoulders, and he was wearing a black hat. My contacts had warned me that Marcell was carrying a gun under that raincoat. With this in mind, knowing how dangerous Marcell was, I called for a backup. This was a time for "good judgment to get the better part of valor."

I watched Marcell from a distance, as he stood in front of a project building at 220 York Street, talking with some men who were "local undesirables." As I watched, one black male who had just walked by me went directly to Marcell and said something to him. Green immediately glanced over toward 190 Sands Street along with the other men around him.

I was standing out of sight behind a wall in front of the building. When I made the call for backup, I told the dispatcher about the situation and told her to tell responding police units to come in the "silent response mode" without lights or sirens. Only two or three minutes after I called for backup, I was "made" (seen)! I watched helplessly as Marcell Green hurried to a parked car on the side of the building and sped away before my backup team could arrive on the scene.

When Green made his dash to the car, I immediately radioed Central with an update of the situation. When the backup team arrived, I told them I had lost sight of Marcell when he drove off in the car. I couldn't tell them which way he went, nor was I close enough to accurately describe his getaway car. It was disappointing for me to get so close to a crucial arrest only to see my suspect vanish from view, while I was helpless to stop him.

Not long after that incident, I heard some more news about Marcell Green. A week or so after he managed to slip away from me, Marcell was killed in a shoot-out with the police somewhere in Nassau County, Long Island, during an armed robbery attempt on a bank. Marcell Green died the way he lived at the age of 32. He exemplifies the dangerous qualities of the repeat felons who have besieged and terrorized black and Latino communities throughout the City of New York. These were also the kinds of people I could expect to meet close-up and face-to-face on a daily basis as a black cop assigned to night patrol in the housing projects of New York.

The two most innocent and vulnerable groups targeted by ghetto terror are the children and the elderly. As the situation grew worse in the projects, I was thrilled when I was finally able to purchase a two-family house in Queens in September of 1979, and move my mother and father out of the Red Hook Housing Projects in South Brooklyn. There had been a great increase in crime against the elderly there.

It seemed like 1978 had come and gone, and as usual, it had been a very busy, tedious year for me. My productivity had continued to increase in terms of both the quality and quantity of my arrests, and I had already received a considerable number of commendations. My commanding officers had begun to place me on special assignments whenever they had serious crime conditions surface in certain difficult locations. On January 5, 1979, I was again called into the captain's office.

"Lewis, there have been an alarming number of assaults and robberies on elderly people in the Red Hook Projects in South Brooklyn. According to our reports, the perpetrator follows his victims to their apartments before committing a 'push-in' assault and robbery. The pattern is all too familiar. These 'push-in bandits' like to come up behind their victims just as they unlock their apartment doors. Then they push their victims into the apartments and attack them inside the rooms before robbing them of whatever cash and valuables they can find."

"Lewis, I want you on this one. You can pick a partner to work with you if you like, but I want to see some results. I called you in on this case because I'm confident you can close it with a solid arrest. I really need to give Central a good report on this case, and fast. This string of violent robberies is getting worse, and I'm afraid somebody's gonna get killed if we don't stop it. Good luck."

I was surprised by the unusual level of senseless violence indicated by the crime reports in this case. Some of the elderly victims had been hospitalized due to the injuries they had suffered during these attacks. The first thing I did after leaving the captain's office was to pull all of the past mugging reports on elderly victims from the Red Hook Housing Project's active case files. I found about 20 reports of attacks in the last two months alone! In almost every incident, the victims could not give an adequate description of their assailant.

As I went through the crime reports, a number of things kept going through my mind. First of all, I kept thinking of my elderly parents, who still lived in Red Hook. I didn't want my mother or father to become an assault and robbery victim. I also kept wondering how much time the original detective assigned to this crisis was devoting to the case. Although I was still basically a foot patrolman, I had been asked to work on cases that were causing public alarm in the past, and each time, I was able to bring to justice the person or persons responsible for the commission of those specific crimes.

I knew the detective bureau was seriously undermanned, and though I had asked to be placed in that bureau many times, my request continued to be denied for reasons unknown or not stated. "At least my superiors know they can depend on me to get results in major cases," I told myself. As I thought about my unsuccessful attempts to become a detective, I became even more adamant in my desire to make an arrest in the Red Hook "push-in robber" case.

As I continued to pour over the reports, one report caught my eye. This report described a brutal attack on an 84-year-old man that just didn't fit the complete picture painted by the other reports. This crime was a little different from the others because it wasn't a push-in robbery. In this attack, the assailant knocked on the victim's door and claimed to be a postman, saying he had a special delivery letter for the victim.

When the elderly gentlemen opened his apartment door, the "postman" handed him what he thought was a letter. When he took it, the assailant struck him in the face with his fist, causing him to fall to the floor. Then the attacker pushed his way into the apartment and hit his elderly victim again, knocking him unconscious. The robber took $40 in cash from the elderly man's pockets along with a gold ring and some other small items of value from the apartment. When the victim's wife returned from the store, she found her husband on the floor bleeding profusely from a head wound suffered in his fall to the hard floor during the brutal attack. She immediately called the police.

I began my investigation by interviewing the 84-year-old victim, named Jesus Belasco*. The head wound he received during the robbery required a number of stitches, but he recovered. Unfortunately, he was unable to give me a useful description of his attacker, so I decided to interview Rene Donner*, a 70-year-old female victim who had been attacked and robbed *twice* by the perpetrator!

During the first attack, the assailant warned Ms. Donner not to go to the police or he would kill her, so she didn't report the incident. Three weeks later, the man attacked Ms. Donner again, giving her two black eyes and a badly bruised face—all for only $11 in cash and some groceries! Ms. Donner had "had enough." She called the police immediately after the attacker fled her apartment. Unfortunately, Ms. Donner was also unable to give me any useful information to help me apprehend her attacker. I ran into the same problem with every victim I interviewed.

Finally, I decided to try the cops assigned to patrol the Red Hook Project. Two of the officers working the familiar four-to-midnight tour remembered an arrest made a year earlier, involving a suspect who liked to mug elderly victims. Based on that information, I pulled and viewed the Red Hook arrest records for the last two years and I finally hit pay dirt!

A 19-year-old black male named Daren Shadow had been arrested four times for assaulting senior citizens! I obtained his photograph from the police photo lab and placed it among five "dummy" photos to create what we call a "photo array." When I began to show the photo array to the various "push-in mugger" victims, one of the victims made a positive identification of Daren Shadow as his attacker. I was relieved and excited. I had identified my prime suspect!

On the sixth of January in 1979, about 24 hours after I was assigned to the case, I located Daren Shadow at his apartment in the Red Hook Housing Project. He was brought to the police record office there so I could interview him. After about 40 minutes, Daren (who had been on parole since October) confessed to mugging more than a dozen senior citizens! He even told me how he set up and committed his crimes!

> "I'd just wait around until I saw them heading for a building. Then I'd just follow them into the elevator and wait. They never suspected me. I just left the elevator when they left, and all I had to do was wait until they opened their apartment door.
>
> "It was beautiful, man...I'd just rush them from behind and put my hand over their mouths so they wouldn't make any noise. The halls are pretty much deserted most of the time, so as long as there's no noise, I could do whatever I wanted. I'd push them into the apartment and beat on 'em a while so they would pay attention to my warnings about calling the cops. Then I'd

*take whatever money I could find on 'em, along with any valu-
ables I saw, and then I'd leave."*

Daren also said he would sometimes disguise himself as a
Housing Authority employee or mailman and knock on the doors
of elderly people he knew lived alone, hoping to lure them into
opening their doors. We later secured a court order and searched
his apartment, recovering a great deal of property which belonged
to many of his victims.

Many of my associates wondered how I won a confession from
Daren Shadow. In retrospect, I think it was because over the years,
I had acquired the ability to win people's confidence, whether they
were criminals or complainants. This ability helped me get information from people who refused to even talk to other detectives
and police officers, and allowed me to solve all kinds of major felonies involving homicides and multiple or serial offenses.

What made Daren Shadow's case so unique was the chronic
and almost pathological nature of his crimes. Due to his past record of robbery and assault against the elderly, the court gave him
six to ten years in jail. Sadly, the story doesn't end there. I told the
assistant district attorney at the time that I thought Daren had a
mental problem, but the comment was essentially dismissed.

Approximately seven years after Shadow's arrest, he was released after serving just over five years in jail. By the summer of
1987, I was working as a detective assigned to serious felony crimes
committed in the Red Hook Projects. Once again, senior citizens
were being assaulted and robbed with alarming frequency. When
two victims died as a result of the brutal beatings they had received, I was called by the captain of the detective division.

"Lewis, I'm getting real worried about all these attacks on the
elderly. It is getting out of hand. It looks like we're not doing our
job. I'm getting a lot of pressure from the chief of the detective
division to make an arrest—and fast! I want you and your partner
to give this matter all of your attention. Now that there are deaths

involved with this mess, these incidents can no longer be considered just a robbery spree. This guy is a killer. *He has to be stopped!"*

The captain was still talking when something suddenly jogged my memory. *Didn't I arrest somebody about seven years ago for preying on the elderly?* I thought. *What was his name...? Now that guy had a history of physically assaulting the elderly too!*

When I was sure about my hunch, I interrupted the captain and explained my theory. I told him, "Captain, if my man is out of jail, then I would bet a year's pay that he is behind all of these attacks." The match seemed almost too obvious. The *modus operandi* in the latest series of assaults and robberies perfectly fit the man I had put behind bars years ago. This time I went to my *own* arrest files, which I had maintained over the years, and pulled out the folder on *Daren Shadow.*

To make a long story short, a number of victims picked Daren out of a police "lineup" without hesitation. After I interviewed him, he made statements to me after acknowledging his legal rights that were used against him at his trial. He was convicted and sentenced to 20 years behind bars. Daren Shadow's case tragically demonstrates why repeat felons should be put behind bars for such a time that they will no longer be a threat to society. Had the prosecutor's office taken my advice concerning the mental state of Daren Shadow, it might have saved the lives of the defenseless senior citizens who died as a result of the assaults they suffered while being robbed.

---

*The names of these individuals have been changed or altered for reasons of safety, anonymity, and privacy, and bear no actual relationship to persons alive or dead. The situations and incidents, however, occurred exactly as described in this book, and in official court records.

# Chapter 5

# Beyond the Edge of Courage

*W*hen you face a life and death situation as a police officer, you also face an inner struggle to keep your innermost fears from causing you to make a wrong decision. It is easier said than done, but you have to control your faculties if you want to make the right decision on whether or not to use *deadly force.* Any time a police officer draws and discharges his firearm in a situation, it should be because *all other options* to control or manage a situation have been exhausted.

I was faced with "the ultimate decision" on June 28, 1977. I realized long ago that when I get out of bed in the morning, I have no idea what is in store for me on that given day. I think if we did know what was ahead, we would rather stay in bed!

It was on a Tuesday, a beautiful June morning. I was scheduled to work my usual shift—the four-to-midnight shift. That year, I was still attending the John Jay College of Criminal Justice, working towards my bachelor's degree in criminal justice. I had to attend two morning classes before reporting for work, and as usual, I had a lot on my mind during those difficult years. Things had not been going well in my marriage. My wife was giving me some serious problems because I had decided to get involved with the church and she was unhappy about it. She retaliated by making life as miserable as possible for me (shortly afterward, she suddenly left my four-year-old daughter and I for a doctor in Virginia).

I kissed my little girl good-bye and left my apartment at around 7:30 a.m. After attending the two morning classes, I left the college at approximately 11:30 that morning and headed for the Red Hook Housing Projects in South Brooklyn, where my parents lived. I was thinking I would feel better about things if I logged some miles doing sprints around the track located at the stadium near Red Hook before going to work.

The John Jay College of Criminal Justice is located at 445 West 59th Street in Manhattan. Since the West Side Highway was being demolished at the time, I was forced to drive through the more congested streets of the city. I drove south on 10th Avenue and turned east on 14th Street, enjoying the change of scenery despite the congestion.

As I crossed Manhattan's famous 5th Avenue and headed toward Broadway and 14th Street near Union Square, I spotted several white males running and shouting, "Help! Police! Police!" Now I became a police officer because I just couldn't ignore people who ask for help. I had a reputation as an "active" or "aggressive" police officer because I responded to people and situations out of a deep instinct of right and wrong. That is where the saying, "Once a cop, always a cop" comes from. If you are out there really doing your job, the job will become part of your being. I couldn't help "being a cop" whether I was "on duty" or "off duty." I think it is the same with any good cop.

I made a quick right turn onto Broadway and hurriedly parked my car on the left hand side of the street in a bus stop. I double-checked my off-duty revolver, ammunition loads, and cuffs, and then sprinted to the corner of Broadway and 14th Street. Turning left, I ran westward towards 5th Avenue. There I caught up with one of the white males and identified myself as a police officer.

"Catch that man in the blue suit!" he shouted between deep breaths, pointing toward two black males walking about 50 yards ahead. One of the men was walking with his arms around the other man, who was wearing a red shirt and tan pants. The rapid exchange between myself and the elderly man was so quick, that I didn't fully understand *why* three elderly men were chasing the black suspect. I took off in pursuit of the man in the blue suit, and I thought I heard the man behind me say the black male had a gun...

As I approached the two black men, I shouted, "Halt, police!" At that point, the man in the blue suit looked over his left shoulder and saw me running towards them. He suddenly began to run, leaving the other man behind. (I suspected that the man in the red shirt was either a friend, or a total stranger enlisted unwillingly to decoy pursuers.)

I was gaining on the suspect, and I again yelled, "Police! Stop!" Then I saw the man reach behind his back and under the blue jacket as he turned left at the southeast corner of 5th Avenue. A wariness came over me, and I felt irritated that there were so many civilians on those crowded streets. *Something inside me caused me to abruptly stop just as I reached the corner.* I quickly surveyed my surroundings as I drew my off-duty firearm—a five-cylinder, snub-nosed revolver with a short two-inch barrel—from the angle holster hidden on the inside of my left leg.

With my gun in my right hand and my badge in the other, I decided to walk directly out into the vehicle and pedestrian traffic on 14th Street because I couldn't see the 5th Avenue side of the building bordering the corner of 5th Avenue and 14th Street. While standing out in the street, I could see the south corner of the building. The man with the blue suit was located only a few feet from the corner with his back up against the wall. He was side-stepping slowly to his left.

He hadn't noticed me yet, because when I stepped onto 14th Street, I stayed concealed behind a street vendor selling hot dogs. (I planned to draw fire away from the vendor and any other civilians in the event of gunplay.) The suspect had his right hand concealed under his suit jacket, and he was staring intensely at the corner, as if he expected someone or something to round the corner at any moment.

I quickly stepped away from the vendor and made sure I was completely on the suspect's "blind side" before I approached him. That is when I saw the gun he was concealing under his jacket. A terribly anxious and painful fear came over me. I felt like something had pierced me right through the heart! My knees seemed to weaken suddenly, and I was aching all over.

I took a deep breath and shouted, "Police! Drop it!"

The man instantly turned his head in complete surprise and stared at me. My eyes were fastened on him, and I could see a kind of smile come over his face. As our eyes met, I saw a cold, hard, fierce look in his eyes as he raised his gun and pointed it at me. In that instant, I knew that he wasn't going to drop the gun. In fact, every fiber in my being knew he was going to shoot me!

That is when I squeezed off two rounds in rapid succession. I watched as the man fell to the ground as if in slow motion, mortally wounded, with his gun clinched tightly in his right hand. There was quite a number of people on the street at the time of the shooting, which took place in front of a technical school of some kind.

Everything in my body seemed to go numb, and my mind was paralyzed in a stupor. In retrospect, I guess I was experiencing a form of extreme emotional trauma as a result of having to shoot the man. In a fog-like daze, I bent down on one knee to take the gun out of the fallen man's hand. While I was in the process of removing the gun, I heard a voice behind me ask, "Are you a cop?" I didn't respond until I heard it for a second time. My mouth just wasn't working right. "Are you on the job?" When I could finally look up, I saw a white man dressed in dark pants and a white shirt with the sleeves rolled up slightly past his wrists, standing a little to my left. He was holding a snub-nosed Detective Special .38-caliber revolver in his hand.

A crowd had already started to collect around me and the fallen man when the man with the gun identified himself as a police lieutenant. After I told him I was a cop, and he saw my shield dangling in front of me from a chain around my neck, he explained that he worked at One Police Plaza where the New York City Police Department Headquarters is located. "Are you all right?" he asked. When I nodded yes, he said he was going to call for assistance on the police radio in his unmarked police car parked on the corner.

By that time, the elderly white men who had been chasing the fallen suspect arrived at the scene. One of the men said he was the owner of a men's clothing store located on East 14th Street. He said the suspect (later identified as Johnny Buck*, a resident of Jersey City, New Jersey) had just robbed his store at gunpoint. He had also taken a wallet from one of the customers, who was also at the shoot-out location.

I recovered the man's wallet from Buck's right rear pants pocket. Several people had witnessed the entire incident, including the hot dog vendor and a schoolteacher, who told me I was very lucky that I shot the suspect before he shot me. The police lieutenant returned and told me help was on its way. Meanwhile, I disarmed the suspect's .22-caliber Ruger 23 revolver. It was fully loaded with six live rounds that could have been sent hurtling at me or at some innocent civilians. The incident made front-page headlines in the *New York Post* and the *New York Daily News*, and was the lead story for most of New York City's radio and television news broadcasts that day.

Later on, law enforcement authorities confirmed that Johnny Buck had been responsible for more than a dozen armed robberies of stores in the 14th Street area over a period of three months. Evidently, he would come into New York City to hold up a store, and then calmly catch a train back to New Jersey. He had done prison time for a number of serious crimes, including assault with a gun, and robbery, and was wanted by police in New Jersey for attempted murder. Buck was a hard-core criminal who died the way he lived.

I didn't make it back home until 1:00 the following afternoon, thanks to all the paperwork and the endless debriefings and interviews conducted by the police brass and the assistant district attorney. (These investigative interviews are standard procedure any time a firearm is discharged, and especially when a suspect is shot or killed.)

I was so restless that I couldn't sleep because my mind was still focused on the events of the previous afternoon. Finally, I called my father and he prayed and talked with me. I also prayed to God that I would never have to go through an incident like that again, but I would face yet another ultimate challenge in the decade to come as you will see in another chapter.

I was summoned to testify before the grand jury, and I told my entire story to them, again as a matter of standard procedure. I was nervous the entire time I was testifying before the grand jury. I don't know why, however. I guess it was just a natural reaction.

I was only asked one question by the grand jury. One of the men on the panel asked, "Why did you shoot the perpetrator?" My reply came quickly, without unnecessary thought: "I shot the suspect to keep him from shooting me." I could only think to myself, *I pray that I never have to go through something of this nature again!* After the hearing, my commanding officer told me to take time off for as long as I needed so I could "get myself together." That was one of the few times I ever remember the police department showing such consideration for me.

On November 25, 1977, New York City Mayor Beame presented me with the police department's highest award, the Medal of Honor "for an act of extraordinary bravery, intelligently performed in the line of duty at imminent personal risk of life and with the knowledge of the danger involved."

While any law enforcement officer faces significantly more risk in the performance of his duties than most other occupations, statistically there are only a small minority of "above average cops" who will readily pull their weapons and fire them in situations where deadly physical force is deemed necessary. (I am not referring to "trigger-happy" or careless police officers. I'm talking about officers who will look right down a hostile gun barrel and return deadly fire with determination, professionalism, and good judgment.) I have been in or around more than a dozen shootings. In seven of those firefights, I had to personally fire my weapon at armed suspects while in "harm's way" myself.

I can't count the number of life and death situations I have faced as a police officer. At one time, it seemed as if I attracted guns and gunfire. Given the 20 years I spent patrolling and conducting felony investigations in New York City's highest crime areas in the housing projects, it stands to reason that I would see more and be involved in more dangerous situations each year than most police officers encounter in their entire careers.

I never cease to be amazed at how news media reporters and producers can arbitrarily portray the normal conditions of an average police officer as something far above average, when there are above-average (and typically non-white) police officers assigned to far more hazardous settings like the projects who go above and beyond the call of duty every day! Yet, given a choice between shooting footage a mile from a TV station or venturing into more dangerous and predominately non-white neighborhoods for a "cop shot," the prime-time news producers usually choose the easier and safer route. Unfortunately, this paints a totally inaccurate and biased picture of law enforcement and crime prevention in any city.

I still remember seeing a national news segment in the late 1980's honoring a white police officer who simply did his duty by comforting a white woman who had been pinned down by debris from a collapsing crane in Manhattan. This man was made a national hero by the news media and television industries, although he was simply doing what any good police officer or human being is supposed to do, and at no risk to himself.

In August of 1977, another police officer happened to write a traffic summons for an illegally parked car and went on his way. When it was discovered that the car belonged to David Berkowitz, the notorious "Son of Sam" murderer, that officer was elevated to the status of hero and national celebrity simply for citing a parking violation! On any other day, most Americans working in urban areas make snide remarks about police issuing traffic citations. "They oughta get those guys out chasing real murderers and rapists instead of bothering working citizens who can't find a parking place."

This irritation of thousands of dedicated non-white police officers around the nation is carried over to the motion picture and television entertainment industries as well. For decades, they tended to portray "courageous cops" as being almost exclusively white males or females. I am glad to see that this trend is beginning to change, but the industry still has a long way to go. There is no question that this nation desperately needs some real-life heroes from time to time, but I fervently wish our media representatives would make the investment in time and effort to find *genuine heroes* at work among us, regardless of their color, economic and occupational status, religious preference, or place of residence.

One thing is sure: There is no comparison between those trying to "play the role" of a cop before a camera and the real thing. When you confront an armed individual, a certain indescribable fear comes over you that defies open expression because it is an internal feeling. Truly courageous cops ride their inner fears. They commit to the danger they face without concern for their personal safety.

Job responsibility is one thing in police work; courage is another. Going "above and beyond the edge of courage" is altogether a totally different ball game. When an officer knowingly goes beyond the call of duty and steps in harm's way, he or she has entered a dimension shared by less than one-half of one percent of all law enforcement personnel.

Sometimes I felt like the cops working the tough housing project beats lived in that dimension *all the time.* In some of those projects, you might be called a hero simply for surviving longer than a week on the beat during certain crime seasons when violence seemed to blossom everywhere.

In many of the housing projects, we encountered *entire families* that were involved in ongoing criminal activity, from the parents down to the youngest child. These situations only made our job tougher, because we had to deal with the whole family during any investigation, instead of just one suspect. One time, I received a call notifying me that a young black male had pulled out a gun in front of one of the Farragut Housing Project buildings at 191 Sands Street. The suspect was still there when I arrived, but the moment he saw me, he dropped the gun and fled. By the time I had picked up the loaded gun he had discarded, I had lost any chance of catching him in a chase.

Since I knew who he was and where he lived, I wasn't worried about apprehending him. I vouchered the gun and wrote up a firearms complaint on the youth, Mark Dobbins*, who was 17 years of age. He belonged to one of the few problem families we had living in the Farragut Housing Projects. The Dobbins clan was a large family including numerous teenage and adult members. Members of the family were literally pushing drugs from their first-floor apartment as well as in the street.

The Dobbins family was so big that the City Housing Authority had to give them a second apartment by knocking the wall out of an adjacent apartment to make larger accommodations. Mr. Dobbins was an alcoholic, while his wife was a sweet church woman *who had no control over the kids.*

During the previous year, I had arrested a number of people for purchasing drugs from their apartment by using "stakeouts." (The first white male I ever arrested was caught buying drugs from the Dobbins' apartment in the Farragut Housing Project.) Whoever was handling the operation for the family was careful to never open the door when making a sale. Buyers had to slip their money under the door and wait until the quantity of drugs they requested was slipped back under the door from the apartment.

Each time, I entered the project building at 191 Sands Street and waited in the stairwell nearest the Dobbins' apartment until someone would come and make a drug buy. I would unscrew the lightbulb in the stairwell, turn my radio down or completely off, and watch everything going on through the window on the stairwell door. Since the stairwell was dark, and the hallways were lit, that window was for all intents and purposes, a "one-way mirror." When a buyer picked up his or her glassine envelope to verify the type and volume of the contents, I would step out from behind the stairwell door, confront them with the illegal goods in their possession, and arrest them.

The Dobbins' apartment had already been raided once or twice by the narcotics squad, but they never managed to find where the family members were storing their drugs. I attribute that to the fact that the Dobbins family was occupying two apartments, so they had plenty of space to hide the drugs.

As I noted earlier, these "family operations" made our daily duties doubly hazardous. At the same time that I was trying to apprehend Mark Dobbins for the illegal possession of a firearm, and unlawful flight to avoid arrest, I was *also* trying to catch his older brother, Joe Dobbins*, in the act of selling drugs in the street.

Mark dropped out of sight when he learned he was wanted by the police for the possession of the gun. I received a tip that he was staying with a friend or relative somewhere in Queens. On several occasions during the weeks following the gun incident, I tried to bust Mark's older brother, Joe, for possession and sale of a controlled substance. It was just hit and miss, but I was determined to get him. Like every other drug pusher I've met, he thought he could develop a foolproof scheme to sell drugs without getting busted by the police. Time was on my side. All I had to do was exercise a little patience and restraint, knowing full well that sooner or later he would be caught in the very act of dealing drugs.

Several months later, in June of 1971, I was working the four-to-midnight tour again when I saw Joe Dobbins enter a building on York Street in the Farragut Housing Project. The manager of that building had received a number of complaints about drugs being sold in the hallways. The management office had notified the police and I sensed I had "caught the scent" again.

I managed to approach the building without being noticed by Joe Dobbins or his prospective drug customers. As I entered the building with my service revolver drawn, I caught Dobbins in the very act of making a sale. His eager customers vanished when they heard me shout, "Dobbins! Put your hands up! You're under arrest." I arrested him and processed his paperwork, stating that I had caught him in the felony acts of "loitering for the purpose of dealing drugs, possession of a controlled substance with intent to sell, and sale of a controlled substance."

On September 1st, I had to appear in the Brooklyn Criminal Court on one of my countless cases awaiting hearings and trials. As I boarded the elevator to go to the fifth floor, I spotted Joe's "long-lost" younger brother, Mark Dobbins, in the rear of the elevator car! I could tell by the expression on his face that he was startled when he saw me enter the elevator. I kept my cool and pretended not to notice him as I entered the elevator. I even turned my back on him to face the front of the elevator compartment. Pretending not to notice when Mark got off at the third floor, I proceeded up to the fourth and got off.

I saw another cop whom I knew and told him about the "disappearing gunman" on the third floor who was "just begging to be arrested," and he agreed to help me. We took the stairs back down to the third floor and quickly located Mark Dobbins in one of the courtrooms! We calmly arrested him right where he sat in the courtroom. He was waiting for a hearing on an unrelated robbery case, but I had another appointment for him that took precedence over his calendar.

Once Dobbins was outside the court room, he told me, "I had a feeling you were going to come for me the moment I saw you get on the elevator! You really threw me off when you acted so cool after entering the elevator." I immediately booked Mark Dobbins on the outstanding "wanted" complaint I wrote up several months earlier. I wasn't about to see him do his "vanishing act" again.

The years started to come and go as my involvement in police work escalated; the hazards of the job increased at the same rate. I was busy establishing an incredible arrest record and feeling the effects of all the wear and tear. The Farragut and Fort Greene Housing Projects received most of my focus and efforts over the years, and I had become a common "name" among both the good and the bad residents at both locations. I became increasingly aware that my life was in jeopardy every time I put on my police uniform and went to my beat.

Any cop who worked the ghettos in the 70's also had to deal with another constant danger that was extremely unpredictable. The racial and social unrest of the 70's was mirrored and magnified by the growth of aggressive and angry black militant organizations such as the Black Panther Party and the Black Liberation Army. These militant organizations didn't care whether a cop was black or white. To them, if you were a cop, then you were a "pig," and the enemy.

Some members of these organizations were extensively involved in criminal activities, and many had armed themselves with sophisticated weapons and were considered very dangerous. I had arrested so many male and female felony suspects in the projects who claimed to belong to these black militant organizations that I wasn't too popular with them.

The Black Panther Party had a storefront headquarters on Myrtle Avenue, across from the Fort Greene and Ingersoll Housing Projects in the early 70's. Cops, whether they were black or white, knew they had to be constantly aware of the presence and activities of such militant organizations, and by no means were they taken lightly. For the most part, these black militant groups waged war on the drug pushers in their neighborhoods since drugs were having such a negative impact on drug abusers and the community at large.

From a black perspective, I have to say that many of the views and plights of those black militant organizations were timely and bona fide. Yet, that put every black law enforcement officer squarely "between a rock and a hard place." There was no question that all American blacks shared the struggle for justice and equality being waged in those turbulent years, no matter what their profession or occupation happened to be. On the other hand, there was no excuse for all the violence perpetrated by the black militant groups.

As political activist organizations, they were total failures, because the extremely hostile position they took against the "white establishment" defeated their cause, even though it was absolutely valid! Meanwhile, crime continued to rise in the inner-city black and Hispanic communities of New York City. Even worse, more and more crimes were being committed with guns. People were being assaulted and killed with firearms more than ever before in the 70's. Many times I came across situations on patrol where guns were being used in the commission of a crime. I was even involved in off-duty arrests involving suspects using guns for felony crimes.

One hot day on July 19, 1974, I had just begun patrolling the Whitman Houses in the Fort Greene Housing Projects. The heat on those hot summer days was unbearable at times. Fortunately, I had learned to adjust to the heat while serving in the United States Air Force during a 14-month assignment in Tripoli, Libya, in North Africa. My post, Wheelus Air Force Base, was located near the Sahara Desert, where some of the hottest temperatures in the world have been recorded. I learned to survive even when exposed to the prevailing winds carrying the heat off of the desert dunes, which often generated temperatures of 140-degree heat in the shade.

Since it was hot, and it was a Friday evening, I made it my business to be out on my post. These were prime factors for accelerated crime activity. There were more people on the streets than usual, and Friday was a payday for many of the working class people who lived in the community. I knew the robbery artists would be out on the prowl, hoping to "take off" (rob) people who had worked hard all week and were finally going home with their weekly pay.

Since the percentage of robberies and muggings always went up over the weekends, I positioned myself at the corner of Myrtle Avenue at the rear of a project building at 160 Navy Walk. I was hoping I would be a visual deterrent for would-be robbers and muggers looking for a quick profit.

At about 5:45 p.m., a man named Jim Dorn* suddenly came up to me excitedly pointing to a man in the middle of the block who was carrying a small paper bag. "Hey, that man stabbed me with a knife several days ago, and the cops want him for assault. He just tried to kill me again! He put his hand in that brown bag he's carrying and pointed it at me! You'd better get him before he kills somebody."

The suspect, identified by Dorn as Richard Layton*, saw Dorn talking to me, and he began to run when I started towards him. I pursued him as he ran towards the campus grounds of Long Island University. While he was running across the campus grounds with me in close pursuit, I saw the brown bag fall off the object in his hand—*it was a gun!*

As I went for my gun, the suspect suddenly dropped his gun— whether by design or by accident—and the weapon discharged one live round. That caused everyone on the campus to start running too! In fact, I ran into a panicked female student as I stopped to pick up Layton's gun. I was glad that I had the gun now instead of the suspect!

I continued the chase after recovering the dropped handgun. Layton kept looking back over his shoulder as I steadily gained ground on him. Suddenly, he ran down into a subway station located on DeKalb and Flatbush Avenues and jumped the turnstile with me right on his heels. I hurdled the turnstile and ran down the steps leading to the train platform where I finally caught up to the perpetrator.

While at a dead run, I reached out and caught the back of the man's shirt and brought him down to the floor of the platform. A uniformed Transit Police officer quickly moved in to help me cuff Layton, who was still busy trying to catch his breath in hoarse gasps. Once again, I was very thankful for my continued track and field training and God's gift of athletic ability. Even though I had just chased this suspect for nearly a mile on a hot July evening in all my police equipment, I wasn't out of breath. It was attributed to my tremendous running ability and condition. After apprehending Richard Layton, who lived in the Fort Green Housing Projects, I called Central to have a police car pick me up at the subway station.

Things had happened so quickly that I didn't have time to notify my radio operator at Central about the incident, so I called in
the report after the fact from the sidewalk entrance to the subway
station. Layton was taken to Brooklyn Central Booking and
booked for assault, reckless endangerment, and possession of a
firearm. He was carrying a small but deadly "cannon" of a weapon.
I recovered a loaded .357-Magnum two-shot Maverick Derringer
from the college campus. This "Derringer" wasn't the little thing
the public often envision. Despite its small handle size and barrel
length, it was a genuine .357 Magnum with incredible power to kill
or maim in the wrong hands. I'm thankful to report that Layton
was eventually convicted and sentenced to jail.

Crime continued to increase in and around the city due to a
number of national political trends that urban residents felt power-
less to change. Along with the continuing racial equality struggles,
the nation was also immersed in the furor over the Vietnam War. I
believed I was in the best position at that time to do the most good
for the black communities in which I lived, worked, and worshiped.

The federal government established certain "anti-poverty programs" in the early 70's, introducing them predominantly in black
ghetto communities across America. The stated goal of these programs was to improve the quality of life for the citizens in these de-
pressed communities. I believe that the programs constituted a
temporary appeasement scheme by certain high government officials to pacify the growing discontent among blacks in major population centers.

The political parties had finally begun to realize that there was
a significant block of voting power in these inner-city ethnic communities. It was to any administration's advantage to have people
in the ghettos think the government was finally coming to their
aid. This would help scale down the outcry against inequality and
injustice against non-white and particularly, black population seg-
ments across the nation.

From my viewpoint working in New York City's housing projects, those so-called "anti-poverty programs" actually proved to be

detrimental to the black communities in the end. The problem was that countless numbers of black youth dropped out of high school and college to take what they considered the well-paying jobs temporarily funded by these programs. These young people did not consider the short-term nature of those programs because their focus was on getting *any* high-paying job, not on how long the jobs would last once the federal monies ran out. The attractive pay enticed thousands of young blacks to forego their education. The result should have been predictable. When the money ran out (and it did), these young people, who had become accustomed to a nice paycheck, suddenly found themselves out of a job with no job skills, education, or career experience to fall back on. Most found it virtually impossible to get another job.

When President Lyndon B. Johnson died and Richard M. Nixon was elected, President Nixon abolished all of the anti-poverty programs. The sudden action plunged a mass of disenchanted and unprepared black youth into the ranks of the unemployed. That in itself created and added to the already deteriorating problems in black communities around the country. Drugs and other criminal activities became a scapegoat and the sole source of significant income for some of the unemployed. Needless to say, the job of police officers like myself became that much more demanding.

> Two of my most traumatic experiences occurred in the late 70's. On Monday August 9th, in the centennial year of 1976, I was on routine patrol at the Ingersoll Houses in the Fort Greene Housing Project. As I walked past some stores on Myrtle Avenue, I heard two gunshots come from a pizzeria there. I had been willingly and unwillingly involved in too many firefights to make a mistake about that sound. This was no automobile backfiring. Any cop who wants to live longer than the length of a tour in an inner-city housing project has to learn to instantly identify the deadly sounds of a "nine" (.9-millimeter handgun), a Special (usually a .32-caliber handgun), and worst of all, any of the varieties of "streetsweepers" or automatic weapons flooding

our streets (including an incredible variety of foreign and domestic military rifles, and the Israeli Uzi, Mac10s, etc.).

I saw several people run out of the store as I approached cautiously with my service revolver in hand. A man came out holding his bloody left hand, and I asked him, "What happened?" Glancing nervously at the door of the pizzeria, the wounded man said, "The crazy owner of this place just shot me!"

I peered into the store and saw a white male standing behind the counter with a gun in his right hand. My heart was already beating fast, but when I saw the man with the gun, I knew I had to do something fast. Taking a deep breath, I dashed into the store, leveled my gun at the suspect and shouted, "Police! Drop the gun!" The man turned towards me and pointed the gun in my direction.

Now I had to make a split-second decision: Should I use deadly physical force and shoot this man before he can shoot me? It is within my rights legally, logically, and ethically. Or, should I take a chance and give him the benefit of a doubt and just hope that when he sees my police uniform, that he will comply with my order and drop the gun? Scores of police officers face this dilemma every day across America. All of the responsibility—and the *risk*—is theirs...and a whole city, state, or nation waits to sit in judgment on the outcome of their split-second decision made in the heat of conflict and in the face of mortal danger.

In my case, I guess I had a feeling about this suspect. I decided to hold my fire. The suspect turned away from me, and I felt some of the tension ease from my body. Yet the man still hadn't dropped the gun as I had ordered. *He's got something to hide; he doesn't want that gun traced for some reason,* I thought. The suspect suddenly darted into the back of the store, but I was right on his heels. I confronted him while he was in the act of placing the gun into a brown leather bag. The moment he saw me and the gun I had pointed at him, he dropped the leather bag onto a table.

"Step back from the table!" I ordered the suspect, as I moved to the table with a quick movement. "Put your hands up. Now turn around and face the wall!" I kept my revolver on the suspect as I

81

picked up the brown leather bag and opened it to find a Smith and Wesson Model 15 solid-frame revolver with a six-round cylinder chamber. The cylinder contained four live rounds and two spent rounds. Again I breathed a silent prayer of thanks to God that one of those live rounds didn't have my name on it. (Sometimes you wonder how long your "luck" or providence will last.)

I closed the bag and moved it out of reach, and then I cuffed the man whom I learned was the proprietor of the store. By that time, two backup police cars had responded, due to an anonymous 911 report that shots had been fired at the pizzeria. The man who had been shot in the hand was taken to the hospital by ambulance. I read the Miranda rights to the suspect, identified as Anthony Salerno*, and allowed him to close up his store and take the cash out of the cash register. Then I took him to Brooklyn Central Booking where he was booked and charged with attempted murder and possession of a dangerous weapon (firearm).

An additional charge of criminal possession of stolen property was added to Salerno's original charges after the routine gun registration check showed a "hit," meaning it was reported stolen in the commission of a burglary in North Wales, Pennsylvania, 13 months earlier.

Kenneth C. Veit, chief of the North Wales Borough Police Department, told me that Anthony Salerno, who was also found to be an illegal alien, might be employed by another person who had ties with organized crime. For that reason, the case was turned over to the Organized Crime Bureau of the New York City Police Department and the United States Immigration Authority for further investigation and processing. Salerno was eventually deported after serving time in jail. Meanwhile, I was back on my beat in the housing projects of New York City.

---

*The names of these individuals have been changed or altered for reasons of safety, anonymity, and privacy, and bear no actual relationship to persons alive or dead. The situations and incidents, however, occurred exactly as described in this book, and in official court records.

# Chapter 6

# Dangerous Disputes and Life "Out of the Bag"

The first ten years of my police career were spent "in the bag" (or *in uniform*) patrolling New York City's infamous housing projects. Just when I thought I had seen the worst of the worst, something even more hideous and inexplicable would take place. Some of the most alarming crimes I encountered were committed in households against family members—usually during the volatile four-to-midnight and midnight-to-eight tours.

One night at 11:30, I was called to investigate a family dispute in which a husband had allegedly assaulted his wife. When I knocked on the door of the apartment, a woman with a badly bruised face opened the door. I could hear strange sounds coming from the bedroom nearby. When I asked the woman what had happened, she said, "Officer, my husband came in at about 10:00 tonight, and he was completely drunk. We got into an argument, and my husband began beating me with his fists! He finally stopped and staggered off to bed. I had had enough!" Then she described the bizarre way that she "got even" with her abusive husband.

"I just waited until he went to sleep," she said. "Then I took a needle and thread from my sewing kit and quietly stitched around my husband's bedsheets, completely pinning his body between the sheets." After taking a deep breath, she continued, "Then I took a pot of boiling water from the stove and poured it directly onto him as he lay in bed, severely scalding him." The man's wounds were so serious that he had to be taken to the hospital for treatment. Both spouses refused to prefer charges against each other, so I referred them both to Family Court.

In March of 1978, I was working the night watch again in the Fort Greene Housing Projects around 1:30 in the morning when I received a radio call from Central. Gunfire had been reported coming from a fourth floor apartment at the Whitman Complex at 75 Cumberland Walk. When I arrived at the apartment, I knocked on the door with my left hand while holding my drawn service revolver in my right. Domestic disputes put police officers at greater risk than almost any other type of incident, and I wasn't about to take any unnecessary risks that night.

An Hispanic woman nursing a swollen eye and a lacerated bottom lip slowly opened the door, still fighting back her tears. "Ma'am, does someone in your apartment have a gun? I have to know the truth, now," I said, while looking over her shoulder to quickly scan the apartment. "My husband came home drunk," she said. "He started beating on me when I asked him where he had been in the seven hours since he had left his job that afternoon. I finally got angry enough to do something about the way he was treating me. I just waited until he finally went to sleep, then I took his .32-caliber pistol and fired seven bullets into his back while he slept on the bed."

Two backup cops arrived, and we discovered the woman's husband was somehow still alive. After I recovered the weapon from the woman along with seven spent shell casings I found in the bedroom, I arrested the woman on the charge of attempted murder. Her husband was fortunate that none of the seven rounds struck any vital organs. When I talked with the man, I could believe it when he told me, "I didn't wake up until after the fourth or fifth shot." The husband later dropped all court charges against his wife.

One incident occurred in the late 70's that really had an emotional effect on me. It happened on a warm May evening when I was patrolling the Walt Whitman Housing Complex in the Fort Greene section of Brooklyn. At 9:30, an urgent call suddenly blurted out over my radio: "There is *a man down* at 102 Monument Walk, apartment 1C! Ambulance is on the way."

By the time I reached the apartment on foot, I found ambulance attendants hurriedly working on a man's face and eyes. The victim wasn't saying much of anything at the time, but a woman and her 12-year-old daughter were crying in the next room. Before I questioned the victim or the woman and her daughter, I had a quiet talk with one of the medical attendants. He said, "Somebody threw a strong alkaline solution—I think it was lye—into this man's face and eyes." I could see the man's face. It had turned completely black from the burning effect of the solution, and I noticed that his eyes appeared to be completely sealed shut before the medical attendants put some type of dressing over them and wrapped his head and face with gauze bandages.

Moving closer to the woman who was sitting in a chair in the kitchen (her daughter standing next to her), I asked, "What happened here, ma'am? Who assaulted this man?" The women identified the man as her live-in boyfriend and said, "He sexually assaulted my daughter! When I got in his face about it, he attacked me. And that's when I threw lye in his face to protect myself! I thought he was going to kill me."

The daughter's account of the incident matched her mother's at first, but my follow-up investigation proved that both of them had lied to me and other police investigators. Despite the woman's claim that she had acted in self-defense, she was arrested for first-degree assault and for possession of a dangerous weapon.

When I interviewed several of the woman's neighbors and her boyfriend, I was given a totally different account of what happened that night. I will never forget the time I went to Cumberland Hospital to interview the victim. The dressing had been removed, and his face was completely disfigured. His eyes had been permanently sealed by the caustic lye solution. I looked at his face and fought to control a sudden rush of emotion as tears filled my eyes. No human being deserved to have such a terrible thing done to them. It was a despicable act.

Although the hospital room had two beds, the other bed wasn't occupied. He had the room to himself. When I identified myself and asked if he felt up to being interviewed, he agreed to talk to me, even though I could tell he was still in pain. As I began to question him about the incident, I could see that he was having difficulty responding to my questions. "The skin on my face is very tight. I just can't seem to talk right anymore." (He didn't know that the skin on his face had been completely burned off by the lye. Doctors had to graft new skin onto his face from other areas of his body.)

"I came home unexpectedly from a trip that day (the day of the incident), and I caught my girlfriend in bed with another man. The guy somehow managed to collect his clothes and jump out of the first-floor apartment window while half dressed. When I started toward my girlfriend, she threw that stuff in my face and I couldn't see after that. My face felt like it was on fire!" The woman's daughter later told me the same exact story.

The woman went to trial and was found guilty of felony assault and sentenced to prison for a number of years. A few months later, I saw the victim being led by a seeing-eye dog on Myrtle Avenue. He was totally blind and had been scarred for life by the lye.

A week after I completed the investigation on the lye attack, I was called into the patrol captain's office. He wanted to interview me and talk about my latest request to be placed in the plain-clothes division (known in law enforcement as "working out of the bag"). As I entered the office, the captain looked up from my personnel folder that lay on his desk and said, "Have a seat, Lewis," pointing to a chair on the left side of the desk. He glanced down at my record for a few more moments and then looked over at me.

"I have been going over your record, Lewis, and it is very impressive." I knew he hadn't forgotten or overlooked the number of requests I had made over the last two years to work "out of the bag." Now he had me really wondering what was going to happen. I hadn't received any kind of reply to my earlier requests from the Housing Police headquarters in uptown Manhattan. I just couldn't understand why my request for plainclothes duty had been denied for so long. At least I knew it couldn't have anything to do with my record, for it spoke for itself.

The captain suddenly broke through my thoughts with the words, "Lewis, I have just received notification from headquarters that as of May 5, 1978, you are to be reassigned to work *anticrime, plainclothes*." My wish had become a reality. This reassignment meant that I had probably gone one step further toward becoming a detective, the dream of all active police officers.

Working "out of the bag" also meant I would be able to move around more freely, without worrying about being closely supervised. Although there were plainclothes supervisors, they did not check up on officers "out of the bag" as much as the uniformed officers. "Lewis, I know that this assignment will put you in a better position to do an even greater job than you did while you were 'in the bag,' " the captain continued. (At that time, I had been awarded over 30 departmental citations for bravery and meritorious police work, including the police department's highest award, the Medal of Honor.) "Report to the anticrime unit supervisor for further instructions," he said, and then after I thanked the captain and we shook hands, he said, "Lewis, you more than deserve this assignment."

I really felt good inside as I walked to the anticrime office down the hall. I couldn't wait to get out of my uniform and into civilian clothes. Then it dawned on me that I would be at greater risk working "out of the bag" than "in the bag." But that comes along with the territory. The identity of a cop who is not in uniform is automatically concealed, whether they are on or off duty. However, I had already made a number of off-duty arrests on the street and while I was in the subways. I quickly learned that I had an edge; I had the upper hand when my police identity was concealed.

Once a cop is taken "out of the bag," he is undercover. As I mentioned earlier, the effectiveness of undercover officers depends on how streetwise they are. I believe there are several levels of undercover work, each requiring certain expertise and natural abilities, as well as a "thick skin." It takes a special type of cop to do undercover work because of the high level of danger involved. Depending upon the assignment, an undercover officer has to possess a number of key street characteristics to survive.

At last I had made the grade after ten years of grueling police work in the projects. Finally, I would get to work undercover. I would no longer be asked to work in or respond to many of the situations I faced while "in the bag." This was a relief, but what I did not know (but would quickly find out) is that my workload and "crime-busting activity" would almost quadruple!

It was amazing to see how drastically things had deteriorated in many of New York City's less fortunate communities in the decade between the beginning of my police career in 1968 to the time of my appointment to the plainclothes division in 1978. The unthinkable occurred in the early 70's when the city actually *laid off* a number of cops from all three police departments—despite upward spiraling crime problems! The department later called back the cops who were laid off and added a considerable number of new recruits to counter the rapidly escalating crime epidemic plaguing all five boroughs of the City of New York. By 1978, the demand for illegal drugs was on the rise as more and more people became addicted. The new pool of unemployed addicts resorted to all kinds of criminal activities to finance their drug habits.

My new assignment brought me even greater responsibility. My Housing Police precinct served 16 city housing projects that were spread across New York City from South Brooklyn's Red Hook section to downtown's Fort Greene section, and from the Bedford Stuyvesant area to the Williamsburg section. Not only did the precinct cover a large geographical area, but the high population of people in each project combined with the steady stream of visitors in those projects meant that hundreds of thousands of people fell under the precinct's responsibility and jurisdiction.

We were also expected to be ready at any time to assist citizens living in the areas surrounding the projects. Housing cops were sworn and commissioned police officers of the City of New York; therefore, we were to enforce the laws of New York State on and off the project grounds as well. When people need a cop, they don't care what department you are from. All they know is that they need help! Many times I had to take action as a peace officer to stop a crime in progress or intervene in emergency situations, even though I was out of the project area or in transit from one project to another.

New York City's Housing Police Department had been predominantly black since its inception. I believe it was for this reason that Housing cops rarely received the press coverage or positive reputation they deserved for the extraordinary job they were doing. It is astonishing to see what was accomplished by the seriously undermanned Housing Police Department from the early 60's to the 80's. By nearly every measure of effective police performance (arrest rates, ratio of people served per officer, percentage of reported crimes resulting in conviction, etc.), no police department in the State of New York could match the service record of the predominantly black Housing Authority Police Department man for man.

Sir Winston Churchill once complimented the gallantry of the Royal Air Force in World War II saying, "Never have so many owed so much to so few." I believe this high compliment could also be paid to the officers who served during the first 20 years of the Housing Police Department's existence.

My new assignment to plainclothes police work wasn't anything new to me. I had worked many special plainclothes assignments over the last few years. In one instance, the Transit Police Department specifically requested my assistance through Housing Police headquarters. Their detectives were trying to solve a homicide that had occurred on a subway train. The prime suspect was alleged to have been living somewhere in the Fort Greene Housing Complex, and their chances of locating and apprehending him were somewhere between slim and none. Somehow their detectives learned about my previous success in locating and apprehending suspects in the projects. Fortunately, I was able to quickly locate and arrest the suspect in that case, working in concert with Transit Police detectives. My numerous plainclothes special assignments and off-duty arrests and experiences really prepared me in advance to function "out of the bag" on a permanent basis.

There is a big difference between the work of a plainclothes, anticrime unit and that of undercover cops who work alone to infiltrate a drug or organized crime ring, or some other close-knit criminal organization. Officers in anticrime units nearly always work with a partner, and they have backup teams as well (this also applies to more specialized antinarcotic teams).

The greatest risks are faced by the lone undercover officers who have to use their skills to personally infiltrate criminal organizations of various kinds. Their lives are continually at risk, because they have to make drug buys, gather evidence, and make the "sting" or final arrest all by themselves. Worst of all, they are sometimes forced to do this without a gun or any identification as a police officer. This puts them at risk both from the criminal element and from law enforcement officials at times. If these undercover officers do carry a handgun, they take great pains to use weapons not commonly used by cops. A "blown cover" or "being made" (being identified as a police officer) can lead to a violent death at worst or the complete collapse of a particular investigation at best.

The first time I entered the anticrime unit office, I greeted everyone. (I already knew all the cops in the unit.) Some of them had a few more years on the force than I, and one or two started their careers the same year I did. There were also several white officers on the unit, all of whom had joined the police force four or five years *after* I had already begun patrolling the projects. (No one seemed to be able to explain how these officers had been able to climb through the ranks so quickly above so many other non-white officers with greater seniority, more experience, and more outstanding service records.)

The unit sergeant looked up when I walked into his office, and he said, "Lewis, I've been expecting you. Welcome to the unit. Pull up a chair so I can fill you in on your assignment. I've been wondering when you would be assigned to the unit. I know all about you and your service record. I'm glad that you have finally been reassigned to us." After we discussed the objectives of the anti-crime program and my role in it, the sergeant said, "I know you will not have any problem working 'out of the bag.' By the way, you will be working with Eugene Assenceo."

Assenceo had been with the force about five years at the time we teamed up in the anticrime unit, so that made me the senior and most experienced officer. We were assigned to work the four-to-midnight tour, unless of course we were working on a case and needed a tour change.

Things really started to jump during my first few weeks of plainclothes duty. I made a number of arrests for a wide assortment of crimes, including "robbery in progress, grand larceny, and possession of guns or drugs. It is amazing to see what you can stumble across when working undercover in a high crime area. People will commit even the most heinous crimes right in front of an undercover cop and be apprehended, simply because they are convinced there are no cops nearby.

We were generally assigned to a specific location in a project to deal with a certain problem, and we were expected to make arrests in hopes that it would curtail the problem. I was never bored doing undercover work. I knew I was actively fighting crime, and the job included frequent "changes of scenery." One day I might be working at a project in south Brooklyn, and the very next tour I would be working across town in the Marcy Housing Projects.

One time my partner and I were sent to the Red Hook Housing Project to investigate an unusual increase in assaults and robberies in that area of Brooklyn. I noticed that most of the robberies took place around the first of the month, at the exact time when people received their Social Security checks. When the first of the month rolled around, my partner and I arranged to work a day tour at Red Hook. At 10:30 a.m., we were walking toward the check cashing establishment located in a store at a street corner just opposite the project grounds. I had information that a number of the recent robberies had taken place in that vicinity.

As soon as we entered the area, I saw a black man knock a white woman to the ground. When she struggled with her assailant to keep him from taking her pocketbook, the suspect struck the woman in the face with his fist. She lost her grip on the handbag and the man fled in the opposite direction from me. I pursued him as he ran into the project towards Central Mall. I quickly began to gain on him, and when he looked around and saw me, he started to yell for help (he didn't know I was a cop).

When I caught up with him, I had to knock him to the ground. He saw some of his friends nearby and shouted to them for help. That's when I pulled out my revolver and said, "This brother doesn't need *any* help." By that time, my partner had caught up with me, and he helped me handcuff the perpetrator and recover the victim's handbag. We notified the woman about the apprehension, and while I booked my prisoner on charges of grand larceny and assault, my partner drove the woman to Central Booking so she could speak to the district attorney and sign a complaint against her attacker.

I had completed processing the arrest and was in my office at precinct headquarters finishing up my reports when I received a call from a white New York City Police officer. The officer introduced himself over the phone, and he said, "I want to personally thank you for apprehending the man who robbed my mother this morning. If I can ever be of assistance to you, please feel free to call on me. You can call me at the precinct or at my home...." That made my day.

As time went on, I made more and more drug arrests and arrests for drug-related crimes such as assault, robbery, and burglary. In police terminology, a "red-light bandit condition" existed at the Marcy Housing Complex. This term was inspired by the activities of individuals who, on very hot days, would stand on street corners at intersections equipped with red lights. The suspects looked for vehicles with open windows, and when the drivers came to a stop, these "red-light bandits" would sneak up on the blind sides of these unsuspecting drivers, put a gun in their faces, and rob them.

Female occupants were usually robbed of their handbags, and if time permitted, of their jewelry as well. Male victims were robbed of their wallets, watches, and rings. After the robberies, the suspects would quickly run into the Marcy Housing Projects and vanish.

Everything came to a head the day some "red-light bandits" managed to rob an off-duty NYPD Inspector who was driving through the area with one or two other city officials. That was when I was sent to the Marcy Projects to eliminate the problem as part of a "joint effort" between all three New York City Police Departments. My partner and I hit pay dirt in only three days by staking out the location. We saw a robbery in progress and managed to apprehend the two suspects only seconds after they pulled the robbery! (I also recovered a gun from one of the perpetrators.) After a few more arrests were made in the days that followed, the "red-light bandit condition" was cleaned up by the joint efforts of the three departments, and the New York police commissioners began to breathe a lot easier.

Since the Housing Police Detective Bureau was undermanned, members of the anticrime unit (we weren't considered "real detectives" yet) were sometimes called upon to respond to and investigate both past and present felony crimes. On January 16, 1979, I was working the four-to-midnight tour at the Williamsburg Housing Complex investigating a drug problem when I received a radio call at 9:40 p.m.: "Unit respond to homicide at 238 Bond Street, apartment 11B." The address was in the Gowanus Housing Complex in South Brooklyn.

When I arrived at the homicide scene, the victim was lying face down on the floor of the kitchen, and the EMT's (Emergency Medical Technicians) were still waiting for the Medical Examiner to arrive and officially pronounce the victim dead. The victim, Jose Remunoz*, was a 16-year-old Hispanic male. His father, mother, sister, and brother were also present in the apartment when I arrived.

This homicide was just the latest of an already alarming number of murders I had been called upon to investigate. These violent deaths seemed to be occurring more and more frequently. Every time I arrived on the scene and saw the body of a "dead on arrival" (DOA) victim, I felt a cold chill pulse throughout my body. It did not matter whether death had come through natural causes or a gruesome act of violence—there was (and is) something about seeing a lifeless human corpse that always affected me.

I've often wondered about this sensitivity to death. I had seen countless numbers of dead and mutilated bodies literally stacked up in body bags when I was serving in the U.S. Air Force in Vietnam. Each and every time I saw the body of a fellow soldier who gave his life in the ultimate sacrifice for America in the Vietnam Conflict, I was shaken. You would think that I would have become accustomed to seeing dead bodies, but not me. Now, as I encountered body after body in the growing conflicts in New York City's housing projects, I again felt that familiar and unwelcome cold chill course through my body every time.

There I was in the apartment, ever aware of the body of a murdered teenage boy lying on the kitchen floor, surrounded by distraught family members, and trying to figure out through objective analysis what had taken place to cause the boy's death. The victim's parents could barely speak English, so I interviewed the brother of the deceased. He explained that Jose had been involved in a verbal altercation with his sister's boyfriend, Lorenzo Estev*, when Estev suddenly began stabbing the victim's back, head, and chest with a kitchen knife. Estev, a 27-year-old Hispanic male, then fled the scene with the murder weapon according to the victim's brother.

As I conducted my preliminary investigation, I also tried my best to console the victim's distraught mother and sister. When two detectives from the 76th Precinct arrived, I gave them all the information I had obtained from the brother and other witnesses in the apartment. After I notified my supervisor over the phone that the detectives would continue the investigation at the crime scene, I went after the suspect.

I went from the crime scene to several locations where I had been told I might find Lorenzo Estev. I was working the tour alone that day because my partner had a court appearance that morning. Everyone I talked with in my follow-up investigation that night claimed they had not seen or heard from Lorenzo, and no one had any ideas about where he might be. After I talked to Lorenzo's mother, I gave her a phone number where she could reach me the next day in case she heard from her son.

The next day, I received a call from a man who claimed to be Lorenzo Estev's brother: "Lorenzo wants to talk to you. Can you meet me at Dave's Bar? That's the one on the corner of Graham Avenue and Broadway in the Bushwick section in Brooklyn. I'll be waiting for you at ten o'clock tonight."

I had teamed up again with my partner, Eugene Assenceo, for that tour. I was relieved, because Eugene was as fluent in Spanish as he was in English. My Spanish was very poor, and I had gone through a hard time the night before trying to interview the Hispanic relatives and friends of the victim and the suspect. At ten o'clock, my partner and I walked into the dim light of Dave's Bar and were immediately met by an Hispanic male who must have been between 38 to 40 years of age.

The man introduced himself as Duke*, Lorenzo Estev's brother. After we introduced ourselves, Duke asked us to join him in a booth near a window. Duke had a good mastery of the English language, and he told us, "Officers, my brother, Lorenzo, is in the Bronx, hiding out at our aunt's house. Listen, he wants to talk to the police about the incident last night between him and Jose Remunoz, his girlfriend's brother."

When I agreed to talk with Lorenzo over the phone, Duke called his aunt's house from the bar. As I talked with Lorenzo, it was clear that his account of the incident was almost the same as that of the other witnesses—with one major difference. He also told me, "You see, Jose was bigger and heavier than me, and he was beating me up pretty good. Then he grabbed me in the groin area and would not let go. It was hurting me real bad, and nothing I did could make Jose break his hold on me. Finally, I got so desperate that I picked up a 15-inch knife that had fallen on the kitchen floor when we were fighting and I stabbed Jose in the back again and again until he finally released his grip on my groin area. Then I ran out of the apartment in a panic and hid in an abandoned building two blocks away from the project all night. The next morning, I was really scared about what had happened between Jose and me. I heard all the sirens and saw the police."

When Lorenzo finished his account of the incident, I told him, "Lorenzo, you need to turn yourself in. Things might go better for you if you do. If you tell me where to meet you, my partner, Eugene Assenceo, and I will meet you tonight. I'll personally take you to the station." He agreed to turn himself in, but he said he wanted to see a doctor because he was still suffering pain in his groin and where he had been hit in both eyes. I promised I would take him to a hospital when I picked him up.

My partner and I immediately left the bar and met Lorenzo at a specified location in the Bronx. When we took him to the hospital, he was checked by a doctor and released. We then took him to precinct headquarters. Assenceo advised Lorenzo Estev of his constitutional rights and he agreed to make a statement. He said he had thrown the murder weapon onto the roof of a furniture store next door to the abandoned building where he had hidden himself the night of the incident. When Estev completed his statement, we took him to Central Booking where he was booked for one count of second-degree murder.

The following day, I went to the location where Estev said he had disposed of the knife. I borrowed a ladder and climbed up on the roof of the store where I found the knife, half-covered with snow. I vouchered the weapon and personally delivered it to the police laboratory for examination of the blood stains to see it if matched the blood type of the victim.

Police work seemed to become more and more demanding. The stress was seriously aggravated by the difficulties I was facing on the home front after my wife had abandoned me and our daughter for another man. Years later, I also found out that she had been having an affair with an ex-detective I once worked with. The court ultimately awarded me the custody of Senice, so I had to devote some quality time to help meet her many needs.

Things really became complex for me in 1977 after I was assigned to work undercover. In spite of the difficulties, I managed to graduate from John Jay College of Criminal Justice in June of 1978, with a Bachelor of Science degree. From that time to this, I have dedicated my life and energies to the study of God's Word and doing His will, both on the job and in my personal and ministerial life. While some critics charge that devout faith in God is a hindrance to police work, I found that my faith greatly enhanced my proficiency, productivity, and efficiency as a police officer in New York City. Through it all, I was especially indebted to my mother and father who helped me fulfill my responsibility to care for my daughter.

My first year "out of the bag" proved to be my most productive year since I had become a police officer. I managed to compile an extraordinary felony arrest record just through the sheer volume and magnitude of the incidents I encountered in the projects. Even a casual examination of the record revealed that I had made an alarming number of "gun arrests." It seemed like every other felony arrest I made involved suspects who were armed with loaded firearms, which greatly increased my personal stress and risk levels. That first year with the plainclothes unit, I exchanged gunfire with a fleeing robbery suspect on the rooftop of a building in the Red Hook Housing Complex and was faced with all kinds of dangerous situations involving armed antagonists.

Three months into 1979, I was matched with a new partner. Michael Hansen was a white officer who had been on the force for only four years. (I was already in my eleventh year). When we first linked up as a team, Hansen told me, "I've heard a great deal about you. They say you're one of the top cops on the job. I know I'm new here, but I want to learn all I can from you about working undercover so I can function efficiently out of the bag." As I shook his hand, I told him, "I appreciate what you're saying, Hansen. If you are willing to adhere to my leadership and judgment as the senior man, then we will get along just fine. I've learned that the only way to survive and make it out there is to watch each other's backside and work as a team."

We hit it off just fine from the very first day on tour. Hansen was also a Vietnam War veteran who had served his country well in the U.S. Marine Corps, so he was very disciplined. That is one thing that is really needed when you are young and inexperienced, and are thrust into dangerous and sensitive conditions in a sometimes hostile environment. This fact was driven home one month later in a dramatic way.

On April 6, 1979, Hansen and I reported to the precinct headquarters for our assignment on the ever familiar four-to-midnight tour. We did not know it then, but that was going to be one of those tours where we would wish we had stayed in bed that day. When we first reported for duty, we had a job waiting for us. We were told to go to Long Island College Hospital in South Brooklyn to interview the victim of an assault and robbery incident that had occurred earlier at the Taylor Wythe Housing Project. After the interview, we went to the 90th Precinct for a follow-up investigation.

While we were conducting our follow-up investigation, we received a radio call from Central to report to the Tompkins Housing Complex between Tompkins Avenue and Troop Avenue in Brooklyn. It was about 7:00 p.m., and the call involved an interview of a young teenage girl who had been the victim of rape, sexual abuse, and assault. After we interviewed the girl and her mother, we left their apartment to search the area for the assailants.

We finally located the two prime rape suspects in the Sumner Housing Complex, located across from the Tompkins Houses between Troop and Lewis Avenues. After we apprehended both suspects, we called for a backup car to transport the two suspects to the Housing precinct because our car was on the other side of the Tompkins Housing Complex.

Hansen and I were talking as we walked toward our car through the Tompkins Projects when our attention was suddenly drawn to the loud shouts of two black males engaged in a heated dispute. As we walked closer to the two men, I heard the man facing our direction (later identified as Melvin Simmons*) shout at the other man (later identified as Bob Riley*), "I should just blow your head off!"

The two men stood about 10 to 15 feet from each other, and we were no more than 25 feet away from them when Riley suddenly picked up a garbage can and threatened Simmons. Then Simmons pulled a handgun from under the red and black jacket he was wearing and fired two rounds at Riley!

My partner and I were directly behind Riley and in Simmons' line of fire. I was close enough to literally see the fire flash from the muzzle of Simmons' gun each time he fired a round! At that point, neither of the two had noticed my partner and I approaching them. Everything happened at lightning speed after the first rounds were fired. I sure wasn't expecting to be caught up in the middle of a gunfight that night while we were walking toward our car. I was again reminded of the kind of danger that law-abiding project residents had to endure every day this type of activity was allowed to continue.

I didn't even have time to think or get scared. I just sprang into action, and my partner followed suit. I instantly drew my weapon and so did my partner, and then shouted to Simmons, "Police!

Drop the gun!" Simmons instantly fired another round at my partner and I, and then turned to run in the opposite direction. Hansen started to return fire, but I yelled to him to hold his fire because there were people coming up the walk who would be directly in our line of fire. He immediately complied, and we began to pursue the armed suspect. I lost Simmons when he ran into a residential building at 65 Tompkins Avenue in the project. By the time I reached the entrance to the 18-story apartment building, the suspect had already been admitted to the building through the locked main entrance by a teenage girl standing in the lobby.

When we reached the front door, it was locked again, but a man quickly opened the door for us and pointed to apartment 1C and said the man had gone into that apartment. I told Hansen to call for backup and a supervisor to respond to our location. Then I went directly to apartment 1C. I knocked loudly on the door and shouted, "Police! Open the door!"

Taking no chances, my partner and I placed ourselves on either side of the door with our guns drawn. My heart was pounding in my chest as I tried to catch my breath and ready myself for any emergency defensive action that might be needed. We were dealing with a "shooter." Life always seemed to take on a totally different feeling and perspective whenever I was facing an armed suspect who had shown the ability and willingness to fire live rounds at me.

There we were, glued to the wall of each side of the apartment door. When we got no response, I took a deep breath and I knocked again. This time, I knocked as hard as I could. "Open up! This is the police!" I could hear the wailing of the police sirens responding to my partner's radio "Code 10-13," an emergency request for police backup that means "police officer needs immediate assistance!" That code will cause police officers to drop everything and instantly respond from every area near the precinct the moment they hear that a fellow officer may be in trouble.

Some of the officers had already entered the building by the time the girl who had admitted Simmons into the building finally opened her apartment door. When I asked her where the man with the gun had gone, she said she did not know. Thinking that he might be holding someone hostage somewhere in the apartment, I asked her, "Is there anyone besides you in the apartment?" and she replied, "My four sisters are home."

I entered the apartment with extreme caution, accompanied by a number of other police officers, and conducted a rapid search of the apartment. One of the young women in the apartment told us the man (Simmons) had knocked on their door and said, "Some men are trying to kill me! Will you let me in so I can call the police?" When they let him in, he ran to a back room and jumped out of the window. The woman said when they heard my partner and I knock at the door, they thought we were the men who were trying to kill the man they had admitted to their apartment. She said they were so afraid for their lives that they didn't come to the door until they heard the other cops in the hallway.

The four women in apartment 1C belonged to a large family who also occupied the adjoining apartment 1B. The window the suspect used to escape our pursuit was on the other side of the building, so I knew he was long gone. After a thorough search of the apartment confirmed the escape of the suspect, I took the necessary information from one of the women, and my partner and I went back to the precinct. We began processing the paperwork on the two suspects we had arrested earlier on rape charges, but I couldn't stop thinking about the man with the gun who had fired at me and my partner. Finally, I told my partner that I was going to get the gunman if it was the last thing I did. I had a hunch that a frank discussion with Bob Riley, the man Simmons had threatened, would help me find my suspect.

By 4:00 that morning, we had completed the arrest procedures and the mountain of paperwork connected to them, as well as a report on the shoot-out with Simmons. I decided to get an early start on the case, so I went home to take a hot shower, change clothes, and see my daughter Senice. Only four hours later, at 8:00 a.m., Hansen and I started to work on the case again. By 4:00 that afternoon, we had chased down all kinds of leads and reached the end of our scheduled tour. And we still did not have our man. I meant what I said, however. It took me two more days of intense police work, but I finally located and arrested Melvin Simmons and charged him with two counts of attempted murder of a police officer and one count of attempting to murder Bob Riley, along with the charge of the illegal possession and use of a firearm.

Guns seemed to be falling into the hands of more extremely young criminals as an epidemic of serious crime escalated in all five boroughs of the city. By the end of the 70's, all three police departments began to add to their forces, including a considerable number of women (in defiance of tradition). However, for some inexplicable reason, the Housing Police Department saw an influx of so many white officers, both male and female, that black police officers gradually became the minority in that department for the first time in its history. I have always wondered if that was by chance or choice—boy, how I wondered. I am the first to state that good police officers come in all colors and races, and in both genders, but such an unusual hiring pattern over such a short period was awfully hard to explain. The growing hints of hidden agendas within the department seemed to increase right along with the danger and volume levels of my undercover work in the projects as we entered the decade of the 80's.

---

*The names of these individuals have been changed or altered for reasons of safety, anonymity, and privacy, and bear no actual relationship to persons alive or dead. The situations and incidents, however, occurred exactly as described in this book, and in official court records.

# Chapter 7

# Saga of the Unsung Hero

The crime situation in the New York City area climbed to an all-time high in the 80's, especially in the 315 city-owned housing projects. There was no question that something had to be done to stop the citywide crime wave, but officials were publicly debating how it should be done, who would do it, and who would pay for it. For as long as I can remember, New York City politicians have used the "crime suppression platform" to win votes, while the crime crisis steadily worsened over the years.

Things finally deteriorated to the degree that the crime epidemic exploded out of the poorer inner-city neighborhoods to rapidly spread like a plague that disrupted life even in the city's most affluent communities. That was when local, state, and federal authorities decided to organize specialized units within each police department to combat the crime condition. These new anticrime units were to be funded by the federal government.

This cooperative effort gave birth to an elite anticrime unit within the Housing Police Department called the "Project Stabilization Unit." This unit was to be manned by the best of the best on the police force. Since the Housing Police force had been manned predominantly by blacks since its inception, the majority of the exceptional police officers with outstanding police service records were black.

I received written notification to report to PSA (Police Service Area) #9 in the 114th Police Precinct, housed in the record office at the Ravenswood Housing Projects. Selected Housing cops from all five city boroughs had been summoned to that location (including a few white officers). Altogether, 30 or more veteran crime fighters from the projects were gathered together in that conference room. The group included such exceptional black cops as Ronald Boyce, Albert Layne, Samuel Goods, Herbert Simon, George Roland, Carl Bolyan, George Robinson, and many others. Everyone was engrossed in conversation with someone else and the discussions were almost exclusively devoted to experiences on the streets. To a great extent, the story I relate in this book is also their story. I knew almost everyone present, and as I moved from group to group, I learned that no one seemed to know why we were gathered in the room that day.

Fifteen minutes after I arrived, a police inspector and a captain entered the room. Silence came over the room when the captain greeted us and asked us to sit down. Then the captain introduced the inspector, whom I already met, and said he would explain why we were asked to come to the meeting. I could see eager anticipation on the face of each officer as I looked around the room.

"Each of you has been chosen to become part of a new and important unit within the Housing Police Department," the inspector said. "This unit will specialize and focus on specific crimes in high crime areas. It will consist of three squads: an undercover squad and two semi-undercover anticrime squads."

A quiet swell of sound filled the room as the men responded to the news, and then the inspector continued, "The undercover squad will be assigned to those areas in the city where drugs and other related crimes are actually creating a hazardous condition for the citizens who live in those areas. The other units will be used to deal with criminal activity in drug-prone locations. They will also concentrate on other felony crimes such as robberies and burglaries. This job is establishing a unique career path for you men, if you are willing to take it. We expect to draw new candidates for the detective bureau directly from this new Project Stabilization Unit."

Even though I was honored to be selected for the new unit, I also felt disappointed. As a veteran police officer with extensive undercover experience and an outstanding service record, I knew that I should have been appointed to the detective bureau long ago, but had somehow been bypassed for nearly a decade. Nevertheless, I was willing to go along with the program because I had no other option. I had already been told (and later experience seemed to confirm) that appointments to the detective bureau were made by "contracts" rather than by merit or outstanding police work, which is a topic I discuss in a later chapter dealing with corruption.

My partnership with Officer Michael Hansen was dissolved upon my appointment to the new Project Stabilization Unit. Although our association was short, we had gone through a great deal together and had learned to respect each other. He told me at the time of my transfer that he was happy he had been able to work with me because he had learned a great deal from me about working and functioning undercover.

My first assignment as a member of the PSU was to the undercover squad. Over the next several months, my squad was assigned to work in projects throughout the five boroughs of New York City. I began to make far more arrests than ever before, which meant I had to make court appearances in all five boroughs. Whenever a drug problem arose in a certain area, I was one of the cops selected to go into the area to find the source and make an arrest.

When a police officer goes undercover, the odds are overwhelmingly high that he or she will encounter some kind of illegal activity. In fact, it is a real "sure thing" in a high crime area. Yet my primary objective as an undercover cop was to make arrests on specific crimes plaguing a given community. Our units, comprised primarily of black undercover police officers, were sent into black and Hispanic neighborhoods to make a high volume of arrests so public officials could appease city, state, and federal authorities and angry community leaders with impressive arrest statistics in high crime areas of the city.

The Brownsville section of Brooklyn was suffering from a burglary epidemic, and my partner, Albert Layne, and I, were sent to solve the problem. We worked a 10:00 a.m. to 6:00 p.m. tour, since 30 of the reported apartment burglaries in the area occurred in the daytime hours when the residents weren't home due to work or other responsibilities.

Layne and I reported to the Housing Police Precinct 2, located on Sutter Avenue in the Brownsville section of Brooklyn, and told the desk officer that we would be doing some undercover police work in the area. This was done to minimize the danger that we might be mistaken as crooks instead of undercover cops. Only on rare occasions are the presence and identity of undercover cops not disclosed to local precincts for security reasons.

After warning the "locals," Layne and I went out to catch a burglar. All the years I had been exposed to criminal behavior and activities in the projects, combined with new, up-to-date investigative strategies I'd studied in my degree work in criminology, began to come together on that assignment. My "street sense" had become so enhanced that, in many instances, I could tell if a person had something illegal on his or her person simply by his or her behavior patterns. I could almost sense if a suspect was about to commit a crime, or had already committed one.

The Brownsville section of Brooklyn was considered a high crime area. It was home to more than 15 large New York City Housing Authority complexes, including a few that were exceptionally large in area and resident population. When we went undercover in these areas, we could enter a drug-infested location in any of these communities and make a major felony arrest 99 percent of the time!

One time my partner and I were riding in an unmarked car near the location where an alarming number of burglaries had taken place. We had already seen a high level of drug activity in the area. When a cop sees a crime being committed right in front of him, he is always instinctively tempted to take action. In this case, we knew any overt police action on our part could jeopardize our strategic purpose for going undercover. So we did the next best thing. I called the desk officer and gave him all the details he needed to put a stop to the drug activity using uniformed and plainclothes police officers.

After several hours had passed, we checked a number of high-rise dwellings, hoping to intercept a burglary in progress; but everything seemed to be normal. At 2:00 p.m., we stopped at a local fast food restaurant and ate in our unmarked car near a vacant lot in the area we were patrolling. Fifteen minutes later, I spotted one Hispanic man and two black men carrying large black garbage bags. Each man carried two garbage bags, and whatever was in those bags was large and heavy. I could also tell by their actions that whatever they had in those bags was *hot* (stolen)!

I turned to Layne and said, "I bet those are our jaybirds." As Layne nodded in agreement, I put my sandwich on the seat beside me and fired up the car. I did not want to alert the suspects to our presence so I drove on past them and parked on the next block. I got out of the car and released the hood lock, as if I was looking for an engine problem under the hood, while my partner watched the men through the mirror on the passenger's side of the car. When the suspects reached our location, I stepped out from in front of the car, and my partner opened his door and stepped out as well. We confronted the three males together, identifying ourselves as police officers.

"What are you carrying in the garbage bags?" I asked. One of the black men said, "Oh, this is my cousin's stereo equipment. We're on the way to his house." Not satisfied, I asked, "What are you doing with the equipment?" He said, "My cousin loaned me the equipment to use at a party I had over the weekend in my apartment." We inspected all six bags and found stereo equipment worth at least $1,800 or more, including two large speakers. I knew the suspects were lying, but I really couldn't do anything about it because I couldn't disprove their story. I was sure these men were junkies and that the property in those bags was in fact stolen. *But I needed proof.*

A police officer cannot legally stop someone without a "probable cause," and their suspicious manner met that qualification. But I had nothing strong enough to support an arrest. We continued to check out the three males by asking general questions about the items in their possession, their names, and where they lived. Yes, we were stalling. Somehow I hoped to hold them until we could find out if there had been any burglaries reported to the local precinct that day. Unfortunately, it was still early afternoon; people had not returned home from work yet, and no theft reports would come in until they did. I knew we could only detain the three for just so long without reasonable justification. I had to do some fast thinking.

This was when I noticed that the garbage bags the suspects were using to carry the equipment were marked, "Property of the New York City Housing Authority." When I asked the men where they got the bags from, they could not give me an accurate answer. I had found my solution. Now I was justified in detaining them for possession of city property, and it would give Layne and I more time to find out who owned the stolen property in those bags. After we called for a backup car, I had the three men load the bags in our car. The backup car transported the suspects to the Housing precinct office, and we followed it. The black male who first claimed that the merchandise in his possession belonged to a cousin continued to cling to his story the whole way.

Once we arrived at the police station, we took the three males and the merchandise into the detective's office and continued the investigation. Even though there was probable cause for detaining the three suspects, time was still a factor—especially because these suspects had not been officially charged with anything. We immediately checked with the NYPD's 75th Precinct, but they had received no burglary reports. I knew I could not hold the three much longer.

At about 5:00 p.m., I decided to take a risk. I told the man who claimed his cousin owned the stereo equipment, "Listen, if your cousin will come here to the precinct office and verify that this property is in fact his, then we will allow you to leave with the property." The man nodded and said, "Sure, I'll get hold of him. But I'll have to go to his apartment to get him because my cousin doesn't have a phone."

I knew the man's story was an elaborate and prefabricated lie, but I had to stall for more time. Everything hinged on my hope for a timely burglary report. The suspect didn't know it, but he played right into my hands when he agreed to have his cousin come to the station house. I was taking a chance by allowing him to leave the precinct. Who was to say he would return (especially if the property *was* stolen as I suspected)?

Forty minutes after I allowed the most vocal suspect leave to bring his cousin back to the precinct to claim the property, what I was hoping for came to pass. A hysterical woman came into the precinct office to report to the desk officer that her apartment had been burglarized while she was at work. I was immediately asked to come to the front desk.

The woman was still very upset when I identified myself to her, so I tried to help her regain her composure so I could interview her. After she calmed down, I asked her to tell me what was wrong (even though I had already concluded that the stolen property in the office was hers). The woman wiped her face with a tissue she pulled from her pocketbook before she began. "Someone broke into my apartment while I was at work," she said between heavy sobs. "They took my brand- new stereo console television. I just got it last week from the department store. It cost me $1,200, and I haven't even made the first payment on it, or on the $2,200 stereo rack system!"

When I asked, "Is anything else missing?" she said she did not know, because when she entered the apartment, she panicked the moment she saw her new stereo items missing and came directly to the police station. "I don't know what I am going to do," she said as the tears began to flow again. (The whole time, I was thinking, *This is going to be one sad story with a happy ending!*)

By the time the woman finished her story about the burglary, my partner told me the suspect I'd let walk had returned with another black male whom he alleged was his cousin. We had already put the lady in a separate room where she was in isolation. I told her to sit tight, and I left the office. When I entered the detective's office, there were now four men waiting for me in addition to two uniformed officers and my partner.

The suspect who returned with his so-called cousin looked at me, pointed to his "cousin," and said, "This is my cousin, and the stereo equipment belongs to him. Just ask him." I nodded, and then asked my partner to step out of the office with me. In the privacy of the hallway, I quietly told him that the lady I met with was not only missing the stereo equipment from her apartment, but she was also missing a $1,200 stereo console television set. "Layne," I said, "We need to have her view all of the property in those trash bags for identification purposes."

When the victim saw her property, she became excited. "Do you have the television too?" she asked. I told her we didn't have it *yet*, but asked her to wait for a little longer and escorted her back to the isolation room. *That lady has made my day*, I thought to myself as I returned to the detective's office where the four unsuspecting burglary suspects were waiting.

Taking the so-called "cousin" into the room where the property was displayed, I asked him, "Is this your equipment?" When he said it was, I asked him where, when, and how much he had paid for the merchandise. Then I asked, "Where are your receipts?" He made a futile attempt to respond to my questions, but I cut him off and told him he was going to be arrested along with the other three men for burglary and possession of stolen property. That is when he blurted out, "I had nothing to do with the burglary! My friend approached me and asked me to do him a favor. He said he would pay me if I would accompany him to the police station to say the stereo equipment was mine."

"I believe you," I told him. "The problem is that you agreed to lie to the police. You can still be charged with a crime and locked up. Now maybe if you agree to cooperate with us and help us recover everything that was taken..."

The man quickly agreed to help, and we managed to recover the television from where it was stashed behind the building in a vacant lot, hidden under a large, dirty, bed mattress. When we saw how big the television console was, we could only wonder, *How in the world did those thieves ever get this thing through the lady's first floor bedroom window without being seen?* The thieves had hidden the oversized console in an isolated area not too far from the complainant's bedroom window.

In that one arrest and through our follow-up investigation, we were able to close over 35 previous burglary cases and recover property taken in many of the burglaries. The three men had been responsible for all of the burglaries, and after their arrest and conviction, burglaries tapered off considerably in that particular area of Brooklyn. It was a good feeling to know that we were able to help a community that had been plagued with such an epidemic of crime. Policemen who *really care* occasionally enjoy the incredible rewards of a job well done. Unfortunately, those who don't care just consider it another day on the job, with their only reward being a paycheck and the power that comes with their badge.

In the early 80's, the brunt of the crime spree fell primarily on the black and Hispanic communities. Most of the violent crimes committed against residents of lower income neighborhoods were being perpetrated by black and Latino criminals against black and Latino victims! We had to do all that was humanly possible and within the law to break the "siege" within these communities.

The number of arrests I was making reached an all-time high during this period, along with the number of departmental decorations I received. I was being called on to work in various precincts around the city wherever certain crime problems had arisen and to investigate hideous crimes in inner-city or public housing areas.

These special assignments allowed me to make all kinds of high visibility felony arrests for homicides and other crimes. I was keeping very late hours, and sometimes I had to work around the clock, getting little or no sleep. This was the work I enjoyed doing, and I had to make the best of it, no matter how rough it got (and it got very rough at times). Many of my ordeals (and those of other black cops in the ghetto) never made the news headlines. I honestly believe that most of the genuinely heroic deeds done by black and other non-white cops went unnoticed during my police career in New York City. Yet that did not stop them from routinely going above and beyond the call of duty on the job. Many of their stories would make even the most gripping television cop shows look like soap operas.

One of the most vicious and terrifying crimes a person could ever be subjected to is the crime of rape. It is possible that the only crime that could supersede the trauma of rape is murder. Rape victims are almost always emotionally scarred for life, and they must live with the haunting fear and outrage of the memory of their savage violation by a ruthless stranger. Most people forget that cops are human too, and many have wives, daughters, and sisters at home. And everyone has a mother. When a rape occurs, our minds automatically bring up the faces of the females who are close to us as we whisper a prayer that they never are victimized by a rapist. In the poorer neighborhoods, there is nearly always an exceptional number of rapes occurring, and far more occur than actually make it to a police complaint record.

On March 25, 1980, I was given a special assignment to work uptown in the Harlem community. There had been an epidemic of rape/robberies in NYHP Service Area #6, which is located in the 26th NYPD Precinct. Two New York City Housing Projects were involved—the Manhattanville and Grant Houses. Over 14 rapes and robberies had occurred between the two housing projects, and the community was up in arms. I was assigned to work with the decoy squad that had staked out the two target areas for the past few days without any luck.

I was told that the matter had "gone political" because several of the rape victims were professional women, such as registered nurses; and the chief of the department sent word to our commanding officer that he wanted the perpetrator apprehended. The description and modus operandi of the suspect made it clear we were dealing with a shrewd serial rapist who liked to rob his victims after assaulting them.

Fourteen rapes had followed the first reported rape in November of 1979. Witnesses claimed the assailant was a Latino, or a light-skinned black man, and most of the attacks occurred late at night. Some occurred after midnight when the victims were returning home from night jobs. There was no particular day of the week to concentrate on, since some rapes occurred during the week and others on weekends. At least three incidents a month on average were reported, although in one month there were four attacks. The month I was assigned to the case, there had only been two reported rapes. The perpetrator would hit and lay low for a time, and then strike again. It was hard to set up an effective plan to catch the attacker, despite the fact that we had a police artist's sketch of the assailant.

One of the biggest problems was that since the perpetrator was working two projects, it forced us to take in a large area of city real estate. Complicating the case was our belief that the rapist preferred to stalk his victims from some vantage point and follow them to their residences. When they entered an elevator in the building, he would get behind them, push the top floor button, produce a knife, and threaten the lives of his victims. Then he would usually take his victims by force up to the roof landing to assault and rob them, and then flee. (There had been a few reported attempted rapes that were foiled when the victims screamed and frightened off their assailant.)

We also had to contend with the fact that there were only enough cops available to cover a small area at one time. For the next few weeks we worked from 6:00 p.m. to 2:00 a.m. Only one rape was reported during that period, and it happened on our day off. Finally, the squad was taken off the case because there were other areas of the city that needed the squad's attention as well, but something in me felt like we were close to a breakthrough. I asked the captain to allow me and another police officer to stay on the case for a few more weeks just to see what we could do, and he agreed. He also assigned a black police officer named George Rolland to work with me.

I knew that we had a smart cookie on our hands, so I had to devise a scheme that would help us locate and apprehend him. For three night tours, we drove around the target area in our unmarked car for a short period, and then we would park for an hour or so in various locations near main thoroughfares. We concentrated on areas that were saturated with public transportation services and heavy pedestrian traffic in hopes that we would get lucky and see our rapist stalking a lone female on her way home. Unfortunately, while we were concentrating on one target area, our suspect struck in a cooperative housing development in another locality. That got me really angry. I knew we had to do something, but what?

If my 12 years of experience on the job taught me anything, it taught me that a good cop has to "think like a criminal" to catch a criminal. Finally, the idea crossed my mind, *This jaybird knows the area real well. It is possible that he might live or may have lived somewhere in the area in the past. Maybe there is a chance he has been arrested for rape or robbery in the past!*

The wheels started to click in my head as my partner Rolland and I discussed the matter on the fourth night while sitting in the unmarked car. Then it hit me. *Why didn't I think of it before?* I had solved several serial crimes in the past in the same way, including

Richard Lewis, left, kneels beside the body of a gunman while holding the assailant's weapon in his left hand. After Lewis chased the suspect down Fifth Avenue near Union Square in New York City, he positioned himself between the gunman and scores of pedestrians and vendors on the street in broad daylight before confronting the armed robber and identifying himself as a police officer. When the man ignored Lewis' shouted command and pointed a gun at him, Lewis dropped the suspect with two fatal shots. A police lieutenant who rushed to the scene stands with gun in hand to the right. Lewis was off-duty and enroute to college classes when he stopped in response to shouts for help from several people in the exclusive shopping area. This act of heroism earned him his first Medal of Honor, the highest honor awarded by the NYPD (then called the New York City Housing Police Department).

New York City Mayor Beame (from right) awards the New York Police Department's (then the New York Housing Police Department) highest award, the Medal of Honor, to Richard Lewis and George Robinson in recognition of their acts of heroism in separate incidents in 1977. The Medal of Honor is awarded only "for an act of extraordinary bravery, intelligently performed in the line of duty at imminent personal risk of life and with the knowledge of the danger involved."

Top New York City officials and law enforcement leaders honored 16-year veteran and two-time Medal of Honor awardee Detective Richard Lewis in April of 1984. Gathered with Lewis at City Hall Plaza (in foreground from left) were his 10-year-old daughter, Senice, and Mayor Edward I. Koch; and (background left) Housing Police Chief John P. Henry, Chairman Joseph J. Christian, and NYC Police Commissioner Benjamin Ward. At the time of this writing, Richard Lewis was still the only New York police officer in history to receive two Medals of Honor for acts of extraordinary bravery in the line of duty.

# B'klyn lad, 12, wounded — gunman shot in chase

A 12-year-old Brooklyn boy was hit in the chest by a spent bullet in the course of a holdup yesterday, and the gunman was gravely wounded by a Housing Authority cop in the chase that followed.

The boy, Khary Whitt, of 335 Sutter Av., was treated for a slight graze wound that failed to break the skin, but the accused gunman, Anthony Green, 20, was in critical condition in Kings County Hospital.

Police said Green had robbed a man of a gold chain at 350 Blake Av., in the Brownsville section, and wheeled to fire his revolver at two housing officers who gave chase.

At that point, Officer Richard Lewis fired a single shot, dropping Green with a bullet in the head.

---

The above news article is a copy of an August 21, 1982, clipping taken from the *New York Post*. In the article, Police Officer Richard Lewis stops an alleged robber with a single bullet fired from his gun.

Senice was especially proud the day her father received his second Medal of Honor from the NYPD in 1984. They took the time to take a special picture "just for them" after everyone else was gone. A writer in the *Housing Authority Journal* commented, "Every dad should have a moment like this." Lewis was awarded the medal after he ran down an armed robber who had just wounded a 12-year-old boy during his flight. The gunman wheeled around in a playground area and fired at Lewis first. "I shot him on the run, and I then took his gun away, cradled his head in my lap, and prayed for him," Lewis recalls. The suspect died hours later of a head wound. "It's just like yesterday," Lewis states. "I have never gotten over the trauma of those shootings" [referring to the two occasions he killed suspects in the line of duty].

THE WHITE HOUSE

WASHINGTON

July 19, 1984

Dear Senice:

I was delighted to receive your letter and the
newspaper articles about the numerous awards
your father has received for his outstanding
dedication as a policeman.  Your message reflects
the pride and love that parents always hope their
children will feel for them.  Our nation is forever
grateful to men and women who, like your father,
devote themselves selflessly to their duty.

Mrs. Reagan joins me in sending our best wishes
to you and your wonderful family.

Sincerely,

*Ronald Reagan*

Miss Senice Lewis
140-16 Latham Lane
Queens, New York  11434

After Detective Lewis received his second Medal of Honor, his daughter Senice wrote a
letter about her father's achievements to then President Ronald Reagan at the White
House. She was delighted when she received a personal letter of congratulations from
the President and Nancy Reagan in the mail.

New York City saw a flood of false business establishments such as this West Indian-owned "grocery and deli" spring up in the 1980's and 90's (above). These "stores" had just a few shelves "stocked" with minimal amounts of legitimate goods, which were walled off from customers by Plexiglas partitions. In reality, this store, or "smoke shop," was used as a front to disguise high-volume illicit drug sales. When Detective Lewis and his anti-drug team raided this illegal drug operation, they caught the suspects off-guard and seized a deadly cache of automatic weapons and large-caliber pistols (below). This photograph was actually taken from behind the Plexiglas partition, where the confiscated weapons used by the drug ring were displayed on the counter. Shown from left are an Israeli Uzzi "street sweeper" machine gun, a "MAC 10" 9-mm machine gun, and a loaded .38-caliber revolver. In most cases, cops have to oppose high-powered arsenals like this armed only with handguns, standard-issue shotguns, and a search warrant.

**Sports Illustrated**

---

TIME & LIFE BUILDING
NEW YORK, N.Y. 10020
212 JU 6-1212

October 18, 1973

Mr. Richard Lewis
168-40 127th Avenue
Jamaica, New York 11434

Dear Richard:

Congratulations on your outstanding showing in the
New York State Police Olympics.

I thought you would like to know that you are being
featured in the "Faces in the Crowd" section of the
October 22nd issue of SPORTS ILLUSTRATED, a copy
attached.

Each person featured in this section of the magazine
receives a special SI Award of Merit trophy which we
arrange to have presented. I have notified Mike Lee
at the Long Island Press. Please give him a call --
OL 8-1234 -- to discuss the details of the
presentation.

Best wishes,

Keith Morris

/pd
Enc.

Richard Lewis' extraordinary speed and endurance made him especially
effective when pursuing suspects on foot. Lewis was training to compete
in the Olympics before joining the armed forces, and later the police
academy. He continued his training after joining the New York City
Housing Police Department, and was featured in *Sports Illustrated* magazine in October of 1973 for his standout performances in the New York
State Police Olympics.

# 'Locksmith' con had pick of jobs —cops

**By RICHARD JOHNSON and LESLIE GEVIRTZ**

AN EX-CON, who told police he learned locksmithing in jail, was arrested early today for committing as many as 80 break-ins and burglaries.

Housing police picked up 28-year-old Miguel Ferran while he was in the process of picking his way into an apartment in the Metro North Housing project in Harlem.

"Some apartments had two or three locks and he could still get in," Officer Richard Lewis said. "This guy is a real pro."

The cops said Lewis told them he had learned locksmithing while in an upstate jail where he was serving time for a previous crime.

Lewis' partner, Carl Boylan, said:

"It's very frustrating. We lock these guys up for one thing, and they teach them how to commit another crime."

"I got the impression from the way he talked about it," Boylan said, "that it was an actual course in locksmithing, not just something he picked up on the cellblock."

"This guy and his friend committed over 44 burglaries in the Carver Houses alone," Lewis added.

Police said Ferran, who had been out of prison for a year and a half after serving time on a murder charge, netted more than $150,000 in cash and merchandise.

While at the E. 102d St. stationhouse, Ferran phoned his sister-in-law and, according to police, told her: "Get rid of the stuff at my apartment."

Housing Authority officers display array of loot recovered in raid on suspect's apartment.

*Post Photo by Joe De Maria*

# NEW YORK POST

**WEDNESDAY, OCTOBER 15, 1980** **25 CENTS**

© 1980 News Group Publications Inc. Vol. 179, No. 281
AMERICA'S FASTEST-GROWING NEWSPAPER

In this photo reproduced from a page of the *New York Post* daily newspaper, Richard Lewis (seated) works with other police officers to sort through $150,000 worth of loot recovered in a raid on the apartment of a burglar nicknamed "the locksmith con." When Lewis and his partner arrested the suspect, he denied any wrongdoing. But Lewis suspected the man was hiding something, and when he examined his large Afro, he found burglary tools and a fake gun hidden in the man's overly abundant hairdo. The capture of the man and his partner solved 44 burglery cases in one housing project alone and made headlines in several major New York newspapers in mid-October 1980!

# B'klyn push-in suspect nabbed

A youth accused of preying on Red Hook senior citizens for months with push-in attacks was arrested yesterday by Housing Authority police.

Derek Sharlow, 19, arrested four times in the past for assaulting senior citizens, is accused of beating and robbing three Brooklyn seniors last week.

But police say Sharlow may be responsible for more than a dozen other attacks in the neighborhood since he was released on parole in October.

One victim, Lena Pittmon, 70, of 426 Columbia St. said he took $31 from her three weeks ago but she never told police because Sharlow warned her to keep quiet.

She decided to go to police after getting two black eyes in an attack Friday because, she said, she feared he'd kill her the next time.

Richard Lewis, the Housing Authority cop who arrested Sharlow yesterday, said he was able to track the youth because his technique — a push-in attack — was always the same.

He!said that Robert Eldridge, 73, of 131 Lorraine St. was the first of Sharlow's victims last week. Eldridge, who walks with a cane, was attacked from behind as he entered his apartment.

Sharlow kicked and beat him before taking $20 from his wallet and fleeing, police said.

Mrs. Pittmon was attacked Friday morning as she entered her apartment. The assailant gave her two black eyes before taking $11 and a bottle of brandy from the groceries she was carrying.

On Friday afternoon, police said, Sharlow struck again at 465 Columbia St.

He said Sharlow persuaded Francisco Santiago, 84, to open his door by waving an envelope and claiming to have a special delivery letter.

When Santiago opened the door, police said, Sharlow hit him on the head, leaving a wound requiring four stitches.

**LENA PITTMAN**

Lewis used solid detective work to crack the difficult case of "The Push-In Bandit," a criminal who was violently preying on the elderly residents of public housing units. Lewis scoured past arrest records looking for a similar crime pattern. His hunch was right, and he was able to quickly make an arrest and solve the case.

# Too Much For Much Too Little

**NEW YORK DIARY**

**Dennis Duggan**

The blood-spattered concrete wall in the second-floor stairwell of the Samuel J. Tilden Houses in the Brownsville section of Brooklyn is a physical reminder of what it means to be cop in the city.

It is a message that is not lost on Det. Richard Lewis, who has been on the Housing Authority force for almost 20 years and is the only officer to twice win the city's highest award for valor, the Medal of Honor. He has been in six shootouts, one of them in 1982 in the Tilden Houses, where last week yet one more officer left his blood on the wall.

Tuesday morning, on the stairwell of the Tilden project Lewis talked about 26-year-old housing officer, Anthony McLean, who was to be married this summer, and who was gunned down in what police call a drug-related assasination.

Those words also were used to describe the murder of Police Officer Edward Byrne in Queens last month. They have become a standard description for why so many people — including cops — are killed by the city's latest epidemic.

McLean died in one of the city's 314 housing projects where more than 600,000 people live — a population larger than that of Bos-

Please see DUGGAN on Page 33

Newsday / Jeffery A. Salter
Housing Authority Det. Richard Lewis

'The most dangerous job in the city today for a cop is to work in the projects. It's worse than being a street cop or a transit cop because inside these projects you are alone and in these stairwells you are a sitting duck.'

— Det. Richard Lewis

This article featuring Richard Lewis appeared in *Newsday* in 1988 shortly after the assassination-style murder of a Housing Police officer in New York's Tilden Public Housing Project—the second such murder of a police officer in as many months.

Then-Housing Police Det. Richard Lewis on the job in the stairwell of a city housing project where he had gone to investigate a killing.

# A Hero Cop on His Own Turf

*And a Man That Kids in the Projects Can Look Up To*

By Dennis Duggan

THESE days if you want to see retired detective Richard Lewis, also known as "Preacher Cop," a good bet is the three-chair barber shop on Sutter Avenue in Brooklyn run by Fred (Deacon) Justice, a man with a sense of humor who offers you a soft drink from a battered refrigerator before trimming your hair.

The barber shop is a popular meeting place in the neighborhood where drugs and crime are rampant. Its walls are filled with pictures of customers, including many of the cops who work nearby. One of the pictures shows Lewis with his buddy Terry McCoy, his partner for years on the Housing Authority police force.

Lewis, 46, shield No. 3135, left the force a year ago after 20 years spent patrolling sprawling housing projects in tough places like Fort Greene and Red Hook. He is a genuine hero and the only cop in this city's history to have been awarded two medals of valor.

He is also a minister and a superb athlete who has been written up in Sports Illustrated for his running ability. There were a few times when that sort of speed helped him capture criminals.

I met Lewis several years ago at his bungalow home in Queens, where he lives with his wife and two children, Lisa, 22, and Senise, 16, a 10th-grade student at Benjamin Cardozo High School in Bayside. Lewis is such an outstanding cop that a book is now being written about him by Lorenzo Carcaterra of Time magazine. It is called "Crack Cop," a title with more meanings than one, and it is believed to be the first biography ever written about a black cop. The big publishing house of Doubleday has first option on the book thanks to Bill Cosby, who has had his books published by them.

"I grew up in the Red Hook housing project myself," says Lewis, "and, when my superiors found out, they sent me there for the last four years I was on the force. Things had gotten out of hand, but, when the word that 'Dickie' — which is what people called me — was back, I was able to put a damper on things."

One reason the kids who lived in the housing projects could relate to Lewis is that he was no outsider — he even knew many of their parents. He had grown up with them. Another was that they respected his athletic ability, that led him to the Police Olympics, where he won several track medals.

But they also knew Lewis was not a part-time cop,

a cop who drove in and back from some other neighborhood each day. In a sense, he was one of their own, and it didn't hurt that he really cared about the kids.

"In the black community, the cops are often seen as oppressors," says Lewis. "I tried to change that image. I gave them rides on my motor scooter although that was taboo, and I could have gotten into a lot of trouble doing it."

Lewis did everything he could to show the kids that cops weren't people out to harm them or to put them in jail. He played baseball with them, and, when they asked to touch his gun, he would remove the bullets and let them hold it. "I took every advantage I had to let those kids know I was there to help them," he says.

Lewis with his daughter, Senise, and his two police medals of valor.

Street gangs and their lure for the young are well-known to Lewis, who was once a member of a street gang. It was called the El Kovans. In those days, the late 1950s, drugs were unheard of. The gangs were organized for street wars. Lewis was arrested once for possession of a dangerous weapon — a knife — and it was after that when he decided to quit the gang scene and do something better with his life.

He still recalls being given a YD-1 card, a Youth Division card, by the police. It was a badge of honor to the kids in his neighborhood, but to Lewis it was a badge of shame.

"The most important thing I ever did in my life was to quit the gang and join the school track and field team. I thought my time would be better spent running after school than running from the cops," says the veteran cop.

Lewis is also a minister, and a few weeks ago I went to the New Testament Church of God in the Bedford-Stuyvesant section of Brooklyn, where he preaches every Sunday. It was a rainy day and attendance was small, but Lewis delivered a lecture on the dangers of drugs and later met with some of the congregation in the basement for coffee and home-made doughnuts.

One of the best-kept secrets in this city is that the majority of the city's black population is law-abiding and deeply religious. Blacks generally get press only when they commit crimes against whites. You have only to go to a black church with someone like Robert White of the Human Resources Administration to understand that the city has neglected a wellspring of decency and spirituality in its efforts to combat the rising tide of drug-related crime.

Lewis often says that "I am a minister first and a cop second." He feels strongly that it was his faith in God that kept him from being killed in any of the six shootouts he was involved in. Two of those led to the deaths of criminals, and Lewis still recalls those deaths with a feeling of pain.

He is not a man you can use strong language around. That's because he feels he is a role model for youngsters and that, if he uses rough language, they will be encouraged to do the same. When Lewis meets with young people, he tells them to forget the drugs that have overtaken so many of them.

"I tell them to get hooked on Christ," he says. "Now that's a real high."

One year after Richard Lewis left the police force, this full-page article appeared in a special anti-drug edition of *Newsday*, featuring a photo of Detective Lewis (while still active with the department) examining the dark stairwell of a New York City housing project where he had gone to investigate a killing.

that senior citizen "push-in robbery" case in January of 1979 at the Red Hook Houses in South Brooklyn.

As I had done in Red Hook, my partner and I pulled all the rape and robbery arrest records dating as far back as 1970. When we finished going through all of the records, I had accumulated a list of over 40 past rape and robbery offenders. I submitted their names on photo request forms and placed them neatly in photo array folders. Then I got permission to work day tours so I could visit each victim with the photos after I notified them by telephone. On the very first interview, we got a hit. The pattern continued with the second, the third, and so on. Eighteen rape victims picked out the very same individual among the 40 photo folders. This individual was a light-skinned black man who had served four years for a rape conviction. Now it was just a matter of locating this man and taking him into custody.

We were all relieved to finally have a prime suspect in sight. Now that we knew who our man was, we were determined to get him. Investigation revealed that he was living in New Jersey with his mother and sister. For that reason, the case was turned over to the detective squad. The suspect was arrested in New Jersey in the middle of the month of May. The following March, the perpetrator was positively identified and convicted of 20 counts of rape, robbery, and possession of a dangerous weapon (among other things).

During our rape and robbery investigation, we also made a number of felony arrests. One arrest in particular was made on May 1, 1980. We were on our way to a rape victim's house that morning to let her view the photo array of suspects, and a few minutes before 11:00, something caught my attention. As I drove by a check-cashing establishment, I noticed two men who appeared to be "staking out" the business in search of vulnerable victims. Since it was the first day of the month, I knew that a lot of people in the area had received their pension checks, support checks, and payroll checks. Since this was an inner-city area, it wasn't exactly overflowing with banks, savings and loan branch locations, or ATM machines. Public housing residents most often came to neighborhood establishments like this one to cash their checks.

I passed the checking establishment and made a U-turn so I could park our vehicle where we could observe the two suspects while remaining unseen. In just a few minutes, we watched an elderly woman emerge from the check-cashing establishment, and we also watched the two young suspects begin to follow her. Not wanting to alert them to our presence, my partner and I followed them from a distance. We saw the lady enter a high-rise at Grant Houses, and we picked up the pace when the two suspects entered behind her.

In a matter of moments, we heard a woman scream. As I ran towards the lobby entrance, the two suspects exited the building at a dead run. One was carrying the pocketbook I saw in the possession of the woman. I went after the suspect with the handbag, while Rolland pursued the other man. They both were apprehended and charged with assault and robbery. Thank God we were in the right place at the right time to catch the perpetrators.

I really felt good after we arrested the serial rapist, along with the other arrests we made while on special assignment. My partner and I received yet another department decoration for a job well done. As I had done in the past, I submitted a request to be reassigned from the plainclothes division to the detective bureau, only to be denied yet again. Ironically, years later a white cop working with a decoy team used the same method I had used in the Manhattanville and Grant rape case to solve a similar rape epidemic in another part of the city. When the perpetrator was located and apprehended, this cop was labeled a hero, the story was published in the newspapers, and he was named as the *New York Daily News'* Hero Cop of the month.

# Chapter 8

# The Ultimate Price for Honor

*Greater love hath no man than this, that a man lay down his life for his friends* (John 15:13).

*For scarcely for a righteous man will one die: yet peradventure for a good man some would even dare to die* (Romans 5:7).

When police candidates take an oath to their state Penal Code and the Constitution of the United States, many don't really understand that they will be putting their very lives on the line to protect the life, limb, and property of others. Most, if not all, are caught up in the ecstasy of receiving an appointment to a police academy, and not much thought is given to the hazards of the job.

The truth of the matter is that police work does involve certain risks, although the odds of ever being in a shoot-out or being shot are very minute for most. Applications for openings in the police force of New York City are still overflowing and now include a very large female population due to the high salary and excellent fringe benefits. Yet the hazards exist and are increasing with each new day.

Most people avoid discussing death because there is something about dying that frightens or turns them off, but for police officers, there is no getting around the subject of death. One way or another, there will come a time in their careers when they will be confronted with the ultimate tragedy of life—death. Whether it be the normal death of an individual through natural causes or an accident, or the violent and premature death of a crime victim or criminal, or even the supreme sacrifice paid by a peace officer in the line of duty, a face-to-face meeting with death is inevitable.

When a cop is killed in the line of duty, the public often seems to become apathetic toward the life that has been taken. It reminds me of the attitude the American public displayed toward the young soldiers who obeyed orders and fought and gave their lives for this country in the Vietnam Conflict. Their wholesale rejection of Vietnam veterans was despicable to say the least. Without fail, the greatest admiration for fallen police officers and support for their grieving families comes from fellow police officers and their families.

The year of 1980 was a year marked by an upward spiraling crime wave and one of the most shocking encounters with death I had ever witnessed. After solving the rape and robbery epidemic in upper Manhattan, it was time to move on. I began to answer assignments all over the city where the incidence of serious crimes seemed to be growing unchecked. I was making major felony arrests almost every time I showed up for work! I was working in Brooklyn, Manhattan, and Queens, so I had court cases in all three boroughs. One would have never thought that serious crimes would escalate as fast as they did with no sign of relief in sight.

I worked as both a detective (without the title or pay) and an undercover anticrime cop. The workload was taxing the mind and body of every cop in the projects, mainly due to the growth of the drug trade, aided and abetted by a dark army of ruthless drug traffickers and local street pushers who polluted the inner-city neighborhoods with their poisonous venom.

Drug dealers and abusers were holding many black and Latino neighborhoods under siege and bringing new levels of violence to the doors of innocent people through ongoing territorial feuds. Rival drug lords waged open gun battles in the streets without concern for innocent bystanders of any age, seriously injuring many and killing some. The greatest tragedies involved babies shot in their cribs and children killed while playing in playgrounds in drug-prone areas. These incidents, along with countless robberies, burglaries, assaults, and other drug-related crimes had me constantly on the go.

July 23, 1980, in New York City was a typically hot and humid summer day. After testifying before the Brooklyn Grand Jury at 2:00 p.m., I proceeded to the Farragut Houses to do a follow-up investigation on a shooting at 177 Sands Street. Later on, I teamed up with Michael Taylor to work the rest of my tour. Taylor was a young black cop with roughly seven years of experience on the job. We decided to drive around the Fort Greene area to look for a suspect in relation to an assault and robbery incident he was investigating.

Shortly after 7:00 p.m., we received a radio call to respond to the Red Hook Housing Project. A man had been shot in the rear of the building at 80 Bush Street. *Eighty Bush Street–I grew up in that building. My family had lived in apartment 5C in that building!* We reached the crime scene in about ten minutes using the siren and emergency lights on the unmarked police car. A crowd had collected by the time we arrived, and a number of people who still knew me from my younger days in the Red Hook Project called out my old childhood nickname, "There goes Dickie!"

The victim had already been declared dead on arrival, and there had been witnesses to the shooting. I knew I would not have too much trouble finding out who had committed the crime because I still knew quite a few people in the Hook, and some were right there at the crime scene. I talked with Officer Maloney from NYPD's 76th Precinct in South Brooklyn, who was the first officer on the scene. Someone had placed a blue sheet over the victim's body, which was lying face down only a few feet from where Maloney and I stood. The Emergency Medical Service personnel interrupted us to say they were going to remove the victim's body from the crime scene for transport to Long Island College Hospital for an autopsy. (My thoughts were jolted again–*That is the same hospital I was born in...*)

Several people from Red Hook whom I knew took me aside and gave me the name and address of the shooter. Two of them had even witnessed the homicide. After my partner and I went to the hospital to talk briefly with the late victim's wife and sister, I called my lieutenant and told him about the incident. He gave me permission to work on the case since I knew the identity and address of the suspect.

We worked until 2:00 in the morning on the case and were hot on the trail of Wright Ebenezzar Walken*, our prime homicide suspect. He managed to elude us that day, so we came in early the next morning at 8:00. By 5:30 that evening, I located and arrested Walken in a house on Putnam Avenue near Nostrand Avenue. He was booked and charged with the murder of Rupurt Smith*.

The summer of 1980 proved to be hot in a number of ways. I was working a great deal of overtime because of the workload placed upon me and other men in the unit. The steady stream of homicides, felony assault cases, and other severe crimes were taking a toll on me, and I did not even realize it. I went on vacation to Aruba for a week and aired out my head. It was the best thing that could have happened to me at the time.

Another great stress manager for me was my continuing participation in the New York State Police Olympics, held every June since 1969. I trained every chance I had, and the running helped release a lot of built-up stress. Over the years, I won more than 60 track medals in the national and international Police Olympics, and I'm sure the exercise has been a lifesaver in more ways than one.

A week after I came off of vacation, I met with the commander of the Project Stabilization Unit. He teamed me up with another black cop named Carl Boylan and asked us to tackle a string of burglaries plaguing PSA #5. Over 35 burglaries had been committed in public housing projects and nearby private developments, covered by the jurisdictions of several New York City Police precincts. These burglaries were unusual because most, if not all, of the apartment door locks had been picked to gain entrance to the apartments. (Most burglars simply used brute force applied to a crowbar to force their way in). More than $200,000 worth of property had been taken so far.

*Here we go again,* I thought to myself. *It's another big assignment. What do they take me for? A miracle worker?* Boylan and I just nodded and went directly to PSA #5 in the heart of Harlem to sign in. Then we pulled all the records on past burglary reports and previous arrests to get all the information we could about the pattern and style of the perpetrators.

As I went over the reports I noticed that the intruders picked two and three locks on some of the apartment doors, which could only mean that these burglars were good. In fact, they had to be professionals. "Boylan, this is going to be a hard one to crack," I said as I looked up from the files. Boylan replied, "Yeah, the way it looks, we'll have to catch these suspects in the act of picking a lock on a door if we want the charges to stick."

We were hoping someone would notice suspicious strangers lingering in the hallways of his or her building and call the police, because we needed a break. I was glad to know this much: My suspect or suspects were willing to pick two and three locks on an apartment door. That told me they had an exceptional knowledge of locks—the kind of knowledge that only locksmiths possess.

The very first day Boylan and I reported to Harlem, three new burglaries were reported. Every entry was made by picking the door locks on the victim's apartment door. Each apartment was dusted for fingerprints and checked to see if the intruders left something behind that would help identify them. My partner and I conducted a follow-up investigation on the three burglaries and had a locksmith employed by New York City Housing remove the lock cylinders from the victims' doors and replace them with new ones. Then I took the removed cylinders to the police lab for examination. I wanted to know if lock-picking devices had being used to pick the locks or if some other instrument was used by the perpetrators to gain entrance to the victims' apartments.

The burglary victims were very upset about their losses from the burglaries, so they were very cooperative when we interviewed them and requested the lock cylinders. I believed the burglars lived or had lived in the area because the burglaries had occurred after the victims left their apartments in the morning. These criminals appeared to be very familiar with the dwellings they were targeting. They sure seemed to know that no one would be home in the apartments they hit. That could mean they watched to see when a tenant left his apartment, or that they knocked on a potential victim's door to see if anyone was home before picking the locks.

The only way to catch a thief is to be present when the thief strikes. That meant my partner and I had to work day tours, which also meant we were almost certain to come across other crimes in progress requiring necessary police action when warranted. During our burglary investigation, we were asked to respond to a self-inflicted gunshot incident involving a Latino man. We were greeted at the door by the man's hysterical mother who pointed to a back bedroom. We found her son lying on his back on the floor near his bed, in severe pain. His right leg was ripped open from the knee almost to the foot, with his bone exposed. It was a gruesome sight. He wore a long, Army green raincoat, and his right arm was halfway out of the coat. When I saw the wound and the coat, I had a hunch. When I looked under the bed, I saw the butt of a sawed-off pump shotgun.

I pulled the gun carefully from under the bed and saw a belt tied around the trigger guard of the weapon. At that point, it was easy to figure out what happened. By then, Emergency Service Unit personnel were on the scene and busily working on the man's leg, and he screamed out in pain as they administered aid to his leg.

It was clear to me that Juan Reposa*, the wounded man, was a stickup artist who was preparing for an armed robbery when he shot himself. He had fastened a belt to the trigger guard of his pump shotgun to make a sling. This let him sling the weapon from his right shoulder. When he put on the raincoat, the shotgun would be totally concealed under his coat and ready for quick action. Stickup artists like Reposa would walk into a business establishment, brandish a weapon from under his raincoat, pump a round from the shotgun, and as the round falls to the floor, announce a holdup. This time it backfired on him, and he became a victim of his own deadly game. When Reposa placed the shotgun under his arm, his belt sling somehow rested on the rear of the trigger itself instead of the trigger guard. When he let the weight of the gun drop onto the sling, it discharged into his right leg.

I arrested Reposa on the spot for possession of a weapon and for the illegal discharge of the weapon. His description fit that of a Hispanic male wanted for several armed robberies committed with a pump shotgun. He was positively identified later and charged with the armed robberies. It took a number of operations and other medical aid to help try and correct the severe injury to his right leg. When he was well enough, the district attorney's office held a bedside arraignment for him, and he was indicted by the Manhattan Grand Jury on several armed robbery accounts. He was found guilty and sentenced to prison after his discharge from the hospital.

Meanwhile, the burglaries began to occur more frequently. We had been coming down hard on some of the local "undesirables," and we managed to recruit one of them as an informant (who played a crucial role in later days). We got a break four weeks into the case when the suspects slipped up and entered an apartment while a female occupant was still home. Fortunately, she was awakened by the sound of her door closing. When she got up to see who had entered her apartment, she saw two Hispanic men in her living room and screamed, startling the two men, and they fled. She gave us a good description of the burglars, who were also seen by other tenants. A police artist provided a sketch of one of the alleged suspects, with the cooperation of the woman who had foiled the burglary, and we distributed the drawing to every uniformed officer on the beat.

One week later, two foot patrolmen found two suspicious Hispanic men loitering in the tenth floor stairwell of a building. One of the men fit the description of our suspect, so the officers took both men into custody and called me over the radio. Boylan and I arrived at 2:30 that afternoon, and when I saw the two men, I knew they were our boys. Now it was up to me as the lead investigator to prove that they were responsible for the burglaries in the area. Our problem was that we hadn't actually caught the suspects in the commission of a crime. My actions at this point could either make or destroy the case.

I had to extract all of the information from them that I could. It wasn't going to be easy because these men were experienced criminals. After I conferred with my partner and several other police officers, I came up with a plan to get us started.

When I entered the station room, the men were both seated with their left hands cuffed to their chairs. I purposely avoided looking in their direction and asked the police officer in the room to step out. Then my partner closed the door. The suspects had already been searched for weapons, but I felt that something wasn't right about these two. I walked over to Raul Treluga*, the most vulnerable of the two, and asked, "Have you ever been arrested for anything in the past?" When he nodded yes with his head, I told him to stand up and began to search his pockets again. Even a small piece of evidence missed in a search can make it difficult to solve a case. As I put my hand in Treluga's rear right pocket, I felt a small straight piece of metal that turned out to be a precision file used to pick locks. "What are you doing with this?" I asked. His only reply was, "I don't know." The trail had suddenly gotten hotter.

When I approached Manuel Figaro*, the other suspect, I could see he was nervous. In fact, he suddenly stood up when I came near him. "No one told you to get up! Sit down," I told him. Figaro had a large "afro" hairstyle, and he was acting very odd. I sensed that he was afraid of something. I purposely stood over him and started to question him about the 45 burglaries committed at Carver Houses, and I noticed that he was trying to keep me away from his head for some reason. I asked him, "What's wrong with your head, Figaro?" and ran both of my hands through his hair. He tried to avoid my hands, and I quickly discovered why. Lo and behold, I found two more burglary tools used for picking locks hidden in his hair! As I showed the tools to Boylan, I thought to myself, *I've got them where I want them now.*

Things fell right into place after my surprise discovery. I was able to connect the two with a number of past burglaries in the Carver Houses and in the Metro North Homes. Both men confessed to their crimes, and we recovered over 1,500 pieces of property, along with a sawed-off shotgun and a .25-caliber automatic pistol from the residence of Manuel Figaro. The value of the recovered property was well over $25,000, and it included jewelry, watches, and cameras; and that was only a portion of the more than $150,000 in property the two suspects had stolen.

Major articles in the *New York Post* and *The Daily News* explained how Figaro, who had been out of prison for a year and a half after serving time on a murder charge, committed more than 75 burglaries along with Raul Treluga. One of the most alarming facts uncovered in the investigation was that Figaro had learned locksmithing in a course offered to prisoners while they were serving time in upstate jails! Both men were convicted and sentenced to long prison terms.

The residents of the Carver Houses and the Metro North development were relieved by the arrests, and the publicity about the "hair burglars" helped give us a great sense of worth and satisfaction for breaking a tough case. Of course, the good publicity helped boost the rapidly declining image of cops in those days too.

For weeks after the burglary arrest, I was busy collecting evidence against the two suspects before their trial date. I had to contact all the victims and return recovered property to the proper owners. Thursday, November 20th, began like any other day. I started work at 2:00 p.m. because of a special investigation, and at 3:15, I was catching up on paperwork with Carl Boylan in an office in PSA #5 when we heard a relatively routine call come over the radio about a burglary in progress in a second-floor apartment at 1851 3rd Avenue, in the Washington Houses. I heard officers respond to the call, and I still remember that the dispatcher's last words were "proceed with caution."

I was in the middle of giving some information to Sergeant Bonepart from PSA #5 when we were jarred by the loud and piercing sound of a terrified man's voice explode from the radio speaker: "*10-13–Officer shot! Please hurry!*"

No one hesitated; this was the real thing. Every officer in the precinct office immediately dropped everything and ran for the police vehicles. As we ran out of the precinct office, we could still hear the dispatcher giving the location of the downed police officer. Her announcement was followed by a flood of responses from police units rushing to answer the officer's call for help. That is the one thing a police officer can bank on. If a call for help goes out, police officers from all three New York City departments will instantly respond to the best of their ability.

This call was from one of the officers who responded to the burglary in progress in the Washington Houses. Boylan took the wheel of the car as I rode "shotgun," and Sergeant Bonepart jumped in the rear seat. We sped down 5th Avenue towards 102nd Street with lights and siren blazing. (In fact, the air was full of sirens blasting from cop cars in response to the 10-13.) Boylan made a left turn onto 102nd Street, went two blocks, and suddenly screeched to a stop because a fire truck had answered a fire alarm and was blocking the street. Jumping the sidewalk, Boylan backed down 102nd Street on the sidewalk, crossed Lexington Avenue, and drove to 103rd Street going the wrong way. He then proceeded down 103rd the wrong way until we reached 3rd Avenue. We made a right, went up 3rd Avenue the wrong way to 102nd

Street, and turned left to go until we couldn't go any further because of the glut of police cars blocking the street.

We jumped out of the car and ran toward the rear of the building, seeing police officers everywhere. Then I saw something that was burned into my memory for the rest of my life. Four white NYPD police officers ran from the building carrying a black Housing Police officer in their arms to a waiting police vehicle to transport him to the hospital. There was no time to wait for an ambulance. All these men knew was that their fallen brother officer desperately needed help, and they were doing what they had to do to get him to the emergency room.

When I saw the fallen officer, I could not recognize him because half of his face had been blown away. I had seen some horrible deaths in Vietnam while serving in the U.S. Air Force, and on the job as a police officer, but none of them had such an impact on me. I will never forget the look of desperation on the faces of those four white cops who were carrying their black comrade, nor will I forget the terrible wound the officer suffered. No one really knows if those determined New York City Police officers knew that the mortally wounded cop was actually dead even as they carried him to the car, but I knew it the moment I saw him. I was in shock as I watched the men pass by me. I tried to render what help I could, but he was, in fact, dead on arrival.

All kinds of things began to run through my mind. My body went numb, and I felt helpless and paralyzed for a few moments. The only thing I can recall from that time is saying to my partner several times, "Did you see his face? Did you see his face? My God, did you see his face?!"

When I entered the building, another cop told me the fallen officer's name was James T. Dunston. The only information we had at the time was that he had been shot point-blank in the face with a pump shotgun. Boylan and I followed a trail of blood leading up the stairs from the stairwell to the crime scene in the second floor apartment. As we neared the second floor, the amount of blood increased. The second floor of the second story was covered with blood. Footprints had been made with blood leading down the corridor, and as I turned left down the corridor, I saw sneaker prints on the floor and a pool of blood in front of the apartment door where Officer Dunston had been shot.

After I talked with two of the detectives at the apartment, Boylan and I helped seal off the crime scene to keep the inquisitive public away from the area. Shootings always attracted crowds. Then we teamed up with other officers at the scene to conduct a search and investigation of the entire building. An officer had dropped his radio down the elevator shaft, so Boylan and I got a master key from the project manager's office and recovered the radio from the elevator shaft. Then we searched the rooftop and the incinerator for weapons or anything that would help us apprehend the three attackers.

Nearly three hours after the fatal shooting, Boylan and I joined other officers at the 23rd Precinct office for an update meeting. We learned that one suspect had been apprehended at the scene on the elevator. For some reason, he didn't leave the building with the other two suspects. A black off-duty detective from the 23rd Precinct noticed the man in the elevator as he entered the car on the eleventh floor. The detective was unaware that a police officer had been shot on the second floor, but he noticed that the man was acting very suspiciously. When the man made a gesture as if he was trying to avoid someone, the detective looked down at the man's feet and noticed that his sneakers were covered with blood and realized something was terribly wrong. He grabbed the man and went directly to the first floor in the elevator car.

When the elevator doors opened, the lobby of the building was crowded with police officers. He took his suspect directly to the Housing Authority Police captain and said, "Captain, this man might be part of whatever has gone down." How right he was. The Hispanic man was positively identified as one of the three suspects who took part in the armed robbery that resulted in the homicide of a police officer.

The first suspect cooperated with investigators and gave them the names of his two accomplices, so my partner and I began to canvass the area for clues and information that would help us locate and apprehend the suspects at large.

I had a gut feeling that the suspects were still hiding near the scene of the crime. Either they were hiding in an apartment or in one of the many abandoned buildings surrounding the neighborhood. Searching abandoned buildings for armed suspects was a hazardous task, but it had to be done. Boylan and I began carefully checking a number of the desolate buildings close to the Washington Houses. (There were quite a few abandoned in Harlem at that time. Many had become places of refuge for homeless drug addicts and criminals, and some were used as "shooting galleries" for junkies. Without exception, they were filled with all kinds of filthy debris, including human waste and hordes of rodents. My stomach turned every time I had to enter these death traps, but it was just one of the less pleasant sides of police work.)

We were still checking abandoned buildings on 103rd Street when a call came over the radio: "Three males with guns in the lobby of 218 East 104th Street." Boylan and I answered the call as backup units for the cops assigned to that beat, but we warned them that plainclothes cops were also responding to the call. We reached the location and found five men in the lobby of the building. Taking the necessary precautions, we approached the five men and learned why they were standing in the lobby. I recognized one of the Hispanic men as the undercover informant I had recruited while working on the burglary case.

We made eye contact, and he gestured to me that he wanted to talk. I pretended that I was looking for him and put my handcuffs on him so the other men would not suspect him of talking with the police. After we walked him to our car and put him in the rear seat, we drove off to a secluded place to see what he had to say.

Once we had parked out of sight in an isolated area near the East River, I began to talk with Juno* about the shooting of the cop. "Juno, do you know two men who go by the nicknames of 'Papo' and 'Chocolate'?" That was when I hit pay dirt. "Yeah, I know 'em. In fact, I just left them not five minutes before you picked me up! That's why I wanted you to take me with you."

I had given Juno my phone number a month earlier and told him to call anytime he wanted to reach me or my partner, Carl. He had called several times to give me valuable information on individuals who had committed serious felony crimes in the area. We always made sure we gave him a 10- or 20-dollar bill after he gave us some good information. He was our unofficial informer. Juno was into small-time criminal activity due to his drug habit, but his assistance was so valuable that I helped him get out of a few minor situations after he had been picked up by police. Every active streetwise cop knows the value of recruiting and developing one or two personal street informants. They come in handy at times, especially in critical times like this one.

Juno confirmed what I had suspected all along: The cop-killers were junkies and stickup artists. Juno said, "I know all three of the guys who popped the policeman. I was just with Papo and Chocolate in an abandoned tenement on 105th Street, the one between First and Second Avenues. I've known them all for a long time." When I asked him to describe the men, he was able to give me additional information that the police did not have before. We had been told in our briefing that the suspect called "Papo" was wearing a blue beret, but Juno said it was a hat with a small brim. He also said Papo was shorter than the 5′ 11″ height we had been given. Juno told me he didn't know the birth names of the suspects, but he could find out for me.

"Hey, those guys are still hangin' at the abandoned tenement on 105th," Juno said. "They're in the basement that we use as a shooting gallery. They were taking heroin when I talked to them about the robbery and shooting incident. They took turns telling me what happened and what they did at the apartment." The information Juno was giving me proved to be the most vital information of the entire investigation, making Juno a primary witness in the robbery and murder case.

After Juno finished telling what Papo and Chocolate had told him in the shooting gallery, I knew I had to get him over to the 23rd Precinct immediately with the information. The office was the command base for the investigation. The information Juno had given me about the suspects' accounts of the attack and the role each man played in the robbery and shooting caused a sensation to run through my body, and I could feel my heart beating faster.

I was the first to learn that the suspect called "Chocolate" had been wounded in two places on his left arm, and he was bleeding profusely from his gunshot wounds. Juno said, "We tried to get him to the hospital because of the way he was losing blood, but he refused to go because he was afraid he would be picked up by the police." Juno also told me that Papo had the pump shotgun, which he had sawed off himself; while Chocolate had a nickel-plated snub-nosed .38-caliber revolver. "We wrapped Chocolate's wrist and forearm as best we could to try and stop the bleeding," Juno said, as he showed me blood stains from Chocolate's wound on his coat.

Juno continued, "Papo showed me how he shot the cop point-blank in the face with the shotgun, and Chocolate how he exchanged fire with the fallen cop's partner." When I reached the 23rd Precinct with my informant, you can imagine the excitement that was created when everyone realized what we had learned from Juno. Unfortunately, bureaucracy nearly destroyed all of our gains. I had to type out all the information I had received from Juno on a "Complaint Follow-Up" form known affectionately as a "DD-5." All through my interview with Juno at the 23rd Precinct, my informant kept telling me, "You had better hurry up and get over to the shooting gallery, 'cause once Papo and Chocolate are finished shooting up, they will leave the building."

When it was finally decided that we would hit the building where Juno said two suspects were hiding, we went prepared with shotguns and all. We hit the location with an army of cops, but we just missed them by only a few minutes according to the junkies we found at the location. The shooting gallery looked just as Juno had described it. I even saw the spot where Chocolate had been bleeding. Now you will always find blood on the floor and walls of a shooting gallery, because junkies draw blood from their own veins to mix with their drugs before they inject the mixture back into their veins using a hypodermic syringe and needle. This process almost always allows blood to drop to the floor or even squirt on the walls. However, the large amount of blood I saw in one spot in the basement of that abandoned building could only come from someone who was seriously injured.

Although my tour of duty was due to end at 10:00 p.m., I was given permission to work overtime by my superior, and returned to the 23rd Precinct. Juno was still waiting there for me. (We purposely did not take him along for the raid.) When he saw that we did not have Papo and Chocolate with us, he said, "See, if you would have went to the location when I first told you about those guys, you would have found them there!"

Juno gave us the address of Chocolate's mother, which really helped the investigation. We squeezed all the information we could from Juno; the poor guy had been with us for more than three and a half hours. Since I knew he would be a key witness in the case, I had Juno give me several addresses and telephone numbers (including his mother's) where I could reach him right away when needed. Then my partner and I gave him about $40 and drove him to another location and released him.

The two murder suspects were picked up early that morning. Papo was picked up at his mother's house on the east side of Harlem. Chocolate was picked up in the Bronx at his sister's apartment in a city housing project. When detectives knocked on the door of the 12th-floor apartment, Chocolate tossed his nickel-plated, .35-caliber revolver out of a bedroom window where it was recovered by the cops who had surrounded the building.

I received a call that day from the chief of patrol. "Lewis, I want to commend you and your partner for the outstanding job you did in the investigation of the cop shooting and for coming up with a key witness to the killing. By the way, all of your inside information about the weapons and the wounded suspect was 'on the money.' " Just before he hung up the phone, he again said, "Good work, Lewis." I thought to myself the whole time, *That was the least I could do for a fallen comrade in arms.*

The day after the killing I spent several hours interviewing James T. Dunston's partner, along with some witnesses from the apartment where the incident occurred. By piecing together the information I gathered in those interviews, along with what we learned from my informant and from the murder suspects' testimonies, I was able to put together a precise account of what actually happened on that fatal day.

The story begins when the three suspects learned from another source that the owner of a small neighborhood grocery store kept a lot of money locked in a safe in his apartment. Papo, Chocolate, and the third suspect, Reposa, were stickup artists who supported their habit by pulling small-time armed robberies around Harlem. They decided to rob the store owner at his apartment in the Washington Houses. The three culprits forced their way into the man's apartment after they persuaded the occupants to open the door by disguising themselves as city housing maintenance men.

Once they were in the apartment they displayed their weapons and corralled everyone they saw in the living room. They stirred up a great deal of commotion when they began to terrorized the owner of the store, along with his wife, brother-in-law, son, and 11-year-old daughter. Meanwhile, the robbers didn't know that the owner had another daughter, who was about 12 years old, in the apartment at the time. She had been in a back bedroom when she heard her mother cry out, followed by Papo's loud threat to shoot her if she did not shut up.

While the robbers concentrated on forcing the store owner to tell them where his safe was hidden, his 12-year-old daughter hid herself in one of the bedroom closets, *taking the phone with her*! The young girl got herself situated in the closet, and though she was very frightened, she showed extraordinary courage as she quietly dialed 911 on the phone.

When the 911 operator answered, the little girl whispered, "There's a robber in my house!" and gave the operator her address and apartment number. The 911 operator tried to get more information from the child and asked for the telephone number she was calling from for a "call back." The little girl was frightened as it was because she was afraid the robbers would hear her, not realizing they were preoccupied with her parents and family in the front room. She gave the 911 operator only her phone number with no more explanation and abruptly hung up. Several seconds later, the phone rang again! It was the 911 operating calling back to verify the little girl's call. For obvious reasons, the little girl did not answer the phone, and the robbers would not let the people in the living room answer it either.

When the 911 operator did not get a response to her call back, she dispatched the job as a "possible burglary in progress." Officer Dunston and his partner Davis received the call. The two cops had it in their minds that they were responding to a possible "burglary in progress," so they weren't mentally prepared to confront an "armed robbery in progress." Had the 911 operator broadcast a "robbery" in progress instead of a burglary, the two cops would have responded with the support of plenty of backup cops on the scene.

The little girl remained in the closet, silently praying that help would arrive soon. She could hear the pain-filled sounds her father made as one of the robbers assaulted him in an effort to make him reveal the location of the safe and money. Then this ugly scene was interrupted by a sudden knock at the door. Papo, who seemed to be the robber in charge, suddenly hissed to everyone, "Keep quiet or I'll kill you!" Then he motioned to Chocolate to look through the peephole in the door to see who was knocking. Then the knock came again and Dunston shouted, "Police!" Chocolate quickly looked through the peephole and confirmed what they feared. They had to think fast. There they were in the apartment with two cops outside the door! Papo decided to let the owner's daughter answer the door. He told her to tell the police everything was all right or he would kill her and everyone else in the living room.

The store owner's apartment was located at the end of an L-shaped corridor. Officer Dunston and his partner, Officer Davis, walked up to the second floor using the stairs located in the center of the corridor, facing the elevators. They exited the stairwell and went to their right down a corridor with apartments on both sides. The long part of the "L" was behind them, and they had to make a left and walk down to the end of the short corridor with a solid wall on one side. The apartment where the suspects were waiting was at the end of this short corridor to the right. This is where the two cops stood on either side of the closed door, trying to figure out if there was a burglary in progress inside the apartment.

Papo and Chocolate pulled the store owner's daughter slowly toward the door, and her relatives were overcome with fear. Then Papo again warned the little girl what would happen if she tipped off the cops about their presence in the apartment. The kitchen was located to the left of the door, and a wall concealed it from the view of anyone standing in the hallway. Papo stepped behind the wall and into the kitchen, holding the shotgun at ready. Chocolate moved two or three steps closer to the door with the girl, placing her squarely in front of the door before flattening himself against the wall behind the door where he would be hidden from view.

After another knock on the door and a second shout of "Police!" the frightened young girl, by now nearly out of her wits, looked at Chocolate in desperation. When he motioned to her to answer the door, she opened the door and faced the two cops. Dunston asked, "Did anyone here call the police?" In her fright, the young girl did not respond, but just stood there silently. Again, Officer Dunston said, "Miss, I asked you if anyone here called the police." Dunston must have known that something was wrong when the girl started to tremble and by the deep fear expressed in her face and eyes.

Meanwhile, Dunston's partner, Davis, happened to look through the crack in the rear of the door and spotted Chocolate with the nickel-plated revolver in his hand. Davis alerted his partner as he pulled his revolver, and a shot suddenly rang out as Papo stepped from behind the wall in the kitchen with the pump shotgun. His point-blank blast leveled at Dunston hit the unsuspecting officer full in the face, dropping him to the floor. Meanwhile, Chocolate fired several rounds at Davis from behind the door as Davis continued to fire into the apartment. Davis could clearly see that his partner and the little girl had been seriously wounded as they lay on the floor in a spreading pool of blood. He was in a serious position himself. He had emptied his gun, and he had no cover in the face of attackers who had superior fire power and unlimited cover. The only thing left for him to do was to retreat. As he ran down the corridor searching for a place to reload and call for backup, Papo fired another blast at the fleeing officer with his sawed-off shotgun, barely missing him.

Davis was now in a panicked frame of mind. He had just been shot at, and he had seen his partner and a young girl fall to the floor after being cut down with shotgun blasts to the face. He desperately ran down the stairs and out the front of the building while transmitting over his radio, "*10-13, my partner has been shot!*"

He gave the location of the shooting and said desperately, "Please hurry!" Meanwhile, the three suspects were still in the apartment trying to figure out what to do next. They did not know where the fallen officer's partner was, so they were stuck in the apartment. The mother and father were horrified at what had just occurred, and the girl in the bedroom closet stayed where she was, terrified with fright after hearing all of the shooting and commotion in the front of the apartment.

Officer Davis regained his composure and quickly reloaded his .38-caliber service revolver on the first floor while Papo cautiously peeped out of the apartment and looked down the corridor wondering where Davis was. He fired a shotgun blast down the corridor, and when there was no response to his gunfire, the men decided to leave the apartment. The suspects stepped over the wounded girl and fallen cop in the blood-covered hallway, getting blood all over their shoes and sneakers in the process. When they reached the end of the hall, they stopped, and Papo looked to his right around the corner to the end of the corridor. No one was at the elevator, and the doors to the stairwells were closed at the center of the hallway. Again, he fired a blast from the shotgun, actually striking the door at the opposite end of the corridor, and again there was no response to his fire. The three suspects ran to the stairwell and carefully opened the door to make sure no one was there. Then they ran down the steps and out the rear door.

By that time, Davis had reached the rear door, and he quickly fired a volley of rounds at the two fleeing cop killers. Papo stopped, pumped another round into the chamber of his shotgun, and fired at Davis. Davis ducked back inside the building, and Papo and Chocolate vanished from sight. The two suspects headed for the shooting gallery on 105th Street where they met my informant, Juno.

In the end, it was Juno's key information that brought the fugitives to justice. A good, honest cop was dead, and his family deprived of his presence for life. The young girl who was also shot in the firefight was taken to the same hospital where Officer Dunston was pronounced dead on arrival. Doctors were able to effectively treat her for a gunshot wound to the face, but only God could heal the inner wounds she suffered. Everyone who saw the crime scene was struck by the gruesome sight of blood and countless bullet holes that seemed to be everywhere. The immediate area of the apartment inside and out looked like a small battle zone, all for the paltry sum of $450 taken by the killers in return for the murder, assault, and robbery they committed.

One year after the incident, all three suspects were tried in the Supreme Court of the State of New York, and found guilty of the murder of Police Officer James T. Dunston, along with a number of other felony charges. All three defendants received the maximum sentence of 25 years to life without parole.

The death of Officer James T. Dunston exemplifies the ultimate price many cops have paid in the line of duty. Officer Dunston was posthumously awarded the police department's highest award for valor, the Medal of Honor. The award was respectfully presented to his widow and two children in a public ceremony. This chapter is dedicated to the memory of all those Housing cops who have sacrificed their own lives that others might live, paying the ultimate price for honor. We salute you and thank you for a job well done. May you rest in eternal peace.

---

*The names of these individuals have been changed or altered for reasons of safety, anonymity, and privacy, and bear no actual relationship to persons alive or dead. The situations and incidents, however, occurred exactly as described in this book, and in official court records.

# Chapter 9

# "Five-O" Street Alert

Crime continued to climb in New York City in the early 80's, mainly due to the escalation of illegal drug trafficking. Illicit drug sales and abuse were on the rise, and New York City found itself in the middle of a gun and homicide epidemic. Guns became the weapons of choice for young school kids as well as the criminals dealing in illegal drugs. More and more young teenagers were being caught up in this violent web.

When the news media began to focus more attention on violent crimes occurring in the five boroughs, public alarm was stirred and this in turn forced the politicians to respond. Their classic response was to put pressure on the police brass to "do something" to get the situation under control (with no additional support, funding, or commitments from the politicians of course).

A drug task force unit was organized within my unit to concentrate on drug dealers and drug abusers. Four other experienced, streetwise cops were placed in the unit with me. I teamed up with Albert Layne, one of the most knowledgeable cops in the city. Layne and I had worked together before, but this assignment was new and extremely dangerous. In fact, any assignment involving drug traffickers is very hazardous, not only to cops but to everyone in close proximity to the activity. Our job was to apprehend drug dealers and abusers.

We would conduct the operation in plainclothes, and we all had to take extra precautions so the local street pushers and their

139

cohorts did not get the drop on us. Nearly all these criminals packed a gun or kept a heavily armed associate on guard nearby. Rival drug pushers were constantly battling for top sales locations, so if one drug spot was doing a big business, it was certain that rival drug lords would try to uproot their prospering rival and take over their location.

By this time, I was becoming aware of some inequities in the police department's structure, but for the time being, I kept it to myself. In view of all that I had achieved, especially in the cop-killing case, I thought that by now, I would have received a gold shield or would have been promoted a step in rank to detective. Like any thinking person, I had the ambition to achieve and progress in my career. Yet despite my best efforts and a growing list of honors and professional achievements, it was becoming clear that for some reason, I was not being allowed "out of my box."

I forced myself to focus all my attention on the job at hand, and I knew it would be no picnic. My unit was posed to be instantly deployed to any area of New York City where a serious drug traffic problem arose. We were assigned a new, light blue, unmarked van that was devoid of any police markings or equipment for our safety as undercover officers.

Since the drug business was thriving, I knew our felony arrests would "thrive" too. There were drug hot spots in nearly every neighborhood in New York City, including the Wall Street business district and along 42nd Street.

Our first target area was in the Brownsville section of Brooklyn. Layne smiled when he heard we were going to the Brownsville area. "Brother, that's like the fox throwing the rabbit into the brier patch. I've not only worked that place, I've lived in the neighborhood! I know everybody who's into drugs and crime." The heavily populated Brownsville area was home predominantly to poor and low-income black and Hispanic families. The many city housing complexes occupied more than half of the total real estate area in

Brownsville. As in every other poor and low-income community around the city, Brownsville had more than its share of abandoned buildings and lots. These dangerous eyesores made the area look like a bombed-out war zone. While the crime situation had always been high, drug trafficking had gotten totally out of hand, and the good people of the community were suffering at the hands of the lawless. I could only feel compassion for the honest citizens who lived in this run-down community plagued with such an over-whelming crime rate.

It is one thing to live in the inner city under such deplorable conditions, but it is another thing to be victimized by the low-life criminals who live there. You almost have to live in or spend a sig-nificant amount of time in a ghetto to really understand the pain, frustration, and constant anxiety plaguing its honest residents. Drug dealers, drug abusers, and criminals held much of Browns-ville under virtual siege around the clock. This was the norm in ghetto neighborhoods all over New York City.

In many places, the elderly were afraid to leave their apart-ments for fear of being mugged and assaulted. They were like pris-oners locked up in their own home, and even most of the healthy, younger residents would not dare to venture out after sundown. The heartless and vicious criminals in these areas would not hesi-tate to inflict bodily harm or kill their victims. They had a way of dressing, walking, and talking that intimidated most people. Expe-rience had proven to me that it takes a tough, hard-nosed, street-smart cop to deal effectively with hard-core criminals.

Chronic drug abusers acquire the "talent" to become patho-logical liars. I've seen them participate in illegal activity, and when I confronted them, they have actually tried to convince me that what I saw was not really what I saw at all. A person who is strung out on drugs looses all self-esteem and self-respect. Those who get hooked on a controlled substance allow their lives to be conquered by that substance. All they live for and care about is getting more of that poisonous substance into their bodies. They will do anything and everything to obtain that substance. They even steal from their own families. Some have even killed to get money to support their addictions.

It doesn't matter whether a person is rich or poor, educated or ignorant, black or white, drug abuse crosses all boundaries. Abusers can be found in rich neighborhoods, middle-income communities, and in ghetto communities. They number in the millions, and as more abusers swell the ranks, they often resort to crime to support their addictions. We all are affected by their criminal behavior. Just as the alcoholics will drink from the same bottle, drug addicts will share from the same needle, leaving themselves more susceptible to deadly diseases such as AIDS and Hepatitis B. If you saw the open ulcers and the swollen bodies of intravenous drug abusers in the shooting galleries as I have, the sight and stench would turn your stomach. These modern-day zombies are truly the "living dead." Every time they shoot, smoke, snort, freebase, or skin pop drugs, another part of their lives is snuffed out.

I came across a Christian tract entitled, "The Psalm of the Addict," that I believe sums up the terror and destruction one faces when experimenting and abusing a controlled substance. These words were written by a dope addict lost in the dream world of heroin:

> "King Heroin is my shepherd, I shall always want. He maketh me to lie down in the gutters. He leadeth me beside the troubled waters. He destroyeth my soul. He leadeth me in the paths of wickedness for the effort's sake. Yes, I shall walk through the valley of poverty and fear all evil; for thou, Heroin, art with me. Thy needle and capsule try to conform me. Thou strippest the table of groceries in the presence of my family. Thou robbest my head of reason. My cup of sorrow runneth over. Surely heroin addiction shall stalk me all the days of my life and I will dwell in the House of the Damned forever."

The tract explained that this "psalm" was written on the front of a card and found in a telephone booth. The back of the card bore this sad, handwritten postscript:

> "Truly this is my psalm. I am a young woman, 20 years of age, and for the past year and one half I have been wandering down the nightmare of the junkie. I want to quit taking dope and I try but I can't. Jail didn't cure me. Nor did hospitalization help me for long. The doctor told my family it would have been better and indeed kinder if the person who first got me hooked on dope had taken a gun and blown my brains out. And I wish to God she had. My God how I do wish it."

So there I was in the heart of Brownsville, working the four-to-midnight tour in the newly formed antidrug unit. We were there for business, and there was plenty of it on the streets. We had already warned the area commanders of the Housing Police and the NYPD that plainclothes units would be working in respective precincts. These commanders told their uniformed officers to stay out of our target area unless they were called to an emergency or to back us up.

When we hit the streets that spring evening in May of 1981, the pedestrian traffic was heavy as usual on Belmont Avenue in the Brownsville section of Brooklyn. The many discount and variety stores in the area made it a favorite shopping location. People came there from all over New York City and Long Island looking for a good deal on every item you could think of. There was even a large fishing coop there that sold every kind of fresh fish to an eager clientele. Business was good, but many of the businesses were now complaining that the growing army of junkies was stealing merchandise and robbing their customers.

The outcry of the merchants and the alarming number of robberies, including purse and gold chain snatching, had brought us to that location that night. All kinds of drug activity were going on.

Also at this location, a building on Powell Street near Belmont Avenue housed the Methadone Maintenance Program, which served hundreds of drug addicts as a part of a court-ordered, "drug-weaning" therapy regimen. Many people who were arrested for possession of a controlled substance in amounts lower than a specified "felony weight" qualified for the so-called "plea bargaining" system in court, and were offered a lighter sentence if they agreed to enroll in a drug rehabilitation program then known as "The Rockefeller Program." (In essence, it was the methadone maintenance program.) Our experience on the street was that more than 85 percent of the addicts who signed up for the program did it solely to stay out of jail. The truth was that they were abusing the program and still using drugs.

Everyone working the drug scene habitually dressed in a way that blended in with everyone else on the streets. Therefore, Layne and I decided to go into the target area on foot to get a closer look at who was doing what. As we approached Belmont Avenue, we immediately spotted several illegal drug activities in progress. We knew once we took action our covers would be blown, so we waited until we had witnessed about four drug deals. We knew the street pushers had stopped carrying their drug supplys on their persons to avoid arrest for possession of drugs. We waited and watched to see where they had stashed their supplies.

We made the call, and when the unmarked van arrived with the backup team, my partner and I pointed to four individual pushers. Layne and I each grabbed one, and the other two were picked up by the other cops. We also arrested several drug buyers who had made purchases and were trying to leave the area. Two of the pushers had their drugs hidden under garbage cans; a third had hidden his stash in a bag under a large rock in an empty lot; and the fourth had hidden his drug supply behind the bumper of a parked car. To say the least, the pushers were surprised when we arrested them and retrieved their hidden drug stashes.

During our first quarter of an hour on the street, we had already made seven felony arrests! This was just the beginning of what would turn out to be a two-and-a-half-year, undercover, antidrug marathon. It was the most dangerous, repulsive, traumatizing, and highly productive time of my career as a New York City law enforcement officer. Our next tour was a repeat of the previous one, except that I personally made six drug arrests and confiscated two loaded handguns. After just a few tours, the entire unit really got into the swing of things. It wasn't hard adapting to our new assignment. We simply had to adapt our strategies for each situation to outwit the criminal mind.

We had to become criminal tacticians to deal with drug traffickers. It was extremely hazardous, and as I would personally discover, it could quickly become a matter of life or death. I quickly lost count of the times I had to run down a pusher when they would break and run on me. Once in a while, this would happen before I could search them for deadly weapons. Almost without exception, when I caught up with these suspects, they were packing a loaded handgun. Many times, I would get into a scuffle with them; and each time, I couldn't help but wonder, "Is this suspect packing a gun? Can I subdue him before he can reach his weapon?"

One evening I noticed a male Hispanic sitting in a parked red vehicle behind an abandoned building near Powell Street. I watched him from a distance, knowing he couldn't see me. A black two-door sedan parked behind the red car, and its driver slipped into the front passenger seat of the red vehicle. I had a gut feeling that these guys were up to no good. I somehow sensed that drugs were involved. I alerted Layne, and we decided to lay low to observe the situation. The men seemed to be engaged in a serious conversation. Then the man seated on the passenger side of the red car walked back to the rear of the black car. He took a key from his right front pants pocket, unlocked the trunk, and pulled a small brown leather bag from the trunk. Then he closed the trunk and returned to the red car.

I had a feeling that their business had to do with what was in the brown leather bag. They appeared to be looking down at something between them on the seat of the car, so I decided it was time for me to take a look myself. I approached the car as if I was just walking by on the sidewalk. When I got close enough, I looked into the car window and saw the man seated in the driver's seat examining a plastic sandwich bag full of some white substance. My heart beat rapidly as I walked away from the car toward the opposite corner and toward my concealed partner. It was a feeling I had experienced countless times before when I faced high-risk felony situations; I felt like my heart was in my throat.

I kept cool as I walked away from the parked cars so I wouldn't tip them off, but they were so focused on what they were doing that they did not look up even when I passed by. When I finally reached the opposite corner, I turned to my right and walked out of sight of the red car. Then I called Layne on my radio: "Layne, it's going down, and it's big time! We're going to need backup right away." Layne quickly said he would have our backup meet us one street over from the location of the suspects. It didn't take long for the blue van to arrive. By that time, Layne and I were together again. We rapidly plotted our strategy and decided to send in four men on foot, while the remaining four officers would stay with the van, ready to move at a moment's notice.

Two men would come up from the rear of the suspects' vehicle, while two others would walk back around the corner and approach the car from the front. That way we hoped we would be able to have a clear view of the two suspects in the car and get the drop on them if they pulled weapons and tried something. When we came up on them, the van was to converge on the car simultaneously, presenting an overwhelming presence of force, and therefore minimizing our risk.

Everything went as planned. We hit the suspects so quickly that they didn't have time to think or retaliate. We seized one handgun and two plastic bags containing a combined weight of a half a kilo of cocaine! The gun found in the brown leather bag with the cocaine belonged to the man in the passenger's seat. We handcuffed and searched both men and placed them in the van for transport to the police precinct office. When we searched the men, one of them was carrying two 9-millimeter magazines, each one fully loaded with 14 live rounds. Yet he wasn't carrying a gun, just $10,000 in cash. (Doesn't everyone carry that much pocket change?) Then Layne and I drove the two cars belonging to the suspects to the precinct where they were also thoroughly searched.

I knew a 9-millimeter gun had to be in that red car somewhere, and I hoped the cops searching the car would come up with it. Yet when the cops had finished their search of the vehicles, they told me they had found no trace of any gun. I asked them, "Could you take another look in the red car? I know the driver's gun has to be in it." They searched again, but to no avail. Finally I went out and searched the car myself, and I found the gun secured in the spare tire.

It was clear to me that these suspects were into big-time drug trafficking, so I turned their names and all evidence files over to the police intelligence unit so a follow-up investigation could be done. Making drug arrests was a long and drawn out process. Although an individual officer no longer had to personally transport evidence to the city's only police lab on 21st Street in Manhattan, the arresting officer still had to "voucher" all seized evidence. (This change was made to cut down on the enormous amount of overtime cops were making.) I vouchered all the drugs, guns, ammunition, and money seized in the arrest, and both suspects were charged with possession of a controlled substance with intent to sell; one man was charged with possession of firearms.

My unit continued to work the Brownsville area for four more weeks, until we had made such an impact that the criminal element began to recognize us. Then we knew it was time for us to relocate for a while, so we were assigned to work the Fort Greene section of Brooklyn. That was when a new name for cops hit the streets:

"Five-O." The name was *borrowed* from a popular television program at the time titled, "Hawaii Five-O."

Layne and I were making arrests on every tour, and I was averaging eight to ten felony arrests a week. One time we were cruising a drug-prone area on Myrtle Avenue near the Fort Greene Housing Complex when we came upon a holdup in progress. A male assailant was pointing a small .22-caliber handgun at the victim, a postal worker who had just cashed his paycheck. Layne and I came up behind the suspect, and we both placed our (rather big) guns on each side of the perpetrator's head. He gave up without incident.

A search of the suspect produced four uncashed welfare checks worth over $900, four Social Services Department identification cards, four Social Security cards, and four medical identification cards for the drug rehabilitation program! He had been arrested previously for a minor drug violation and had copped out to the Rockefeller Program when offered an ultimatum in a plea-bargaining situation.

Many repeat drug offenders took advantage of drug programs in New York City because once they were enrolled in a drug program, they became eligible for public assistance. This man had devised a slick scheme to collect several checks and other benefits from the city (in addition to his "income" from armed robbery). Our search uncovered a written list naming the locations, dates, and times he was to report to each welfare center and medical center to sign for his checks and pick up his methadone. He used the Department of Social Services I.D. cards to prove to welfare that he was going to the medical center for his drug rehabilitation medicine (which he more than likely was selling to pay for his drug of choice).

By the way, I met this young offender again about five years later after his release from jail. At that time, he was getting his life together and was working toward a bachelor's degree. I was delighted to see that this man had made some positive progress in his life. When I had arrested him years before, I admonished him about abusing his God-given talent and ability. I told him the energy and knowledge he wasted engineering that scheme to steal from the government could be channeled into doing something constructive and rewarding in his life. I thank God that he listened to me and did something to turn his life around.

Gradually, the nation's entire network of federal, state, and local law enforcement agencies began to work together to quell the rise of drug trafficking and drug abuse in the 80's. The drug abuse epidemic had permeated every segment of society, and it was destroying the very fabric of America's families, social structure, and economic stability. Nearly every law enforcement and court system was being overrun with drug arrests and arrests for drug-related crimes.

On any given night, the police booking and court system in New York City would be backed up with drug arrests. To make matters worse, the drug dealers we faced began to get younger and younger, and much more bold and violent. This new breed seemed to be more openly hostile to the police than ever. Not only did we have to take the necessary precautions in dealing with local street pushers, but the drug addicts themselves seemed more likely and willing to violently resist arrest, and many were high from the drugs they were abusing.

Every variety of controlled substance was available for sale or abuse on the streets of New York. Certain areas offered specialized substances like phencyclidine (known on the street as PCP, or "angel dust"), LSD ("acid"), and hashish, just to name a few. The most popular drugs, including heroin, cocaine, barbiturates, amphetamines, and marijuana, could be found almost anywhere in all five boroughs. As the days, weeks, and months passed, we found ourselves working all five boroughs—uptown, downtown, across town, or in the center of town. If you named it, we were there. And if we hadn't been, we soon would be.

I had cases in criminal and supreme courts in all five boroughs. If I wasn't in court testifying on a previous arrest case, then I was in one of the five boroughs' central booking offices processing a new arrest. The only time I was not making an arrest was when I wasn't working. At times, I couldn't help but make a collar even while off duty!

By now, our unmarked van was known by drug dealers and junkies all over the city. As soon as our van was spotted entering a neighborhood, the alert would go out: "Five-O! Five-O!" That forced us to think of a scheme to keep the van from spooking the criminal element on the streets.

One hot Friday afternoon in June, my unit had been assigned to work the four-to-midnight tour up in Harlem around 114th Street near Lenox Avenue. Our new scheme placed Layne and I in the target area on foot in advance. When the other officers came through the neighborhood in the dreaded blue van, Layne and I watched unnoticed as all the drug dealers scrambled to their secret hiding places to retrieve their stashed drugs. As they retrieved their drugs, we arrested them on the spot!

On this particular day, I walked down one side of 114th Street while Layne took the other side. As soon as the blue van turned onto the block, the word spread like wildfire, "Five-O! Five-O!" I couldn't resist helping the effort a little. As I passed a suspected drug pusher, I whispered to him, "Five-O!" and he immediately stepped back into the lobby of the building behind him. I signaled to Layne that I was going in to check out my suspect in the building.

I entered the lobby as if I was glad to get out of sight as the blue van drove by, and then I approached the man in the building and said, "Hey man, whatcha got?" His only reply was, "Quarters." Then I said, "...of what? Coke or heroin?" He blinked and said, "Heroin." A quarter of heroin came in a glassine envelope and could be bought for about $40 in those days. "How much do you have?" I asked, and he said, "How much do you want?"

*This guy must have a good supply on him,* I thought to myself. Then I pulled out my own money and pretended to count: "One hundred...two hundred..." As I counted the money, the suspect pulled a brown paper bag out from under his shirt and started counting out glassine envelopes containing the white heroin powder.

While he was busy counting his supply of glassine envelopes, I looked around and saw my partner standing to the side of the entrance door. Then I put the money back into my pocket and pulled out the police shield hanging on a chain around my neck. I didn't say anything to the man; I just put my shield in his face. He seemed puzzled for a moment. First he looked at my shield, and then at the drugs he was holding in his right hand. He appeared to be under the influence of an intoxicant of some sort, and was slow to react. When he finally realized I was a cop and that he was busted, he tried to run on me; and that is when I knocked him to the floor. My partner ran into the lobby when he saw the scuffle break out.

Layne was about 6' 6" tall, and he weighed about 270 pounds. He put all of his weight on the suspect who weighed about 130 pounds soaking wet. Incredibly, the suspect seemed to lift my partner up as he tried desperately to pick himself up from the floor. I had to help hold him down when he tried to keep us from handcuffing him. When we finally got the cuffs on him, we recovered about $1500 worth of heroin. We later learned that he had been high on PCP, better known as angel dust. That explained his almost supernatural strength and dazed appearance.

Phencyclidine, commonly called PCP or angel dust, is a hallucinogen. It causes illusions and hallucinations, and it distorts a person's perception of time and distance. It sometimes makes abusers exceptionally strong. That was what my partner and I experienced with the heroin dealer. After I processed the pusher through Manhattan Central Booking, he was lodged in a holding pen at Central Booking in NYPD headquarters at 1 Police Plaza.

At times, the court system would be backed up for two days or more because of the enormous number of arrests being made by cops all over the city. As the number of arrests I was making continued to increase, so did my overtime. I was averaging well over 100 hours of overtime a month! The job was getting more and more hazardous for me and my partner because of the countless close calls he and I had faced. Our unit was not too well liked by the criminal element throughout the city for obvious reasons. Our big sweeps would put a huge dent in the illegal drug activity in any given neighborhood, so we were most certainly considered bad for the drug business in New York City.

While the good people in the communities were happy we were doing such a great job, the drug pushers had become so enraged by our curtailment of their illegal drug sales that they were making anonymous and threatening phone calls to various precinct headquarters about "those undercover cops with the unmarked blue police van." The callers usually threatened to shoot a police officer in retaliation for the arrests the undercover police were making.

When the Staten Island borough received a number of threatening calls, our supervisors took the calls seriously and kept us out of that particular target area for a time. Naturally once we were allowed to go back into that area, we went in like excited cowboys on a roundup! Everyone we could get our hands on who was selling or buying drugs got arrested. Sometimes we each had five or more collars going to Central Booking at once—just like a real roundup in the West.

On April 1, 1981, my unit was again working in Staten Island. We were returning to our target area after an early meal when we came upon a fistfight between two young men. I yelled to the cop driving the van to stop. When he did, I jumped out along with my partner intending to break up the fight. As we approached on foot, I saw a woman (whom we later identified as the mother of one of the young men) walking towards the two men. She was cursing at one of the men, and as she neared them, she shouted that she was going to kill him. The man broke away from the woman's son and started to back away from the woman. That is when I saw the woman reach into her handbag and pull out a handgun!

The man turned and ran for his life when he saw the weapon. The woman fired once and missed him. That is when I ran up behind her, grabbed the gun, and disarmed her with a martial arts technique. She was arrested and booked on attempted murder, criminal use of a firearm, and possession of a deadly weapon. The story made the *New York Post* and *The Staten Island Advance Newspaper*.

That year alone, I made over 100 arrests involving firearms. During the two and a half years I spent in narcotics, I made close to 1,000 arrests, of which more than 800 were felonies! The money I made from all the overtime I put in caught the attention of several best-selling New York City newspapers, and resulted in a number of articles profiling myself, Layne, and a number of other cops from the three police departments. These articles highlighted the number of arrests each individual cop had made in a year's time, and the amount of money we made. That particular article noted that I had personally made over 400 arrests that year, and earned more than $25,000 in overtime money. The public response to the article was overwhelming. The consensus was: "If those cops make that many exceptional arrests, then they deserve the overtime money and more!" Such is the life on the "New York City Five-O."

# Chapter 10

# A Shook-up Generation

Charles Dickens wrote in the book entitled, *A Tale of Two Cities*, It was the best of times, it was the worst of times." If I have learned anything, it is that while circumstances are caused by people, people also change because of circumstances. Since my early childhood, and especially since I became a police officer in New York City, I have seen that people interact with the things and circumstances around them from the time they enter the world to the time they depart. It is more important than ever for parents to train their offspring from birth to do the right things in life.

Children today cannot look to or depend upon movie or sports celebrities to be their heroes or role models. Too many of them get caught up in negative and perverted things that destroy their lives. The true heroes and role models in a child's life should be his own parents, grandparents, or near kin—in that order. Anyone else is subject to fail them. Kids really need heroes in their lives; it is vital that they have someone they can look up to.

In the beginning of the 80's, I saw a new breed of criminals surface. They were younger than the norm, and they were more aggressive and vocal. Their rationality or ability to reason and control their raw impulses was minimized and substituted by unchecked violence. Their focus of life seemed to be limited to the materialistic love of things and the uncontrolled involvement with drugs and sex. Immorality was running rampant, just as it runs rampant in

155

our society today. Unfortunately, the very young or the vulnerable are always the targets, products, and victims of illegal drugs, sex, and violence that are plaguing communities like a malignant cancer.

Everything seemed to take a sudden turn for the worse. Music started to get louder and more violence-prone. Heavy metal music, punk rock, rap music, and alternative music all took their turns at bat to promote permissive sex, drug use, and overt violence against cops, other races, the opposite sex, or whoever or whatever happened to "be in the way." It had a tremendously devastating effect on the younger generation. Even the way the young teenage and adult males began to dress was intimidating. The oversized clothes featuring pants without belts hanging below the waist was a style copied directly from the style of convicts in prison. As these dangerous new fads were introduced to black and Hispanic youths in the ghettos, and to young people of every race, color, and economic position across the country, the angry influence of the culture on teen behavior started to take its toll on our communities. Young teenagers started to experiment with dangerous drugs, and many died the first time they experimented with controlled substances; and young teenage girls began to have babies at an alarming rate no one had predicted.

The government's solution to the drug and crime crisis was to require that stiffer prison sentences be given to convicted felons, that more "bigger and better" houses of detention be built, and that more cops be put on the streets. Although I personally believe that these "solutions" to the overall crime problem will never truly solve our problems, we shouldn't stop trying by any means.

According to the New Testament writings of the apostle Paul in his Second Letter to Timothy, "This know also, that in the last days, perilous times shall come" (2 Tim. 3:1). We are certainly living in such a time when danger seems to be lurking all around us. We can attest to the fact that things have taken a turn for the worse, and there is no evidence that things will get better. There is no question something has to be done to stop the crime epidemic sweeping through the cities of our nation. Yet the wrong decisions could prove to be counterproductive or lead to an even greater catastrophe.

One of the greatest institutions ordained by the Creator God is the family. Both the husband and wife are to play vital roles in the lives and upbringing of their children. It has been proven that communities with a high percentage of broken homes will also have an exceptionally high crime rate. Whenever the family structure breaks down, children become uncontrollable, and the social order as a whole gets out of control. When children are raised in a dysfunctional environment, it affects their personality, disposition, and overall behavior.

Children living in neighborhoods where all kinds of criminal activity take place right in front of them sometimes become involved, either as victims or as participants. The illegal activity may be happening in their homes, not in the street. You would be surprised and shocked by some of the things innocent kids are exposed to in their own homes through the deviant actions of one or both parents, or of an older brother or sister.

As a police officer, it was my unpleasant duty to respond to homes where children had been neglected for days by a mother who was strung out on a controlled substance. That mother would do drugs in the presence of her children with their father and friends. Without any concern for the welfare and safety of her children, she would smoke crack cocaine and marijuana, freebase cocaine, and shoot up heroin, right in front of them every day. This same scene was repeated in countless codependent homes in the ghettos and even in well-to-do neighborhoods across America.

Since one of the terrible side effects of the abuse of an illegal substance is its tendency to rob abusers of their power to reason, an entire generation of kids have been exposed to all kinds of filth. Some children even have had unseemly things forced upon them by their intoxicated parents. Some were given deadly drugs or alcohol, or they would get a contact high from inhalation of the smoke from crack or marijuana users.

I am especially saddened when I see a drug-abusing mother who isn't employed apply for and receive support from the Department of Social Services for herself and her baby. The problem isn't the assistance; the tragedy is that the woman will invariably use the support money to support her chronic drug addiction. If a survey could ever be taken to measure the number of city, state, and federal welfare dollars used to purchase illicit drugs over the years, the total sum would be astronomical.

When several generations of children are subjected to a downward spiral of increasingly harsh treatment and abuse, then at one point, a generation will arise that thinks there is nothing wrong with indulging in the same illegal activities they were exposed to by their parents. Their behavior is likely to become a vicious revolving cycle, passed on from generation to generation, unless something positive is done to nip it in the bud.

It is frightening to see the very young engaging in a career of crime. Many of these young people are dangerous and ruthless. Their hostile and even depraved behavior is generally attributed to how and where they grew up. The streets are becoming more dangerous than ever, as the law violators get younger and younger. One 13-year-old boy I arrested for selling cocaine at the Saint Nicks Housing Project in Harlem had ten glassine envelopes of cocaine (selling for $10 each) in possession, along with $500 in cash.

With the new antidrug push came even more diabolical drug-pushing strategies. Local street pushers started employing minors under 16 years of age to sell their goods, since underage drug offenders were generally sent to the family court's juvenile division where they nearly always got off with a "warning" from the judge. Given the relatively large amount of money the kids were paid for their efforts, most considered the inconvenience of a "warning" well worth the trouble.

The Saint Nicholas Houses were located in the heart of Harlem, only a few blocks from 125th Street and the famous Apollo Theater. They were also one of the primary drug hot spots in

New York City. Its central location encouraged drug users from all over the city to converge on 125th Street. My unit had busted so many drug dealers and buyers in the area of the St. Nicks Projects that they could almost smell our blue unmarked van coming into the area.

The drug pushers began to work in three-man teams. One man would steer potential buyers to a second man who collected the money for the particular type and amount of drugs requested. Once he received and counted the money, he would tell the buyer to see a third individual, who might have on a certain identifying piece of clothing and would be standing or seated off a ways from the others. The man who collected the money would use his fingers to signal to the man holding the drugs how much "product" the buyer should receive.

At first, the drug pushers were convinced their new scheme was foolproof, but they found out the hard way that it wasn't when all three members of team after team were arrested and charged with acting in concert in the sale and possession of a controlled substance. On several occasions when assigned to work the Saint Nicholas Houses, I would go to the roof of one of the 18- or 20-story buildings and spot the drug dealers selling their goods. Then I would alert my partner and the other cops in my unit by radio and identify who was doing what on the street. This worked for a while until I was "made" when a pusher noticed me looking down on them talking on my radio. From that point on, the pushers in that area started to watch the rooftops.

I countered their defensive move by getting a large cardboard carton from a supermarket that was big enough to cover my upper body, and made two holes in the side of the carton. This time, when I reached the various rooftops of buildings overlooking the drug-prone locations, I put the empty box over my head and rested it on the edge of the rooftops. I was able to watch the drug pushers carry on business as usual and enjoyed a good laugh. The pushers still looked up at the rooftop, but they never paid any attention to the box on the ledge. And they couldn't figure out how they were still getting caught selling drugs.

Unfortunately, I noticed that as soon as one pusher was arrested, another would soon take his place! It seemed as if they were inexhaustible in numbers. As the demand for certain drugs increased, so did the number of local street pushers. We noticed that the number of guns and the amount of violence on the street also escalated to an alarming level at the same time. Greedy drug pushers started ripping one another off, and openly feuding over prosperous drug locations. Deadly drive-by shootings began to flare up all over the city.

I witnessed two of these shootings from my rooftop location, and the unit was able to locate and apprehend the perpetrators on a variety of felony assault and weapons charges, including a homicide. Drug-prone neighborhoods across the city were being terrorized by these ongoing feuds between drug thugs. People were afraid to walk in areas of their communities where drugs were being sold. Not only did they fear for their own safety, but for that of their children.

Drug trafficking had become a 24-hour, 7-day-a-week business. A shoot-out could occur at any given time, day or night. A great number of the drive-by shooters were young teenagers with no regard for innocent people who might get caught in their cross fire. Even small children playing in designated play areas were being cut down in street gun battles. My job as an undercover narcotics cop had suddenly become even more dangerous because this new young breed of drug dealer and abuser was far more aggressive and callous than those of the past.

The generation of the 1980's and early 1990's had become high-strung, highly volatile, and uncontrollable. We were sent to the Williamsburg section of Brooklyn to help curb the high concentration of drug activity and mostly Hispanic gang activity. Street gangs were a big problem in many large cities across the nation at that time, and the violence they were known for was bad enough.

However, once they started to get into drug trafficking, the violence rapidly escalated.

The Williamsburg section was heavily populated by Latinos and was home to several gangs. Two gangs in particular, the "Homicides" and the "Dirty Ones," were the most notorious and violent of them all. Although they both were predominantly Hispanic, each gang also had a few black males in their membership. Gangs have existed in New York City since 1827, and I can still remember how prevalent they were when I was a child growing up in the Red Hook Housing Projects in South Brooklyn. As I mentioned in a previous chapter, I had once been drafted into a black gang from the projects called the "El Kovons" during my teenage years.

The gangs in my time were violent, and many young men and women were killed in intergang rivalries; but there is no comparison between the gangs of my youth and the violent young gangs of the late 80's and early 90's that I encountered as a cop in New York City (and especially the gangs in Los Angeles). Today's gangs are involved in all kinds of criminal activity, including the distribution and sale of drugs and gun running. Like the feuding drug dealers, these gangs are incredibly violent. These young teenage and young adult gang members are universally hostile to rival gangs, police, and anyone else who will not succumb to their demands. They have been known to terrorize whole communities.

Street gangs and individuals involved in illegal drug trafficking now use far more sophisticated weaponry than the police. Military-style automatic weapons, like the 9-millimeter handgun, the Tech 9, and other high-powered automatic weaponry, have become the weapons of choice on the street, and the average cop on the beat with a service revolver and night stick is totally outgunned by the very people he was sworn to control.

While every city borough had some gang activity, at this time the most activity occurred in Richmond, Brooklyn, Bronx, and Manhattan (which had the worst activity of all). The majority of the gang activity was taking place in the confines of the 90th Precinct, where there were a number of city housing projects. The gangs in and around the Williamsburg Housing Complex had concentrated their efforts in drug trafficking and extortion (but they committed their "fair share" of rapes, robberies, burglaries, and homicides). It was not hard spotting gang members; their "colors" were a dead giveaway.

It wasn't until I got involved in the undercover investigation of the Williamsburg gang members that I realized how vicious they were. To hear and read about them was one thing, but when you came face to face with them, all of a sudden a new reality set in. As an unwilling 14-year-old member of the "El Kovons" street gang decades earlier, I was expected to show my face whenever they called meetings. Most of the time, the members just hung around the park or community center where they would talk jive and drink cheap wine. Sometimes the older members would play fight with the younger members. The gang members who showed no fear when confronted with danger were said to have a lot of heart. I thought a few of those guys were just *plum crazy*.

Comparing that behavior to the behavior of the modern gang members I had to deal with, there was a difference between then and now like the difference between night and day! While gangs in the 50's and 60's might have carried homemade "zip" guns featuring a single .22-caliber round, the weapon of choice for many gang members today is an Israeli-made "Uzi" submachine gun or "street sweeper."

The gangs of my time would fight for a reason most of the time; the gangs in Williamsburg did not need a reason to do anything they did. If they wanted something, they just took it upon themselves to go after it. They would instantly use violent retaliation on anyone who refused to yield to their aggression. Any comments about these gang members "just being kids looking for a good time" did not apply. These guys were willing participants in a highly-organized criminal organization, and never let anyone tell you differently. They killed simply because they felt they had to, and because they liked the feeling of power it gave them. Most of them used their poverty as an excuse. My answer was simple: "Well, we were poor too, but we didn't go around dealing drugs and shooting Uzi's through the streets at little children, pregnant women, and innocent bystanders."

I believe those of us in the older generations led a more moral life because our parents were there. Eighty percent of the kids in gangs today have never seen their fathers! That is unbelievable. Our education system was also stronger because it was built around discipline. We couldn't wear garrison belts to school. In fact, we couldn't even wear jeans. You had to take a certain amount of pride in yourself, and that pride and discipline eventually paid off. They gave most young people a positive sense of direction.

That kind of life seems so strange and foreign to me now after spending so many years in the neighborhoods fighting gangs, drug lords, and crack users. Fortunately, we started to have a great impact on the two Williamsburg gangs. We arrested many of the members for all kinds of felony crimes, including robberies, rape, drug possession and distribution, assault, gun possession and use, and homicide, plus other serious crimes. We were getting to know a large number of the gang members by their street names.

When it was learned that one of the gangs had broken into a National Guard Armory on Marcy Avenue and stolen a number of M-16 automatic rifles and ammunition, we joined forces with other state and federal law enforcement agencies to crack the case and arrest those responsible for the break-in. A break in the case came when a vicious gang war broke out between two gangs. M-16 rifles were used in a street brawl, and several gang members got shot, as well as an innocent bystander. (One of the gang members took a bullet in the leg, went to the hospital to have the bullet removed, and then left the same night and headed back to the streets for more fighting!)

It didn't take us long to locate and arrest most of the youths involved in the fighting after we received an anonymous tip telling us where they were hiding out. We also recovered most of the stolen M-16s, along with a large cache of other weapons and ammunition.

After spending about three months in the Williamsburg area, we were finally able to put a big dent in overall gang operations. Along the way, we had to dance on a few hard heads to send a clear message to the others, but my partner and I managed to gain their respect. We even challenged them to several games of handball during our off-duty hours. (We still had to be on our guard while engaged in a friendly game of handball because these guys were unpredictable and couldn't be trusted.)

People live in fear of gang members, and for good reason. They love hurting people. I used to have a pretty violent temper, but it was nothing compared to the anger these guys are hiding within. My temper would have gotten me killed if the gangs of my day were as bloodthirsty as today's crews. I once went to a gang funeral at the Ponce Funeral Home to pay my respects to a Puerto Rican boy who, at the age of 16, had been shot and killed by a rival gang. The gang members spotted me right away and called out, "Five-O!" It was okay for me to be there that night because of the funeral; the gang members considered the funeral home to be a "neutral" site.

I wasn't surprised to see that the slain boy's parents had no say in how their son's funeral was conducted. This was strictly a gang "social function," and the home boys were out in force. They paid tribute to their fallen friend by tossing knives, their colors, and other memorabilia directly into the deceased boy's coffin according to gang tradition. I even saw someone toss a small handgun into the coffin. The older people were petrified, and I just stared in amazement. Things had definitely changed.

# Chapter 11

# For the Love of Money

There is a popular saying that voices the cynicism of our age: "Everyone has a price, and anyone can be bought." That saying could be the motto and prime operative strategy for anyone who is heavily involved in illegal drug trafficking. There is another statement that profoundly describes the reason for the seemingly endless escalation of illegal drug trafficking and violence around the world. These words date back to the first century: "For the love of money is the root of all evil" (1 Tim. 6:10a). The saying comes, of course, from the Bible. Ever since money was money, men have relentlessly pursued the power it represents. Some of these money-seekers have resorted to any and every kind of depraved and even murderous tactic to obtain it. Their heartless actions revealed a shocking disregard for life, limb, and the property of others. Money, and the possession of it, was all that these individuals lived and died for.

I believe that the God of creation gave man dominion over the earth, but after man's fall from grace, he allowed himself to be dominated by the very things he was given authority to rule. Men and women have literally become subject and slave to the raw resources we were given to utilize. We have become addicted and enslaved to the possession and abuse of countless minerals, natural foods, plant substances, and chemicals produced by the earth.

Much of this book describes the havoc caused by our slavish craving for organic substances that we originally received from the earth for the healing and preservation of the body! I am referring to the vast array of natural substances we call drugs. Most of these are derived from natural plant and mineral sources, and others are synthesized from chemical substances in imitation of naturally occurring substances. What God gave us as a treasure trove of helpful and healing substances has become the greatest destructive force in human history through human abuse and misuse.

The power and influence that the love of money has on human beings motivate fortune-hungry and power-seeking men and women to market highly profitable but illegal drugs at any cost! The vicious illicit drug trade has contributed enormously to the high rate of crime and corruption plaguing virtually every nation on the earth. The disastrous impact of drug trafficking and abuse has so radically altered and shaken our society as a whole that this epidemic can be characterized as the ultimate evil in the world today!

The only way to grasp the devastating impact the illicit drug trade and drug abuse has had on the world over the centuries is to look carefully at its roots. Drugs have been used and abused by human societies for thousands of years. Archaeologists have unearthed evidence proving that the ancient Babylonian, Assyrian, and Egyptian empires (to mention a few) used drugs for a number of medicinal and religious purposes.

The modern science of pharmacology (the science of drugs) began when men first learned that the fruit, leaves, flowers, bark, and roots of specific plants, trees, and herbs possessed certain properties that could powerfully effect the human body and mind. From that growing body of folklore and primitive medicine, men learned to systematically record and use those properties as drugs to improve life both physically and mentally. Yet those same drugs that preserve or improve the quality of life when the human body is out of balance can have a negative and sometimes devastating effect on the mind and body when used out of their prescribed dose or purpose.

For centuries, China was considered to be one of the wealthiest and most self-sufficient nations in the world. Her complex society had been built upon principles of moral responsibility, personal restraint, and reason. Blessed with an industrious people and rich in natural resources, China became one of the most prosperous, independent, and self-sufficient nations on earth. The Chinese worked for centuries building "The Great Wall" around her borders to keep the secrets and wealth of the empire within, and the destructive ways and by-products of other societies out.

Although foreigners were prohibited from entering into China, the British eventually managed to gain some limited trade with China by the 17th century. The British were already established leaders in international drug trafficking because of colonial holdings in some key drug-producing areas of the world. When it was discovered that the Chinese had a weakness for an addictive narcotic drug called opium (also called "black dirt" at that time), English traders began to flood China with that drug. England used the drug, which was derived from the dried juice of the Eurasian opium poppy fields of India, one of the British Empire's colonies, to infiltrate the fortified empire of China. Thousands of Chinese became addicted to opium, and opium dens very similar to today's "crack houses" sprang up all over China. Opium abuse and addiction quickly began to overwhelm the nation, and history records that English drug traffickers and the Crown became rich at the expense of the people of China.

In the early stages of abuse, opium induced a euphoria, but habitual use left its victims mere burnt-out husks of their former selves. The final stage of addiction was marked by insanity and cruel death. Wherever the addicts gathered and smoked the opium, they would cough and spit. In their weakened state, they unknowingly became infected with such deadly diseases as tuberculosis and influenza, and they quickly spread their contagion to others, both addicts and non-addicts alike.

Drug trafficking flourished in China right under the noses of her queen and her judges, politicians, and police—sometimes even

167

with their assistance. The British traders were able to corrupt many of them with money. When the Chinese government finally woke up, they again closed their doors to all foreign trade and destroyed thousands of crates of raw opium stored in British warehouses in Canton.

England immediately responded by declaring war on China (just as the Latin American drug cartels and traffickers have waged war against legitimate governments and law enforcement officials today). This was when the cultural and scientific isolation of China began to work against them. The English navy, with modern warships of iron, brutally defeated China's outmoded and outgunned fleet of wooden warships. Britain seized the island of Hong Kong. The Opium War lasted from 1839-1842 and ended with a treaty in which Hong Kong became the central point of England's drug trade. Criminal societies like today's Mafia quickly joined forces with foreign smugglers to disperse profitable drugs like opium throughout the known world.

When a civil war called the "Taiping Rebellion" broke out in China, (at a cost of 30 million lives), chaos reduced China to such a critical state that European states such as England, France, Germany, and Russia stepped in and carved up China like a ripe melon, with each taking a piece for their own benefit.

By the end of the 19th century, China had more than 22 million opium addicts. When Mao Zedong's communists crushed opposition and seized control of the country, the continuous internal strife was ended, but at a great cost. The conflict again took 30 million lives, and all foreigners (including devoted missionaries) were ordered out. Mao did away with China's opium problem by brutally eliminating the traffickers and abusers.

As brutal as Mao Zedong's revolution may appear, history shows us an even more grim and vivid picture of the reign of terror brought about by the tyranny of unchecked drug trafficking and abuse. It has been said that history has a tendency to repeat itself.

If you doubt the truth of this statement, then look very closely at the way drug trafficking and abuse is destroying our society in this nation.

Drug trafficking is a vile, deadly business that is incredibly lucrative. It is raping our society. The despicable "glamour" of the power and wealth surrounding the drug trade attracts the scum of the earth with its potential of instant riches. My years as an undercover narcotics cop forced me to live and operate in an altogether different world, where the entire demeanor of men and women was changed as they succumbed to the deadly allure of drug addiction and distribution.

Illegal drugs were introduced to inner-city black communities for one purpose only—to make money. The profiteers who first brought these drugs into black neighborhoods could have cared less for the welfare and quality of life of the residents. Some believe there is evidence that the first drug traffickers fully intended to confine the drug sales (and the addiction they would surely produce) to blacks or Afro- Americans. If that was the plan, we all know now that the plan backfired and spread to society as a whole. Yet the immeasurable damage drugs have done in black communities in particular, and in America as a whole, is tragic, irreparable, and alarming.

The illicit drug trade in New York City finally got so out of hand that its police departments had to take more drastic measures. Drug traffickers on every level were now "killing to kill." They had proven they were willing to do anything to protect their stores of controlled substances from the government authorities, from their competition, and from robbers. They would even resort to cold-blooded murder to make sure the poison they were marketing could reach the streets and bring wealth to their pockets.

Their deadly "products" have destroyed lives and killed countless numbers of human beings. Heroin, at one time, was the primary "drug of choice." Ironically, heroin was first introduced in

1874 as an antidote to help break the addiction of Civil War soldiers who became hooked on morphine, which was the main painkiller used by doctors at that time. The use and abuse of heroin became very prevalent, quickly creating a well-established illegal market. Heroin is a narcotic produced from the juice of the poppy plant grown in vast quantities in the "Golden Triangle" of Burma, Laos, Thailand, as well as in Mexico and India.

Heroin eventually slipped to second place when cocaine experienced an explosive and deadly rise in popularity. While heroin is taken by injection, sniffed, or smoked, cocaine is administered in all those ways plus one more. The actor-comedian, Richard Pryor, made national headlines when he was injured and disfigured while allegedly "freebasing" cocaine. This is the most dangerous form of use, since it involves treating the cocaine using a heated and highly volatile ether mixture to produce intoxicating vapors that are inhaled. Pryor was severely burned when the mixture presumably exploded in his face.

As the demand for cocaine and other addictive drugs increased, I found myself arresting large numbers of aliens who had entered the U.S. illegally to deliver and sell mass amounts of controlled substances. Opportunists from the West Indies, South America, Africa, and other areas were pursuing their "American dreams" at the expense of American taxpayers and certain Americans' growing appetites for substances such as cocaine and marijuana. Many West Indians, being black, easily entered black communities and set up make shift "stores." These crafty drug traffickers would simply place a number of name-brand products in the windows to conceal what was really being peddled inside the "store."

These pushers trusted no one. They put up Plexiglas partitions with small holes designed to allow the passage of money and drugs while offering some protection to the drug pushers. These makeshift stores sprang up in black neighborhoods all over the city; but the locals quickly discovered the true nature of these "businesses," and the complaints began to pour into the police precincts. My unit was ordered to put these "entrepreneurs" out of business. The fact that these West Indian drug dealers were heavily armed made our new assignment extremely hazardous.

When a "store" was located, we would park our car in an inconspicuous area and watch the activity for a while. Two "lookouts" were usually positioned outside near the entrance. Many times, we would apprehend some of the buyers a few blocks from the store after their drug buys, just to enhance the felony charges on the dealers. Then Layne and I would enter the store and each of us would make a drug buy before returning to our command post. This was done to get a positive identification of the pusher or pushers.

When we were ready to raid the drug spot, two cops would pick up the lookouts, and the rest of the unit would simultaneously rush into the store with a battering ram to knock open the locked Plexiglas door so we could reach the seller and the drugs. We made sure there were officers covering all doors and windows in the back and on the sides of the building to prevent escape. Then we would voucher all the drugs and money we had seized as court evidence.

The numbers of these stores continued to increase, and they became known as "smoke shops." It seemed like the more we hit, the more would spring up! Several times we exchanged gunfire with one or two fleeing perpetrators before they were captured while trying to exit their buildings. We recovered quite a few guns in our efforts.

On one particular smoke shop raid, I made a buy from a man and woman operating the shop. Then I joined the raiding team for the rush into the shop. This shop was unique because the Plexiglas partition was only partially finished. When we rushed in with guns in hand, the male suspect attempted to bend down behind the counter. I jumped over the counter and landed on top of him just as he reached for a nickel-plated, sawed-off, double-barreled shotgun. I wrestled with him until my partner helped me take the gun away from him. That was a close call. The cocaine, marijuana, and money we confiscated from the suspects turned out to be worth quite a large sum.

Many times we would hit a smoke shop thinking we had closed it down, only to learn that someone else had reopened the shop only a few hours later! That was discouraging to me and the other cops, but we would hit the spot again when we were assigned to work that specific location. This cycle went on until the police were finally given the authority to padlock a drug premise after it was raided.

Drug trafficking had become a violent and sophisticated business. The people who ran the smoke shops usually had a number of them in a given black neighborhood. Their business was so profitable and brisk that many of them stayed open 24 hours a day, 7 days a week. These profiteers literally organized dealers to work in shifts, while other people were assigned to make drug drops and money pickups from the sales locations. Sometimes, we were fortunate enough to catch the individual making the drops and pickups, and that was indeed a bonus catch.

The corrupting power of the "love of money" wasn't restricted to drug dealers and drug addicts. Many times police squads would raid a drug spot but fail to catch the sellers, who would leave large quantities of drugs and untraceable cash behind. Although the seized property was supposed to be vouchered in the safekeeping of the court, most of the time the money (and even the drugs, at times) were simply taken and kept by crooked cops.

Cops often see things happen among their associates that aren't correct and that they don't like. They all face the temptation to turn their heads and ignore it, or even worse, to join in. Undercover narcotics work is not only dangerous, but it can become very tempting to a corrupt cop. In my opinion, there is nothing worse that a rogue cop. They are even worse than the most hardened career criminal. A cop gone bad has sunk into an abyss. There have always been bad cops and law enforcement officials. They may have become vulnerable because of selfish greed and succumbed to the criminal tactics they were sworn to fight, or bitterness may have led them to do things they would never have done under normal circumstances.

Before I started to work in narcotics, I saw cops routinely subject themselves to graft. It came in the form of a free cup of coffee, a meal, or any number of things or services that required monetary payment but were given to cops free of charge. However, the cops who received these free goods and services were expected to reciprocate by "looking the other way" when those same business establishments were in violation of the law. Cops have sold their very souls for filthy lucre.

When I was working in uniform at the Fort Greene Housing Complex, I used to go to a popular restaurant located in the downtown section of Brooklyn, in the confines of the 84th Precinct. I saw cops and detectives from the 84th and 88th Precincts eat meals and walk out without paying. When I finished my meal and proceeded to the cashier to pay my check, I'd notice the cashier would look at the pins on my uniform collar to see if I was from one of the two NYPD precincts. I would remark to the cashier, "I am with the Housing Police Department. We pay our way."

The acceptance of small-time graft can quickly lead to big-time corruption. Narcotics work seemed to birth a type of wholesale corruption by rogue cops on levels I had never imagined. Some drug dealers I arrested tried to bribe me with money so I would let them go or help them get rid of their drugs so it couldn't be used as evidence in a court of law. They were always shocked when I turned them down and warned them that they would be charged with trying to bribe a police officer if they ever tried it again. One dealer told me, "Man, you sure aren't like those white narco cops. They would have taken the money." While that may be an unfair accusation against white cops in general, it does point to a terrible integrity problem in New York City law enforcement.

It took an honest cop named Serpico to expose the corruption of criminally corrupt cops in the late 60's and early 70's. Serpico's life was placed in serious jeopardy because he had the courage to report the corruption rampant in the New York City Police Department. Because of the widespread police corruption, the city government formed an investigation unit called the Knapp Commission, named after Judge Whitman Knapp. The commissioner's office succeeded in uncovering a large number of rogue cops who were "on the pad" or "on the take" (receiving bribe money or involved in extortion). Some were prosecuted for their crimes and sent to prison while others were fired from the police department. There were a few black rogue cops among those who were prosecuted, but the majority were white.

Some black cops thought that to be accepted by white cops, they had to take part in the things that they did, even if it was criminal or violated departmental procedures. Many of the rogue white cops would shake down drug dealers for their stash of drugs and money, only to resell the same drugs in the same community! Not one of these rogue cops would have sold those drugs in his or her own community, yet they were willing to do their dirty work in black communities, and then leave work and go home outside the city.

I remember many times, as we sat on drug-prone locations gathering evidence and arresting buyers, we ended up arresting both white and black court officers, correction officers, postal workers, transit workers, and many other people with good government jobs! I felt bad about it, but I had a job to do. In my opinion, those people had put themselves and others in jeopardy.

Cocaine was used in relative moderation and was called the social drug of the rich and well-to-do in the 60's and 70's. In fact, cocaine was even used in Coca-Cola® until the turn of the century. (The formula was modified to use the cola nut instead, which has a high caffeine level.) It wasn't until the early 80's that cocaine

174

started to become a problem drug. Today, the use and abuse of cocaine has escalated into America's number one crisis.

Over six million people use cocaine on a regular, daily, or semi-regular basis. Over 25 million people have experimented with cocaine. What is not known is how many died from their first ingestion of cocaine. We do know that more than two million people are addicted to cocaine, including high-ranking government officials, government employees, movie and sports figures, clergy, judges, lawyers, teachers, law enforcement officials, doctors, and commercial airline pilots. I could go on and on with a long and "distinguished" list.

The money made from the sale of cocaine is so astronomical that people are willing to risk their lives to traffic the drug. In 1966, cocaine sold for $7,000 a pound. At the time of this writing, it is selling for over $24,000 a pound—up to three or four times as much as an ounce of gold! Consider this: One ton of cocaine is worth one billion dollars, and more money is made in one year from the sale of cocaine than is earned by all three major American auto manufacturers combined! This incredible amount of money has led countless numbers of local cops and people in sensitive areas of government to become enticed and entangled in corruption.

Competition became so keen that drug traffickers were always trying to come up with ideas that would attract potential buyers to their product; because users quickly learned that not all cocaine was the same. Cocaine for street use is extracted from the coca leaf in two steps. First the leaves are placed in a press or steel drum along with sulfuric acid and are crushed into a mash called pasta (cocaine sulfate). This pasta is then further processed by adding a solvent, hydrochloric acid, to eliminate other chemicals. The result, cocaine hydrochloride, is sold in crystal form or chopped into the more familiar white, odorless powder.

Cocaine made from South American base is about 97 percent pure. After it is sold and resold, it is "cut and recut" and other substances are added to increase its volume before it hits the street.

Many of the dangerous chemicals used to refine the cocaine are still present in the powder also when it hits the street.

The local street level competition became more rigid as the number of pushers increased. Some pushers began to sell more potent cocaine than their competitors so their coke would be in demand, and then they carefully "branded" it with a distinctive name or insignia on the outside of the glassine envelopes, such as "Death Wish," "Dynamite," "Black Gold," or "Playboy Bunny." Abusers would begin to say, "Yeah, get Death Wish; it'll give you a better hit." That brought would-be buyers looking for that particular "brand" of cocaine in the neighborhood.

Controlled substances or drugs fall into five categories: (1) Narcotics, (2) Depressants, (3) Stimulants, (4) Hallucinogens, (5) Cannabis. Heroin, a narcotic, has no medical value at all. Cocaine is a stimulant that is also used as a local anesthetic. Hallucinogens have no medicinal value whatsoever, and only the chemical, tetrahydrocannabinol, derived from cannabis category (marijuana) has value. It is used as a cancer chemotherapy anti-nauseant.

Frankly, people abuse drugs to get high—period. Major drug traffickers are always experimenting with new kinds of organic and dangerous synthetic drugs, because new types of drugs are their "insurance" that they will always have an active moneymaking product to market. Drug traffickers are heartless, insensitive, and dangerous killers who play by their own rules. Their only concern is that they make money at any cost. They hawk their drugs with no concern about the welfare of the abuser (no matter what their age). If you have the money, they will sell you their poison.

Local street pushers often give young kids a "free ride," which means they give them free samples of their drugs hoping they will get hooked, and therefore gain more customers. This is why I believe everyone involved in drug trafficking, from the top drug lords to the local street pushers who sell their goods to the individual addict, should be charged and tried for murder! In reality, that is what they all are. They are murderers who sell substances that rob the abuser of all human values, including his personal dignity and physical life.

Cops working narcotics faced an uphill battle all the way. I really believe the police departments in New York City were making headway through their joint antidrug efforts in early 1984. Then a new drug hit the streets in the Bronx during the fall. The drug was called "crack," and it was an especially virulent form of cocaine. Crack was a "freebased" form of cocaine processed from cocaine hydrochloride, which was further processed into crystals known as "rocks." The drug was then packaged in transparent vials resembling large vitamin capsules with a small colored cap. Crack revolutionized the cocaine drug trafficking business overnight.

The potency of this new drug was so great that a person only had to experiment with it one time to become addicted to it! The word *crack* either came from the crackling sound it made when it was smoked, or from its occasional resemblance to cracked paint chips or plaster. On the street, there is a saying about the potency of "crack" that goes, "One time is too many, and a thousand times is not enough."

The greatest quest of any drug abuser is to find the one drug that will produce the ultimate high. Most drug users I've dealt with started out smoking marijuana, contrary to popular reports and pro-marijuana groups. Then they graduated to a more powerful drug, and so on it goes. Then came "crack." Crack was sold on the streets in small vials at purity levels between 60 and 90 percent. Although the amounts varied, the small vials usually contained about 100 milligrams of crack, which cost approximately $10. Larger vials containing 250 milligrams cost $25, and 500-milligram vials cost between $40 and $50.

A $10-vial containing 100 milligrams of cocaine could provide one, two, or three inhalations when smoked in a pipe, depending on how deeply the user breathes. The lower price per dose attracts countless crack buyers while giving pushers and dealers a substantial profit. Since crack users often crave more immediately after smoking, they purchase more cocaine in the crack form than they would have if they had used the traditional cocaine hydrochloride form of cocaine regularly.

The endless desire for a more intense "high" without the complications and dangers involved in freebasing cocaine with ether, or injecting cocaine with hypodermic needles, combined with the fear of and universal spread of AIDS in the drug community, has been the impetus for the smoking of crack as an alternative form of use.

The euphoric affect produced by smoking crack is far more intense than that produced when cocaine is ingested through inhalation. And it is at least equal to, if not greater than the "buzz" obtained through injection. Crack hits the addict's system in a matter of seconds and usually lasts from five to ten minutes. Then the user may experience a restless irritability accompanied by severe depression and an almost insatiable craving for more crack. That is one of the reasons the drug is extremely dangerous. Cocaine and crack cocaine also cause an abuser's heart to beat more rapidly. It often triggers irregular heartbeats, and may trigger a cardiac arrest leading to death. Countless numbers of people have died from their very first experience with crack, and others died after the second, third, fifth, or even the tenth abuse in a single day. Crack addiction is like a never-ending game of Russian roulette. You never know if "the next time" will be your last time.

The addictive power of crack produces such a continuous and uncontrollable craving that the abuser has to take the drug just to keep from getting sick. God made the human body an extraordinary, complex, beautiful, and complete machine with an incredible immune system and all the necessary qualities to heal and sustain itself. But there are limits to its ability to adjust to foreign substances.

When a person first ingests a foreign substance such as an illicit drug or alcohol, the body will reject that irritating substance. When a person gets sick from an impure substance taken into his body, it is a sign that the body is rejecting a poisonous substance as a matter of survival. However, if the person persistently continues to ingest that impurity, the body will start to adapt itself to that foreign substance. In fact, it will begin to crave the very substance it first rejected. Addiction is the end result.

No one dreamed that the sale and abuse of crack cocaine would take root and spread as rapidly as it did. So-called "crack houses" and crack apartments sprang up all over the city. In some locations, a user could both purchase and smoke the drug on the same premises. In others, a user could only purchase the drug but was not allowed entry to the building or room.

Crack attracted a level of violence that raised the consciousness of society to the menace and danger of drug abuse. By then, shootings (and drive-by shootings in particular) were occurring 24 hours a day, 7 days a week! Not only were children and people shot in the streets, but now many were getting cut down in their own homes! Street dealers seemed to get younger and younger, and to double in numbers overnight. They still used weaponry that was more sophisticated and had greater fire power than what most cops carried, but eventually police departments across America began to change to 9-millimeter weapons to enhance a cop's overall performance ability.

Homicides and gun-related assaults suddenly increased at a tremendous rate, and too many innocent people were getting killed, injured, and crippled by feuding drug thugs. So the New York City Housing Police Department, along with the NYPD, had to reorganize some of their patrol procedures to combat the crime crisis brought about by "crack." I was assigned to investigate the problem, and what I thought would be somewhat of a relief from the work overload of the past few years proved to be just the opposite! Although the high numbers of arrests I had been accustomed to decreased considerably, the stress and frustration levels increased dramatically.

I found myself responding to calls where young children had been terribly abused by drug-abusing parents. I even dealt with "crackhead" mothers who were prostituting their own daughters to get money to buy drugs! Then I had to investigate all the instances where infants were shot while asleep in their beds or children were gunned down while playing in an outside play area. People were more afraid than ever to come outside of their apartments. It seemed no one was safe anywhere in drug-prone neighborhoods.

The heartless scum and cold-blooded murderers who sell illicit drugs and guns to children, young adults, and adults in and around our communities are dangerous in more ways than one. The expensive cars, gold jewelry, and designer clothes that they flaunt before kids in every poor neighborhood are all but irresistible. Kids tend to admire their lavish and flamboyant (if short-lived) lifestyles, and many strive to emulate them by selling drugs when they get older.

In the 20 years I spent as a cop and detective in New York City, I saw some little children grow up and make something out of themselves despite every obstacle, and I have seen some turn to a life of crime and drug abuse despite every opportunity to succeed. In any case, the degenerate drug dealers and murderers that are loose in communities across the nation (especially in the black communities) must be stopped at any cost! Their next victim could be you, or a friend, or a member of your family.

# Chapter 12

# Black Man With a Gun

When I first entered the New York City Housing Authority Police Department, I had high expectations of becoming the best cop that I could possibly be. I had a few run-ins with the police in my youth, and one of my brothers was severely beaten by a police officer, as I described earlier. So my experiences with the police in general, along with all the things I'd heard, read, and witnessed about police brutality, murder, racism, and abuse caused my feelings about cops to be very grim. For some odd reason, I still thought that maybe I could make a difference.

From 1962 to 1968, I was a member of the U.S. Air Force. The Air Force provided what was termed "three hots and a cot," which meant you were always assured three meals a day and a place to sleep. Although I was confronted with racism in the Air Force, I thanked God for the overall experience. I benefited from it in many ways, but above all, those years in the service made me a better person in every way.

I had some serious fights with white airmen who made racial remarks, and I learned through personal experience that blacks were subject to discrimination in promotions, assignments, and punitive actions. For obvious reasons, I did not think twice about leaving the service when my enlistment was up. Most of the serious physical altercations between blacks and whites were carefully shielded from the public, especially those that took place in Vietnam where I served. One of the most discouraging experiences for me was when I would train a white airman with less time and rank

181

than myself, only to see him be promoted over me. This happened many times. Many black sergeants would train white subordinates, and a few years down the road, the same white airmen or soldiers would be of equal or higher rank than the black individuals who trained them.

It wasn't until I joined the police department that I really appreciated my military training, discipline, and experiences. Being a cop in the City of New York is one thing; being a *black cop* in New York is a totally different ball game. I had many white friends during my childhood and early teen years. We regularly played together and, on occasion, ate and slept at one another's homes as kids will do. Some of my white friends had parents who were prejudiced, and I can still remember those friends calling me a "black nigger" when we would have altercations. A fight would almost certainly ensue in those days if a white kid referred to a black friend as a "nigger." It wasn't until I went into the service that I found out what racism was really all about.

I was much wiser when I became a cop, but I had no idea I would witness all kinds of racist acts being committed by white cops of every rank. I saw discriminatory acts perpetrated against my own people, and to my surprise, I personally became the target of systematic organized racism throughout my career. I realize how inflammatory and biased my claim sounds, and I wish it could be softened or moderated. But to do so would force me to embrace a lie.

I believe that a majority of white police officers either willingly or unknowingly have a low opinion toward blacks in general. Perhaps it is a bias engendered by our culture or by upbringing, but the point is that it is there. It comes out in everyday speech and actions, and it can't help but surface in the performance of duty from time to time. On one occasion, a white detective said to me, "Well, I think all the blacks living in city housing are on welfare." He lived outside the New York City limits, of course, in a predominately white area. He was shocked when I told him, "That's interesting. My sources indicate that there are more black professionals living in city housing projects holding better jobs than cops *and* making greater salaries than you could ever imagine with your finite mind!"

I am afraid that most white cops assigned to black or Afro-American communities throughout this country could care less about the people they have sworn to serve and protect in those minority neighborhoods. I thank God for every exception to that frightening generality.

Sadly, the negative attitude exhibited by many white cops towards black communities doesn't end there. It also extends to black police officers. Many times, when I heard white cops of various ranks making offensive remarks about my race, I would confront them (and nearly end up in a physical confrontation). I was hot-headed in my youth, but I had learned to curb my anger in most situations as a police officer. However, it was my faith in Jesus Christ, along with the personal discipline I acquired in the martial arts and as a soldier, that kept me from losing my cool (and possibly my job).

As a rookie in the police academy, I was shocked at some of the suggestions the firearms instructor would make. One time he bluntly told his class of future law enforcement officers, "Shoot first, and ask questions later. *You* be the one left to tell the story." Perhaps that helps explain the mentality of white cops over the years who shot black cops in the back without warning while these non-white officers were performing their duty.

My class of academy rookies was also told, "Always carry a large pocket knife to use as a *throwaway*." A "throwaway" could be used if you "accidentally" shot a perpetrator and later found out he was not carrying a weapon. (This might happen on a regular basis using the firearms instructor's guidelines for police action.) Throwaways (which were not limited to knives) could be placed on the perpetrator so that the shooting would appear to be justified. I was bewildered by the things I heard. I could not help but think of all the innocent people who had been carelessly or maliciously gunned down by cops who callously planted weapons on their life-less bodies just to cover their own carelessness or abuse of power. That kind of talk can inspire cops to be "quick on the trigger" and encourage white cops with a racist bent to overreact in situations involving blacks.

Without question, racism is one of the most divisive and deadly problems facing American law enforcement. Blacks have traditionally suffered from the hostilities of racist white police offi-cers (who tend to be the most dominant members of any local force or precinct). When the first black candidates were finally ad-mitted to the police department in New York City, they were still treated with indifference at best, and outright disdain in most cases. The few blacks who were fortunate enough to be appointed were given the lowest assignments and routinely denied any chance for advancement.

Perhaps the worst manifestations of this smoldering racism hidden in the ranks of New York City's law enforcement organiza-tions are the shootings of black policemen by white policemen. In the early 80's, I was working with Albert Layne on a drug problem in and around projects located between Park and Lexington Ave-nues on 115th Street in Harlem. We were working undercover, and in those days, all plainclothes cops had to wear a secret item on their person that would identify them as a police officer to avoid being shot by other cops.

We had watched two black male suspects make some drug sales in the middle of 115th Street. Our backup had already ar-rested several of the buyers out of sight of our suspects, so we de-cided it was time for us to move in. The dealers "made" us as we approached them, and they took off running. One suspect ran to-wards Park Avenue, and I took off after him while Layne pursued the other one. I chased the dealer as he made a right turn at the cor-ner of 115th Street and Park Avenue and crossed Park Avenue un-der the train trestle. By then, I was right behind him and closing fast.

184

When the suspect crossed the street again, I was directly behind him and I knocked him to the ground. Then I pulled my gun and told him not to move. I was in the process of handcuffing the pusher and had gone so far as to draw both of his hands behind his back. He was lying face down in a prone position, and I had one of my knees on his back. I had my handcuffs in one hand and gun in the other when I suddenly I heard a loud voice yell out from behind me, "drop it!"

When I turned to see what was going on, I saw a white male in plain clothes leaning over the hood of a black car with both hands on his gun, which was pointed directly at me. I didn't have much time to think, but I knew that if I dropped my gun, there was a good chance the suspect would pick it up and shoot me! I made my decision and yelled, *"I'm on the job!"* and flung the police shield hanging around my neck to my back, continuing to cuff the drug dealer. By that time, my partner came on the scene and pulled his gun. (Now I liked Albert Layne, but I *really liked* Layne that day!)

The unknown white cop simply put away his gun, jumped in his car, and sped away without bothering to identify himself. I just thank God that he did not shoot me. I was extremely upset about the incident, and all I could think about was all the black cops before me who were doing the same exact thing I was doing and... bang, bang, they were dead at the hands of white police officers.

The 70's denoted the low-water mark of interracial relations between black and white cops. The increasingly racist attitudes and actions of a majority of white cops helped alienate countless numbers of black and Hispanic cops as well as civilians. Eight black cops were shot by white cops in that decade alone! These incidents were labeled "tragic mistakes." Because of these "tragic mistakes," two black officers lost their lives, three more were permanently disabled, and three others were seriously wounded—and all of these outrageous incidents were needless.

I was a black officer who had almost become another statistic, and I was outraged by this parade of racially-motivated incidents, as were the majority of black cops in New York City. All of us couldn't shake the thought in the back of our minds: "*It could happen to me.*" These shootings created such a furor that on March 19, 1973, Sgt. Howard Sheffey, then president of the Guardians, the black police officers' fraternal organization, declared, "White policemen are shooting at black people too fast. And it's very strange that these 'tragic mistakes' seem to happen only to black people." Even after black cops went to extra lengths to identify themselves, these so-called "tragic mistakes" did not cease.

On April 3, 1972, a black detective was shot to death by a uniformed white officer after chasing a suspect. When the white officer arrived on the scene and saw a black man with a gun, he opened fire on Detective William R. Capers, killing him. The police department's investigation concluded the shooting was a "mistaken identity case," and the white officer responsible was found to be without fault.

March 5, 1973, Officer Irving E. Wright, the brother of a prominent black New York City politician, was shot and killed by two white officers while chasing an armed man who had just robbed an all-night grocery store. The white cops said they "saw a black man" running down the street chasing another man. The two officers approached Wright from behind and opened fire without warning, notice, or any command to surrender, mortally wounding him. The medical examiner's report stated that Officer Wright received multiple gunshot wounds *in the back.*

On June 7, 1973, a black detective named William B. Jakes was shot once in the abdomen by a white uniformed cop while on a stakeout. Detective Jakes was involved with a 25-man team composed of units from the FBI, NYPD, and the Queens district attorney's office responding to a tip that weapons were to be delivered to black militants in the East New York section of Brooklyn.

Detective Jakes and his two partners had taken their assigned post with shotguns on the roof of a building. Someone made an anonymous 911 call reporting that there were unknown strangers on the roof. Two uniformed white cops from the 75th Precinct, who were unaware of the stakeout, were dispatched to the scene. They went directly to the roof and found the door to the roof partly open. As they pushed the door open, they saw a shotgun and a black man in plain clothes. One of the white cops fired three rounds through the opened door without warning or challenge, striking Jakes once in the abdomen. Jakes survived the gunshot wound, and the white cop was vindicated from any wrongdoing by the police department.

Another black cop, a detective named John White, was shot by a white detective on December 14, 1973. Both men were unknowingly chasing the same car thief, and both officers were in plain clothes. Detective White was the first to stop the suspect (who was white). He ordered him to get out, spread his legs, and lean against the side of the car. Then he begin to frisk the suspect in the same way police frisk suspects from Los Angeles to Boston. When the white detective came on the scene, he said he saw a "black man with a gun" that was aimed at a white man.

This detective took it for granted that Detective White was the car thief and immediately opened fire without warning! White was struck in the back of his right arm, and he dropped his gun and ran hysterically into the street in an attempt to get out of the line of fire. He didn't see his assailant and didn't know who was shooting at him. As he ran he shouted several times, *"I'm on the job!"* (a code phrase used by all undercover and off-duty cops to identify themselves to one another). It didn't help. The white detective continued to fire at Detective White, hitting him in the neck. Then the white detective approached the seriously wounded black cop and began to frisk him as he lay bleeding on the asphalt. That is when he discovered Detective White's police shield and realized that the "black man with a gun" was actually a black police officer.

Not only were the white cops gunning down black cops, but they were also killing black youths without justification. On April 10, 1973, a white police officer shot and killed a young black college student named John Brabbam. When the officer was indicted by a Brooklyn grand jury for the killing, the policeman said he had stopped Brabbam in a routine auto inspection, and claimed the student had threatened him. The officer, who had already drawn his gun from its holster (for a "routine auto inspection"?), fired his gun and killed the college student, allegedly recovering a toy gun at the scene.

An investigation was conducted by the police department, and the district attorney's office later established that the same toy gun had been seen in the officer's possession *a day prior to the incident!*

Another white police officer shot and killed Clifford Glover, a black ten-year-old, on April 28, 1973. That officer was the first New York City police officer to be charged with murder.

On September 15, 1974, a 14-year-old black boy named Claude Reese, Jr., was shot and killed by a white police officer who was responding to an alleged burglary in a tenement basement in the Brownsville section of Brooklyn. Reese was at the location working with several other young people who were cleaning the basement for the purpose of having a party. The officer and his partner entered the basement with their guns drawn. The young black youths were so startled by the two white men with drawn guns that they tried to run out of fear. That is when the white officer shot and killed Claude Reese. The officer later claimed that the boy had turned and "pointed something" at him. No weapon was ever found, despite a thorough search of the building.

(Ironically, an incident almost identical to the Claude Reese killing occurred in that same section of Brooklyn 20 years later. On January 10, 1994, 17-year-old Shuaib Abdul-Latif was shot and killed in an incident in which cops alleged to have been responding to a call of a "man with a gun." Shuaib was also in a basement of a tenement building when a half-dozen cops stormed down the steps with guns drawn, causing the occupants to panic and run for cover. A cop fired at the kids without warning, killing Shuaib as he ran for cover.

Two days after that shooting, I went to the scene of the shooting to investigate the incident at the request of Al-Amin Abdul-Latif. The police claimed that they thought Shuaib had a gun. Once again, as in the Claude Reese case two decades earlier, an extensive search of the building failed to turn up a single weapon. While I was standing in front of the building conferring with Ali-Abdul Karee, a Housing Police van filled with white police officers drove by slowly as the white cops made some heckling and disparaging remarks. Then they drove off. "You see, that's how those white mother 'so-and-so's' are," remarked one of the teenage girls I was interviewing. As a retired detective, I was ashamed to say that I could identify with what she was saying.

Peter Bailey wrote an article in the November 1974 issue of *Ebony* magazine entitled, "You Can't Tell the Cops From the Robbers," in which he said, "No one [in the police department] can give any adequate explanation as to why no white [plainclothes] officer or off-duty officer has ever been shot by black cops or even why no black officer in civilian clothes has ever been shot by another black cop." The truth was starting to come out...

On November 25, 1976, 15-year-old Randolph Evans, a black youth, was shot to death by a white police officer who had responded to a call of "a man with a gun" along with five other officers at a project in the East New York section of Brooklyn. The call proved to be unfounded, and as the officer left the building, he met Randolph Evans. They had words and the officer suddenly drew his service revolver and fired one round point-blank into Evan's head, killing him instantly. That officer became the third white police officer in three years to be indicted for the murder of a black youth. As in the previous cases, the white officer was acquitted of the killing.

On November 5, 1977, a white officer was found guilty of criminally negligent homicide for the beating death of Israel Rodriguez, a Hispanic suspect he had arrested. This was the first time a white police officer had ever been convicted of homicide. The conviction was attributed in part to fellow officers who had the courage to do the unthinkable and break the unwritten "blue code of silence" and testify against another police officer.

Most of the incidents involving white officers shooting black officers and civilians are never reported by the news media. White officers have even stopped me when I was driving my car while off duty. They became abusive until I identified myself as a police officer and left them speechless. One time, while I was working the night watch as a plainclothes detective, two white officers tried to pull me over for no apparent reason. When I refused to stop, they put on their vehicle's emergency lights and sirens, so I also switched on the emergency lights and siren of my police vehicle. They finally got the message and stopped their pursuit.

The shooting of black cops by white cops had all but ceased until November 11, 1993. Derwin Pannell, a black New York City Transit plainclothes cop, was in the process of effecting an arrest along with his white partner. He had his gun on the suspect and was in the process of handcuffing him when four uniformed white officers came on the scene and opened fire on Pannell *without any warning whatsoever.*

Pannell was wounded in the neck, and luckily, he was wearing a bulletproof vest which saved him from further injury or death. The four white officers *fired a total of 21 rounds* at Pannell. Their excuse was that they didn't know Pannell was a cop. In reality, when they came on the scene, all they saw was a "black man with a gun." They never took the time to think that just maybe he was a cop. Evidently, they made no effort to evaluate the actions of a cop who was obviously following standard police procedure. Incredibly, these four professionally trained police officers, with a combined total of 21 years of service on the force, failed realize that Pannell, who was clearly holding handcuffs and working in tandem with a white officer, was merely taking actions they themselves performed almost daily!

Black police officers from all three New York City Police Departments had formed a union in the 70's called the "Grand Council of Guardians" to give black police officers a stronger voice in the public arena, along with greater power and influence in the police community. The Guardians were outraged at the shooting of Officer Pannell and at the way the Transit Police Department was handling the incident.

Erick Adams, vice president of the Grand Council of Guardians at the time, told the media, "Derwin Pannell was not a black cop the day he was shot. Historically, we have been stereotyped. He could have been a victim of a crime, but no, *he was a black man with a gun* in America, and that equals *criminal*." The police department heads chose to call the Pannell shooting "friendly fire," a term adopted by military officials in Operation Desert Storm to describe (and justify) the actions of allied forces that fired on one another after mistaking them for the enemy.

Only nine months later, while the Pannell shooting was still fresh on the minds of black cops throughout the city, yet another black Transit cop was shot by a white cop! On August 22, 1994, an off-duty white NYPD cop named Peter Del-Debbio shot Desmond Robinson, a black undercover cop, five times in the back while Robinson was performing his duty. Robinson said he had just stopped chasing a suspect in the New York City subway. "I relaxed and stood still for at least three seconds, thinking everything was all right," he recalled. "Then I thought, *Oh my God, what did I miss?* Suddenly I was on the ground looking at my gun in front of me, and 'bang...bang!' "

Peter Del-Debbio had opened fire on the black plainclothes cop without warning, while Robinson was standing with his gun in hand and his back towards the shooter. To add insult to injury, while Robinson lay face-down on the floor seriously wounded, Del-Debbio came up to him and fired still another round into his back! It was only by the grace of God that Robinson survived his wounds.

The outrageous nature of this shooting was topped off by the attitudes and actions of New York City Mayor Guiliani and Police Commissioner Bratten, who infuriated the membership of the United Fraternity of Black Law Enforcement Officers and the black community at large. Again, the term "friendly fire" was purposely used to undermine the seriousness and motive of the incident. It was utterly ludicrous to even suggest that the last two shootings were acts of "friendly fire" or "tragic mistakes." At the time of this writing, a jury has found Peter Del-Debbio guilty of second-degree assault, and Police Commissioner Bratten has publicly announced his resignation.

The term *friendly fire* was being used out of context by police officials to justify wrongdoing. It refers exclusively to soldiers or military commanders who willingly direct artillery shelling or air strikes on *their own position* to keep their base position from being overrun by enemy forces. (This happened many times in the Korean and Vietnam Wars.) This is done with the knowledge that there is a good chance some of their own men may be wounded or killed by the "friendly fire." But there is a big difference between voluntarily calling down fire on your own position and being shot in the back by somebody. Anything else is "hostile fire," even when the one doing the shooting happens to "be on your side."

Anytime someone begins shooting at another person without warning, they have already decided to kill that individual. The use of a firearm constitutes deadly physical force. There is no acceptable explanation for white cops shooting black cops in plainclothes—especially when they were clearly in the performance of duty. In every incident involving the shooting of a black cop, the victim was shot without warning and from behind.

Any white cop who comes upon a scene where a black or non-white cop is in the process of effecting an arrest or dealing with a criminal situation simply has to take a few seconds to evaluate the actions of the individuals involved. Any officer who comes upon a questionable scene unannounced and unnoticed has the time to find adequate cover and confront an individual—whether black, Hispanic, white, or green—in the professional manner every police officer is trained to do.

If every white police officer who has fired upon a black police officer had given that black officer the benefit of the doubt, he would have quickly discovered that "the black man with the gun" was, in fact, a black cop. Unfortunately, the general attitudes and actions of white cops toward black cops and civilians today still belies an ongoing undercurrent of racism in local, state, and federal law enforcement agencies across America.

Countless black law enforcement officers, including myself, have encountered situations where we could have "shot first and asked questions later" as other white officers have done. In many instances, I have observed certain individuals from a safe vantage point to see what they were up to, and once I was satisfied that they were in fact cops, I went about my business; and they never knew another cop was in the area. Unfortunately, certain racially motivated white cops know that historically, they have been able to get away with a great deal of abusive behavior in black and non-white communities, so they take every opportunity that comes their way to abuse their power and authority as law enforcement officers with relative impunity.

The nation was shocked at the beating of Rodney King by Los Angeles policemen, but this is merely one prime example among many incidents of the actions of racist white cops. I wasn't surprised when it was revealed that at least two police supervisors were present during the entire beating. Had it not been for the person recording the abusive actions of the cops on a VHS-camcorder camera, there would not have been any record of the incident. These officers didn't simply decide to beat a black man to a pulp with their supervisors present that day; this was "business as usual," like another day at the beach.

The way the Los Angeles police department and district attorney's office handled the Nicole Simpson and Ron Goldman murders merely exemplifies the white backlash against black suspects in the overall law enforcement and due process system. Regardless of whether O.J. Simpson was guilty or innocent of the murders, that case reeked of racially-motivated actions, motives, and bungling. Every experienced detective knows a case can be won or lost by the way the initial investigation is handled. A highly-sensitive murder case forces detectives to take extra care to "go by the book."

# Chapter 13

# Alone in Death's Face

*W*hen a cop wakes up and gets ready for work, nothing is farther from his mind than death. Human beings don't want to think about death; it is not a popular subject for discussion. We block it out of our minds, even though we are dying every second. Yet cops are confronted by death 24 hours a day, 7 days a week, as they witness gunshot and accident victims declared dead on arrival (DOA) or when they face life-and-death situations.

I have never talked with other officers about getting into a shoot-out or being shot, nor have I ever heard other cops engaged in a similar conversation. Cops just don't talk about life-and-death situations until they are *in one.* By the end of 1981, I had already been in five shoot-outs and had killed one individual while in the line of duty. While I know that man has always feared death because of the unknown, I have also learned that you just can't prepare for death. It may come when you least expect it (except in the case of suicide). One thing is for certain, we all have an appointment with death. Yet some people choose lifestyles that cause them to die before their appointed time, and which also may place the lives of others in jeopardy.

As a person, and in my profession as a police officer, I have always had a high regard for life. I have faced many life-and-death situations, and each experience has left an everlasting impression on me. A cop is trained to respond to and function in a crisis efficiently and effectively, even under the most adverse conditions. It

195

only takes one incident to severely test your training and capability and push you nearly over the line of life into death, in the twinkling of an eye.

My partner and I were walking on Belmont Avenue in the Brownsville section of Brooklyn on a hot July afternoon in 1981 after being assigned to investigate a severe drug and robbery epidemic. We had just exited a restaurant on Mother Gaston Avenue when something caught my eye that really disturbed me. I called Albert Layne's attention to a woman a few yards in front of us who was nodding over a baby stroller. The situation was especially heartbreaking because the baby, who was just over a year old, was seated in the stroller with his head back, looking up into the face of his nodding mother, a heroin addict who was on a drug high. You can't help but to grieve at sights like that. My compassion went out for that child.

I went over to the woman and shook her a few times until she came out of her stupor, and then I walked away. "That poor child has to suffer just because his mother is a junkie," I told my partner. "That's the way it is," Layne said as we turned the corner onto Belmont Avenue.

While we were still on Belmont Avenue, we saw a drug sale go down. The buyer, a young Hispanic man, was unaware that we were undercover cops, and he walked directly toward us with his drugs in hand. Layne grabbed him as he walked by, and the drug seller, who was also a male Hispanic, saw the arrest and quickly stepped back into a nearby apartment building. "I'm going after him," I told Layne.

When I reached the building and went inside, I saw the suspect at the rear of the steps, where the basement door led to the basement staircase. I approached him while shouting, "Police. Don't move!" I didn't pull out my gun, only my shield. From my position, I couldn't see his hands, but I knew he was doing something with them. I came up on him quickly, and the way he suddenly whirled his body and moved toward me made me feel sure that he had a gun, and that he was going to shoot me!

A strange feeling came over me, and my mind had already anticipated being shot. My body reacted to the suspect's movements as if I was about to suffer the devastating shock and trauma of a bullet fired from his gun at close range. Thank God, it did not happen. The dealer quickly pushed past me and tried to run, but my partner stopped him at the door. "Boy," I said to myself, "I thought I had bought it." I'll never forget the feeling that came over me that day. It was a mixture of paralyzing fear and a strange anticipation of getting shot. In a corner behind the door leading to the basement steps, I found a large number of glassine envelopes containing a white substance that turned out to be heroin. Both the buyer and the seller were arrested and charged with the purchase, and the sale and possession of a controlled substance, respectively.

Guns and shootings were becoming the norm with drug dealers and street crimes, which created an added hazard for undercover cops in particular, and police officers in general. One incident caused my antinarcotics team to take extra precautions when dealing with all drug offenders. We made a drug sweep in a drug-prone location one hot August Friday evening in the Williamsburg section of Brooklyn.

Our usual method was to drop off three men at each end of a targeted block (including my partner and I). When both teams were in position, Layne and I would always walk a few yards ahead of the team shouting, "Five-0, Five-0!" When the drug dealers heard the alert, they would hurriedly try to leave the area, and some would even toss their drugs into what they thought was a secret location like under a car or under the steps at the entrance of a dwelling. Of course I could see them, and my team would immediately apprehend them and their drugs. Dealers or buyers who ran from us would be caught by the oncoming team from the other end of the block. The van followed behind us as we picked up suspects. We would quickly handcuff their hands behind their backs and place them in the back of the van along with the drugs they had tried to throw away.

On this particular roundup, we had worked especially fast because of the unusual number of drug dealers present. We hadn't even taken the time to frisk the suspects for weapons. We were headed back to the precinct house in our van, along with eight handcuffed suspects, in the rear when we suddenly heard a loud thump on the floor at the rear of the van. One of the suspects yelled, "Who threw that ball?" I told the driver to pull over and stop, and he also motioned to the cops in the unmarked car following us that we were stopping.

When Layne and I got out of the van and looked under the rear seats with a flashlight, we spotted a 9-millimeter automatic handgun on the floor! It was fully loaded with 15 live rounds. That gave us all a good scare. We couldn't help but think about what could have happened if the person with the gun had decided he did not want to go to jail. We made everyone get out of the van and conducted a thorough search of each prisoner. We found another fully loaded .38-caliber handgun, and a 9-millimeter ammunition clip containing 14 additional live rounds matching the clip that we found in the first handgun, which made it easy to identify the owner of the 9-millimeter pistol. We learned a good lesson from that incident, and we never put a prisoner in the van again without thoroughly searching him or her for weapons. The year 1981 was another record year in arrests and number of guns seized. I discovered I had made over 400 arrests that year.

I had been in a number of life-threatening situations in the past, like many cops. I thought I had seen the worst of things. That is what I thought until February 15, 1982, that is.

It was Monday, and I was working the 2-to-10 night tour with Layne at the Tompkins and Sumner Housing Projects in Brooklyn. It was about 6:20 p.m., and the entire antinarcotics team was with Layne and I in the blue unmarked van. All of a sudden we heard two shots ring out from the direction of the projects; then we saw people running away from the rear of a building at 10 Lewis Avenue.

The driver stopped the van and we all jumped out and started to run toward the gunfire as more shots were fired. I sprinted ahead of the team, and as I approached the area where we'd heard gunshots, I saw a young black man running towards me, and carrying a huge black radio (or "boom box"). I figured he must have been involved in the shooting, so I shouted to him, "Stop! Police!" The suspect suddenly darted to my right, and I followed closely behind him until he came to a fence. He instantly dropped the radio and scrambled up over the fence.

Still behind him, I climbed the fence and pulled my revolver before I again ordered the young man to halt. That is when he wheeled around and fired a round at me, catching me totally off guard! All I can remember doing in that split second was saying, "God, don't let him shoot me." Things began to happen even faster. Even though I had been taken by surprise, I returned fire, completely emptying my service revolver at the fleeing male. Another member of the team also fired several rounds at the suspect. I always carried two guns, so I slipped the empty revolver back into its holster, and pulled a second gun from my shoulder holster, taking time to check to see if I was shot. (Considering the way my adrenaline was flowing, I could have been shot without realizing it. I didn't want to drop dead from a gunshot wound if I could help it.)

I again picked up the pursuit of the suspect and gained enough ground to aim my revolver at him. I would have shot him had it not been for two young ladies who stepped into my line of fire, causing me to lose the suspect when he ran into an abandoned building on Broadway. By that time, the area was swarming with cops. A thorough search of the abandoned building failed to turn up the suspect. Several hours later, I received a call to report to Cumberland Hospital in the Fort Greene section of Brooklyn. There was a gunshot victim there who fit the description of the black male I had pursued earlier. I picked up two persons who had been robbed at gunpoint by the suspect I was pursuing and took them to the hospital. Perhaps they could identify the gunshot victim as their assailant.

The two robbery victims could not make a positive identification of the man in the emergency room, nor could I. It was too dark outside at the time of the shoot-out, and the lighting was poor where the incident had occurred, so I didn't get a good look at the face of the suspect. However, a uniformed cop who had also exchanged shots with an individual that night positively identified the wounded man in the hospital as the suspect.

Several months later, after nearly 14 years on the police force, I was finally assigned to the detective bureau. I still was disappointed because I wasn't given a detective's gold shield right away (which I should have received years before). "You will receive it in due time," was the only remark the chief of detectives made to me. I just shrugged and told myself, "Well, you're in, so make the best of it." My partner, Albert Layne, turned down his appointment because he was happy where he was. Making all those arrests meant a great deal of overtime and money. Anyway, he was going to retire soon and felt it would be more beneficial for him in the long run to stay with the narcotics squad.

My first assignment as a member of the detective bureau was to work with the robbery task force. I had only been in the detective bureau for two weeks when the unthinkable happened to me again.

When I entered the room that held the grand jury, it wasn't as if I had not been here before. I had appeared before grand juries in all five boroughs hundreds of times, but this time was different. I had killed a man. Six years earlier, I was called to appear before the Manhattan grand jury under similar conditions. It was "deja vu" all over again. The two eldest members of the jury wiped droplets of sweat from their brow, their starched shirt collars wilting in the humid heat of the courtroom. An assistant district attorney studied his notes, his blue Bic doing a nervous tap against the scarred wooden desk. The judge, his deep-creased black robe hiding a sweat-drenched, blue-on-white shirt, opened his case book and looked toward the 12 members of the grand jury, making eye contact with the nervous-looking, brown-haired woman in the front row. One of the jurors shifted in his seat, a hand defending against a muffled cough. It was 9:37 a.m.

As I walked past the lawyer's table, police shield number 3135 hanging from the chest pocket of my jacket, I nodded in the judge's direction and avoided the gaze of the jury. Placing my left hand on a tattered Bible, I raised my right hand and swore to tell the truth, the whole truth...

As a rule, cops hate appearing before grand juries on cases involving them personally. They always feel on the defensive, as if both their actions and their motives are on trial. I knew I would have only a few minutes to paint a picture of the shooting incident that left a man dying with a bullet wound from my gun. I would have to convince 12 total strangers that I was left with no choice but to use deadly force and take a man's life. I had to convince them that my actions were those of a reasonable man, that as a trained police officer I did all I could to avoid gunplay and had only acted to defend my own life and those of innocent bystanders.

I sat in the witness chair with my hands folded across my lap, staring straight at the assistant district attorney. By 10:24 a.m., I had answered the assistant D.A.'s questions about my numerous citations, the Medal of Valor, my standing in the community, and the respect I had earned in the city's housing projects. Within seven minutes, the assistant D.A. had neatly worked his way up to the day of the shooting, August 20, 1982. As the young attorney walked away from me, walking slowly and casually toward the jury, he asked the most important leading question of all: "Detective Lewis. Please, if you will, as best as you can recall, tell the court what happened on that day, during your tour of duty...."

The story I told that grand jury is the same story I am about to relate to you.

It was late August, and brutally hot and sticky due to the high humidity shortly after noon, when I left the NYCHPD Precinct Service Area 2 on Sutter Avenue with my partner, Robert Brown. We got into our unmarked car and hit the streets as part of a 12-member robbery task force looking for a male suspect who was grabbing women as they were returning home from work and mugging them. His pattern was to follow his victims home and strike when they entered their places of residence.

We had a photo of the suspect along with a decent description, so myself and Brown were on our way to interview some of the mugging victims and have them view a photo array in hopes of getting a positive I.D. on the suspect. We had driven for ten minutes when our right front tire blew out. Brown's choice comment was, "They should take all these cars and flush them down the river."

"It's okay," I said. "There's a gas station right over there. Pull in. It won't take but ten minutes to fix." So we pulled into an old Mobil gas station. It wasn't the cleanest of stations, but it was the best at the time. I don't think there was a single spot of cement that didn't have a grease or oil stain on it. The station was right on the corner of Sutter and Mother Gaston Boulevard. Since I couldn't handle hanging around the grease, the dirty dogs, and the smell of gas and smoke, I told Brown to sit tight. "Brown, the first woman we're planning to interview lives right around the corner from this station. I'll save us both some time by walking over to her house and showing her the photos now. Maybe she can identify her assailant. I'll meet you in front of this building. Grab yourself a cup of coffee," I told Brown. "I'm sure this place has a coffee machine." Brown smirked and added, "And I'm sure it's clean too."

I left the gas station and walked west on Sutter Avenue toward the woman's building. There was a city park and a school directly across the street. Then I heard two loud shots ring out, back to back. I heard some screams and saw people running in my direction from the park. I ran back to the gas station and yelled out to Brown, "*Shots fired in the park!*"

Brown dropped his coffee and jumped into the unmarked police car—it's flat tire still unfixed. As I ran across the street toward the park, I took out my snub-nosed, .38 Detective Special revolver with my right hand, and displayed my shield with my left. (As I mentioned earlier, anytime a black man with a gun in his hand is running in public, he had better have a shield in his other hand.)

I was running with every bit of speed I could muster toward the park. *Bam! Bam!* The screams grew louder, and there was a panic on the street. One shot thudded into the left front door of a parked car less than three feet from me as I ran by. I heard the shot and sound of the projectile as it struck the car and "hit the deck" so hard that I banged my knee.

I could tell by the sound of the bullet hitting the car that it came from a large caliber gun. *Nine millimeter, most likely*, I thought to myself. I took cover behind a car and checked out the scene. The park was fenced in, and there was a littered alleyway between the park and the school. A young man ran by behind me, but when he saw my drawn gun and the shield hanging from my neck, he suddenly stopped and said, "Keep your eye on the guy in the gray-hooded parka. I just saw him rob a guy."

I focused my attention on the man in the parka and saw the gun in his right hand. He was looking around and trying to play it cool, but there was a strange look on his face. Slowly, he put the gun in the waistband of his trousers, pulled the parka over it, and began to run. I took off after him, leaving him a 75- to 100-yard lead. I didn't want to alert him to my presence, preferring that he leave the scene without any idea that he was being followed by a cop. I was wearing casual jeans and a safari jacket, so I didn't look too much like a cop.

This guy was a fast runner who could really move. I was really glad I had kept up my daily six-mile training regimen. I didn't want to lose this shooter—not now. I was gaining on him, and his lead was cut down to 50 yards when he suddenly crossed the street and entered another playground area right in the middle of the projects. It was fairly empty, with more benches than trees. I was only 25 yards from the suspect and moving fast when he headed toward a bench where a couple of girls were sitting. As he was passing them, they happened to notice me behind him with my drawn gun and police shield. One of the girls yelled out to him, "The cop is behind you! The Man! Five-O—behind you!"

The man suddenly stopped and reached into his pants. Then he pulled out his gun, spun around, and pointed it directly at me! There was no place to run for cover, and there was no time to take aim or even think. Everything happened so fast that all I could do was point my gun and pull the trigger. I hit the suspect on the first shot.

I watched the man go down, and I started to shake. He went down like a wounded animal. The bullet struck him on the left side of his head, and the swelling started immediately as blood flowed through cracks in the concrete and under the bench toward the grass. I went over to him, took the gun from his hand, and knelt by his side. "Don't move, son," I told him. "Please don't move."

He was just a boy. He couldn't have been more than 17 years old. I cradled his head in my lap and looked at his face, half-covered with blood. "Please God," I began to pray. "Please Lord, don't let him die. Please, don't let him die. Please Lord. Please..."

It seemed as if my whole body had gone completely numb of any feeling. When I looked into the suspect's eyes, I realized that he didn't have much time left. My senses were all but gone. I just couldn't look at him anymore. I took my jacket off and rested his bloody head on it, then I waited numbly for the emergency service units to arrive. Then I walked away, and my partner pulled up in our car with the flat tire.

Brown came up behind me, put his arm around my shoulder, and stayed with me for a moment. Then I handed him my gun and shield, along with the suspect's gun. "I quit, Brown," I told him.

"I've had enough. I can't do this anymore. I can't shoot anybody ever again, especially a kid."

Brown stopped me as I walked away and grabbed both of my shoulders. "Listen to me, Richie," he said. "If that gunman had had his way, it would have been me leaning over your body. He was a dangerous guy. He wouldn't have thought twice about bringing you down. So stay cool, my friend. Stay very cool."

The scene was flooded with cops from both the Housing Authority and the NYPD 73rd Precinct. They searched the guy's pockets and found a handful of jewelry and rings. They also found 20 live rounds of ammunition on his body. The suspect was Anthony Green, and he was a known "shooter" in the area. He was known as "Two Bodies" on the street, which meant that he had killed two people.

As I leaned against a patrol car, my body was still shaking and sweaty. My legs and back ached, my head felt fuzzy, and my arms seemed to weigh a ton. I couldn't focus on the scene. All the faces were blurs, and the sounds echoed. It was my second shooting in a year, the seventh face-to-face shoot-out of my career. *I can't go on anymore. I just can't take another person's life*, I thought. I shook Brown's hand and thanked him, and walked away alone to a waiting car.

Back in the precinct, I was taken into the captain's office. He had my gun and the spent round on his desk. As I watched, he replaced the spent round with a live one, and I couldn't understand why. That was not his function. That was the job of an Emergency Services police officer.

While I was there, the captain received a call from a deputy chief and I heard him say the shooting was justified, and that the police officer had followed proper procedure. Judging by the tone in his voice, it almost sounded like he wished that weren't the case. (I had always wondered if the department would try to pin something on me if they could. I wasn't well liked because I had spoken out on some racial issues involving biased treatment of black cops.

A few of the top white bosses had labeled me as a "renegade cop." I was black, and good at what I did, and no one could touch me with accusations of corruption or poor performance in the line of duty.)

After that, I endured endless rounds of interrogation and questioning from department officials. I couldn't help but wonder whether the slain suspect was the culprit, or me. Then, the department lawyer showed up and started asking his questions. Later still, the assistant D.A. assigned to the case came by and did the same. All in all, I was in that examination room for 16 hours. (Now I know what criminals feel like.)

While I was there, another cop working downstairs filled out my report sheet. He wasn't supposed to, but he did it anyway. The biggest problem was that he made a mistake. He put me down as the "complainant," not as the arresting officer. No one noticed the error until I was called in with a court summons a few weeks later. I wasn't being called down as a cop; I was being called down as a civilian! I tossed the subpoena in the garbage, called the D.A.'s office, and cleared up the problem. Even so, I still felt uneasy about the whole situation. There was no doubt that the whole incident had been handled badly, even improperly, almost as if I were at fault. It seemed to be a trend that had only started when I joined the bureau.

I found out later that the commanding officer of the detective bureau had actually tried to give the credit for the arrest to one of his white detectives! He didn't care for me because in the past I had made his detectives look bad on numerous occasions while working as a plainclothes cop; I had solved cases they couldn't. I had become convinced by his actions that he would do almost anything to jam me and keep me from becoming a top-ranked detective.

From that day on, I learned to be more careful—very careful. I had learned that even one mistake, one wrong comment, even one typographical error, could cost you your job, your pension, your name, and everything else you had worked so hard to earn. You could lose it all "just like that," and nobody would care.

After I answered everyone's questions, I was taken to Brookdale Hospital—the same hospital where they had taken the suspect I shot. The doctors checked me over and cleared me in a little over an hour. While I was there, police officials began to grill my partner at the station house for his version of the shooting incident. I could have left the hospital and gone straight home, but instead, I went back to the precinct station. I wanted to know more about the kid.

One of the cops investigating the suspect told me the gunman had wounded a 12-year-old boy in the chest with one of the shots he had fired during a robbery. He was also a suspect in three separate homicides, as well as a known thief and murderer. There were several wanted cards out on him (called "61's"). He was basically a "bad guy" who had often bragged about the "two bodies" he had on him, so the neighborhood people didn't care much for him. Usually, after a shooting like this, there was a big neighborhood to-do. Not this time. The people seemed relieved to be rid of him.

One incident did occur, but it was a minor one. It seems that a few months earlier, an Italian cop from the 75th Precinct had promised to retaliate against the gunman and "nail him." The neighborhood knew about the threat, so a large group of blacks, mostly family members and a few community activists, had crowded into the 75th Precinct making a lot of noise and claiming that the shooting was racially motivated. My partner, Brown, went down to talk to them. It took him a while to get them to quiet down and get their attention, but once he did, he told them what many didn't want to hear: it wasn't a white cop who did the shooting; it was a black cop, and it was entirely justified. They left quietly soon after that.

The chief of detectives didn't want to give me time off the following day. He said I had to take vacation time. (This wasn't standard police procedure or policy. It was just another outward proof of his racist attitude. Fortunately, my immediate supervisor took it upon himself to tell me to take as many days off as I needed to get myself together.)

I called my oldest brother from the station and said, "Jimmy, can you come down and pick me up?" He was an accountant for the Housing Authority and handled the police payroll. "Yeah, I'll be right there Richie. I heard about the shooting over the radio. I've been real concerned about you, man." After Jimmie drove me home, he was so worried about me that he wanted to stick around until I fell asleep. (By this time, I had gone without sleep for about 26 hours.) I told him, "No Jimmie, I'm okay. I just want to stay up and think for a while. I need to be by myself." After he left, I called my parents' house and talked with my baby daughter, Senice; and then I tried to get some sleep.

I tossed and turned for an hour or two, and finally I got up and put on my track clothes. Then I headed for the street. I started to run, and I just kept on running. I ran for 20 miles or more, and I ran all the way through Kennedy Airport. As I ran, I relived every detail of the shooting again and again, trying to justify it in my mind so I could live with it.

As I ran, I also thought about my ex-wife, and how she had done me wrong by abandoning me and my daughter, Senice, for another man. I thought about the job I had chosen. I was a cop, a Housing cop, the toughest job in the world in my opinion. I kept on running and thought about the drugs that came so easily into the housing projects I was paid to keep clean.

I ran to the point of exhaustion, with my mind reeling from the flood of thoughts and images of all the kids I'd seen on drugs, living on their own, seeing their lives destroyed before they ever began. I thought about the "black on black" killings involving drugs and guns. *More blacks have been killed by other blacks than by all the cops put together across this nation.*

I ran and I ran, and in the end, I thanked God that I was alive. I thanked Him for my call to the ministry that fully complemented my profession as a cop. Then I kept running until I couldn't run anymore. I ran until I saw the sun rise behind me marking the start of a new day.

On April 27, 1984, New York City Mayor Edward Koch presented me with a second Medal of Honor "for actions above and beyond the call of duty, without concern or risk of my own life." The new medal joined the previous medal I kept at home, which was awarded in September 1977. I was the only New York City cop ever to have earned two of these medals in one lifetime, but somehow something was eluding me. Mayor Koch said to me, "You are the bravest man I know," yet I was afraid for my city, for the youth, and for my people. Whether the mayor knew it or not, my own department had done all it could to stain my name in the incident, and the sickening feeling I had felt as I cradled that teenage boy's head in my lap still came back from time to time.

# Chapter 14

# Corruption From Within

**M**y father and mother raised me to be an independent, self-motivated man, and I've always had a healthy dose of ambition. I was taught to study and work hard to achieve excellence in life. My father always told us, "You all have the qualities it takes to be somebody in society. But remember: Acquired knowledge is something no one can ever take away from you. When a man is educated, he can see things a little clearer than one who is not. You won't be easily fooled or deceived by people who mean you no good. It makes you a free independent thinker. Since you are black, your knowledge will be your greatest asset."

I was taught from early childhood to stand for what was right and not to allow anyone to walk over me. My parents lived a true Christian life and taught us sound Christian ethics. My father and mother worked hard to support and raise five children in a loving and caring environment, and they passed that work ethic along to us. I never looked for anyone to give me anything; earning an honest day's pay was the only way for me. Whatever I chose to do, I would put my whole heart into it and was determined to be the very best at whatever I did.

My career as a police officer, apart from the really important work on the streets and serving honest citizens, also introduced me to the sad world of corruption, prejudice, and internal police politics. I reluctantly came to realize that corruption was one of the prime reasons blacks and other non-whites were routinely held back regarding career advancement.

211

I realize that many, perhaps even a majority of my readers will be white, and this chapter and others that describe unjust conditions in law enforcement are not to be an indictment on any race or economic group. It is an indictment against racism, regardless of the individual it is controlling and influencing. It is simply an unfortunate fact that this nation has a history of racial inequity that can be traced back to the public institution of slavery, which flourished in this nation from its founding to the Civil War, only a little over one and a quarter centuries ago.

I discovered evidence that corrupt police officials, most of whom were white men in upper levels of authority, openly displayed preferential treatment toward family members or promotion candidates of the same race. This was not just the work of a few individuals undermining the system. This was the inner structure of the system itself, where corrupt activities were rampant.

The corruption had gone on so long that it was considered "business as usual." Many, including myself, learned the hard way that anyone who "stepped out of line" and did not play their game would have the "troops" called out after them. The average law-abiding person looking in from the outside might see or hear about these things, and then ask themselves, "I wonder if the blatant acts I saw really happened? After all, isn't this department supposed to uphold the law, not break it?"

A unique and unwritten code of apartheid was alive and well-entrenched in the New York City Housing Authority Police Department, where discrimination against black officers appeared to be the norm, not the exception. Whites held the majority of positions in the power structure of all three New York City police departments, despite the fact that the majority of officers in the Housing Police Department had been black and Hispanic from its inception. When I became a cop, I was placed on the inside of the "blue line." Yet as far as "fair and equal" treatment was concerned, I quickly learned that white cops received preferential treatment in assignments, promotions, and even in disciplinary matters. A two-tiered system existed, one favoring whites, the other playing against blacks. The individuals who instituted that type of conduct would go to any extreme to cover up their illegal actions.

Police work for black officers had always presented special challenges within the police department itself, as well as in the communities they served. Most, if not all, had to contend with biased or racist attitudes and political tactics of one or more superior officers, meaning they always received the toughest and most hazardous assignments and were expected to perform under substandard conditions. Black police officers eligible and overdue for promotion to a high position in the department were generally treated like secondary or second-rate officers, which perhaps reflected the overall inequities of the American society as a whole.

During my tenure with the New York City Housing Authority Police Department, I was passed over for promotion for more than 14 and a half years before I was finally promoted to 3rd grade detective. I found out the hard way that when you are black, merit doesn't matter. If this sounds harsh or a bit bitter, it is because I am still trying to come to terms with the inequities I experienced. I had run into the same type of racial corruption in the U.S. Air Force in the 70's. (I pray that it has changed for the better now.)

Anyone who dedicates his life to a demanding profession such as law enforcement, and who gives more of himself to the job than is normally required, should receive some kind of recognition for his sacrifice. I'm not saying *special recognition*; I'm referring to equal recognition apart from race, gender, or economic background.

I became very frustrated and disheartened when I saw white officers with considerably less time, experience, expertise, and arrests promoted to detective over me.

Many of the black officers I served with told me about the long history of injustices and denials they had suffered at the hands of their white department heads. They said, "Less deserving white officers were promoted and appointed over us as though we never existed." When I made direct inquiries about why I hadn't been promoted to detective year after year, I was always told, "You have to wait your turn, Lewis." When I would pin my superiors down to question why specific white officers with less seniority and inferior service records evidently "had their turn" and were promoted ahead of me over the last decade, they were always at a loss to give me a truthful answer. Now I know why. There wasn't any.

I became so discouraged with the situation that I conducted my own investigation to find answers. How could discrimination go on like "business as usual" when there were supposedly so many procedures in place to ensure fair treatment? That is when I found out how corrupt the inner structure of the police department truly was. I learned that many white cops used outside influences such as politicians and influential or prestigious family members and friends to get promoted. This method of using outside assistance for preferential treatment in assignments, promotions, and disciplinary matters was known as "having a hook."

These outside individuals, or so-called "hooks," would use their position to make "under-the-table" verbal deals with high-ranking police officials responsible for making assignments and approving promotions. Some of the deals actually involved monetary gains, while others hinged on reciprocated favors in the form of assistance to a ranking official in obtaining a high position for himself, or some other kind of payment. Acts of this nature gave some key police superiors greater power and protection than the public at large would ever know under normal circumstances. While these corrupt practices might be difficult to hide or disguise in many typical police organizations, the massive size of the three New York police departments (which were larger than most state law enforcement agencies) created an ideal cover for massive corruption. Anyone who dared to speak out was immediately dismissed as a self-serving "whiner" and troublemaker.

In my case, when I began to speak out publicly concerning the department's illegal, double-standard personnel practices, the feelings my white superiors felt toward me really changed for the worse, especially those in key positions. Everything was fine until I began to speak out against specific instances of unjust treatment of black cops. Fortunately, I had the backing of the Guardians, the black policemen's fraternal organization.

Another fortunate source of support and encouragement came from a totally unexpected source. The number of newsworthy arrests I had made rose so high in the 80's during my antinarcotics undercover days that an article appeared in *Newsday*, one of New York City's top newspapers, on October 10, 1984. Dennis Duggan, a top-rated white journalist and columnist, wrote an article entitled, "Honored Cop Wants Rewards With Medals," which gave a brief summary of my life and achievements on the force and my plight within the police department.

A few weeks later, an NBC news reporter named Ben Farnsworth came out to my house to interview me. I simply told my story; no embellishment was needed. It had taken over 14 years—even with numerous citations, including two Medals of Honor—to make detective 3rd grade. When I finally made it, there were white officers with less than seven years on the job and far fewer achievements already sharing the rank of 3rd grade detective with me. A few officers with ten years of service had already been promoted to 2nd grade detective. A grade one detective, the highest detective rank attainable, earned a salary equal to that of a police lieutenant.

One would have thought I had committed the ultimate crime because I dared to take a stand for equal justice. The truth is that to the predominately white police establishment, my years of service and Medals of Honor meant nothing. I had upset their apple cart. I had dared to break the unwritten "blue code of silence." Perhaps worst of all, I had rubbed the top brass the wrong way and embarrassed them by exposing the truth.

One friendly police supervisor warned me privately, "Watch your back, Lewis, because the department heads are out to get you." I had been labeled a maverick and was blackballed by some of the so-called "untouchable bosses." Evidently the unwritten "blue code of silence" meant that non-white officers were to stay in their place and stand idly by while others walked all over them. At least, that seemed to be the consensus of those in charge.

I had several young black cops ask me during my ordeal at the hands of high level police supervisors, "What do you do when you are passed over for career path assignments and promotions? Do you stop producing? Do you do just enough to get by?" My answer was a duplicate of my actions: "No, do *more* work, make *more* arrests, always keep your activity way *above* the average! I've learned from past experiences that as long as you continue to do a good job and make sure your record is kept clean, nothing much can be said. You can't give 'the man' ammunition to use against you. If you stop producing and you get into a situation where your personal file is used as a factor in determining the outcome of a matter, a poor record can be used against you."

In the beginning I suspected it, but now I had independent verification from third parties in the management structure: There was a conspiracy against me by the department heads. I also knew from my military training that when you know how your enemy conducts his business, you can always stay a few steps ahead of him.

My greatest source for the strength I needed to withstand the organized hostilities waged against me by certain high-ranking department officials came from my faith in God. As a minister of the gospel, I was absolutely convinced that if I took a stand for right, I could withstand any persecution that came my way.

One of my greatest disappointments was the discovery that there were a few black supervisors who were being used in the vendetta launched against me. In many circles in the system, you will always find blacks being drafted by corrupt white authorities to "side" with them. As long as some blacks will go along with corrupt white leaders and "share" in their actions, the actions will be accepted. These black bosses may go along with the program because they don't want to rock the boat. Even though they have the position and the power to help their own people in advancements and other areas, they will not. On the other hand, many white bosses go all out to help their own.

I was kept abreast of the conspiracy against me by a number of black supervisors who were in my corner and by a few blacks who were working in headquarters. I was dismayed to discover that the conspiracy against me seemed to have a snowball effect with certain white supervisors in and out of the detective bureau. I noticed from the beginning of my days in the detective bureau that my immediate supervisor tried to appease the chief of detectives by attempting to belittle my performance as an investigator; this was in spite of the fact that I was always one of the top detectives, in terms of felony arrests made and cases closed, right up until I retired from service. Inexplicably, however, my quarterly evaluations were always "average" in contrast to my performance, which was said to be second to none.

Any police officer knows that police activity and results constitute three-fourths of any objective evaluation report for a police officer. The other 25 percent of the evaluation report concerns less important but necessary skills such as report writing, court testimony, investigation skills, attitude, and so forth. If the performance evaluations had been used as a genuine evaluation tool, then all officers—whether black, white, Hispanic, or any other race or gender—would have gotten an even break and an equal opportunity for advancement.

Unfortunately, these evaluations turned out to be yet another instrument used by the department to keep blacks from advancing beyond 3rd grade detective. (No, I wasn't the only one.) Supervisors were grading me in certain areas they had never witnessed for themselves, such as my testimony in court. Criminal cases aren't closed when suspects go free, so my testimony before juries and judges,which was followed by a long string of convictions, spoke for itself. The only logical conclusion was that someone was trying to keep me from making 2nd grade detective.

Every time my superiors tried to downgrade my overall performance, I would prove them wrong. On several occasions, I anticipated hostile actions in advance; so I went to assistant district attorneys and judges to obtain letters from them offering independent comments and assessments of both my report writing and my ability to testify effectively and intelligently before the court.

The assistant district attorneys and judges universally commended my report writing and testimony in criminal court cases. A final blow to my hostile superiors came from my professors at the John Jay College of Criminal Justice where I had earned my bachelor of science degree. They provided letters commending my writing ability. That really got to my opponents, especially the chief of detectives. He made an extremely derogatory racial remark to me, and I told him and the other white inspector present, "You guys will never make a 'nigger' out of me!" They didn't take too kindly to my reply, but that was their problem.

All through this harassment, my expertise and performance as a detective was not hindered. Certain officials tried their best to break me, but their best wasn't good enough. I was determined not to let them do to me what they had done to so many black cops before me. By God's grace, I was able to perform my duties despite the extreme pressure I felt day after day. My greatest consolation through it all was my personal faith in Jesus Christ. As so many Christians of all races had done before me, I found solace in the Word of God, as I recalled various Scripture passages such as, "Greater is He that is in you, than he that is in the world" (1 Jn. 4:4b), and "If God be for us, who can be against us?" (Rom. 8:31b) These spiritual truths gave me an inner peace and assurance that I would preserve even in the worst of times.

From the day I first started to expose specific examples of corruption within the police department, I experienced resentment and retaliation. These only intensified over the years as my service record continued to win growing public attention, and as the inequity of the bias against me became more and more apparent.

When a number of cases that I solved won wide coverage by the news media, the publicity seemed to irritate the chief of detectives to no end.

At one point, bureau officials even went so far as to relieve me of an arrest I made and assign it to another detective. When a man who was working on the roof of a public school in the Fort Greene project area was shot in the head, the case was assigned to an investigator who was unable to turn up any leads. Several weeks later I made an arrest in an armed robbery case, and from that arrest I received information about the shooting of the roofer. I was able to locate and apprehend the suspected murderer and recover the rifle used in the shooting.

The day my partner and I notified our supervisor of the arrest, the chief of detectives also had to be informed because this was considered a high profile case. When the chief of detectives discovered that I was the one who cracked the case, he reassigned the previous detective (who had already ended his workday six hours before) and had him come into the office and take credit for the collar. He knew the case would be covered by the media, and he didn't want me anywhere near it.

First of all it is a violation of written departmental procedure to call a detective back to duty when he has just gotten off duty. Second, any officer who makes an arrest and personally recovers evidence must follow through with the entire case, since he has all the particulars surrounding the arrest (and therefore can testify under oath as an eyewitness). The reassigned detective would have to use information obtained from a second party (me) pertaining to the arrest and testify *as if it were his own*. If he was called to testify in court (which was almost certain) concerning statements made by the defendant, the recovery of the evidence, or how the arrest was made, the detective would be forced either to commit hearsay or even perjure himself before the court.

In this particular case, the detective did just that; his statements were challenged by the defense and the case was dismissed!

It made me wonder who the real criminal was in this instance—the suspected murderer, or the detective who falsely claimed to have located and arrested the fugitive...

I am sad to say that the conspiracy against me finally reached such a level that I filed complaints against the police department with the State of New York and the Federal Department of Human Rights. Then someone from departmental headquarters alerted me that my personnel records had been sabotaged. I knew then that it was time to take action. What I found after reviewing my file was that a number of positive things, including copies of commendation and appreciation letters written by citizens and officials of the City of New York, were missing from my private personnel folder (in violation of law). At first, I was upset about the whole situation, but I had to face reality—I was fighting the system.

On September 12, 1986, the captain in the detective bureau handed me a letter written one and a half months before (on July 31) by the deputy chief of the Housing Department which read:

Dear Detective Lewis:

In your complaint forwarded to the State Division of Human Rights, you stated that "corruption is prevalent in the Housing Authority Police Department."

As you are aware, Department Procedure #110-21 mandates that Police Officers becoming aware of corruption involving any member of the department must immediately contact a supervisor assigned to the Internal Affairs Bureau. You are hereby directed to contact the Internal Affairs Bureau forthwith, with the specifics of your allegation. In addition, you may also contact the office of the special State Prosecutor regarding this matter.

Very truly yours,
Marvin Krivitzky, Deputy Chief

I guess they thought they had me in a corner. I contacted the Internal Affairs Bureau right after I finished reading the letter and learned that the chief of I.A.B. was expecting my call. He ordered me to come up to his office immediately, which was a sure sign it was a setup. Little did they know that I was ready for them; I had done my homework. Although they never wanted to own up to it, I knew the record showed that I was one of their top investigators by all objective standards of measure.

While I was working on my assigned cases, I also investigated a number of the bosses on the job, gathering information and data whenever the opportunity presented itself. I even had something on the chief of the Internal Affairs Bureau. I was well prepared for them. If they wanted to open Pandora's box and expose the corruption, I was willing to accommodate them.

The chief of the I.A.B. was black. His "interview" consisted of one question: "What is the corruption you referred to in your Human Rights complaints?"

I said, "For one, racism." He quickly replied, "That's not corruption."

"I beg your pardon! Webster's Dictionary states that racism is one of the highest forms of corruption because it corrupts the morals of man and causes inhumane treatment of one human being towards another."

I didn't have to stop or even start with the topic of racism. I quickly moved on to the fact that a number of top police bosses were going to the John Jay College of Criminal Justice on city time. If that wasn't good enough, I also mentioned the "sweet deals" some of the top brass had made with politicians and other influential people in return for special favors. Then I asked a probing question of my own: "What about the double standards that exist concerning black and white cops? I have all kinds of statistics to affirm and reaffirm the existence of an ongoing two-tier system supporting racial bias in promotions and punitive actions." I asked why certain white cops had been allowed to get copies of the questions for the sergeant and lieutenant candidate exams weeks before the tests were scheduled—and received no reply. Then I went into the evidence revealing an active conspiracy against me. I noted that the chief of the department had refused to grant my request for an audience with him in flagrant violation of Patrol Manual Procedure #015-1, which stipulated that officers may "apply for interview with the Chief only when action or relief cannot be obtained by other means."

Several times I paused and asked him if he had the tape recorder on, because they always taped internal affairs interviews. He never replied; he just looked at me. I took that as a cue, and told him how a police sergeant called my house when I wasn't home and upset my 11-year-old daughter. I bluntly reminded him that the sergeant in question was from his very department, and then I reminded him of our previous discussion about the incident.

I also listed a number of incidents in which I was denied a change of tour to make an arrest or do follow-up investigations on active cases in progress. One case in particular occurred on August 28, 1984, when my immediate supervisor refused to change my tour so I could do a follow-up on a robbery and attempted murder case I was investigating.

Two days later, "Investigation Inquiry #117" was sent from the executive officer of the detective bureau to the very sergeant who had failed to approve my change of tour request! Unknown to him, my sources had already given me a copy of this letter, and I watched him read it. I already knew he wasn't going to say anything to me about the inquiry. I was laughing to myself as he read the letter. A couple of times he glanced up at me where I was sitting at my desk against the wall, but he didn't say a word. The captain's letter read:

Subject: **COMPLAINT AGAINST DETECTIVE RICHARD LEWIS #754.**

On Wednesday, August 29, 1984, at 1304 hours, the undersigned received a call from Yvonne Dunson (452-7257). She called to complain about Detective Richard Lewis #754 assigned to Police Service Area #3 Detective Squad.

She went on to say that one Steven Warren robbed her on August 3, 1984. Since that time, Warren and a male accomplice tried to shoot her brother who filed a complaint at the 81st Precinct, P.D.C. #4871.

Steven Warren and the robbery complainant, Yvonne Dunson, appeared in court on Monday, August 27, 1984, with A.D.A. Pat DuBois and the robbery case was adjourned until September 19, 1984. On Friday, August 24, 1984, Detective Lewis had informed Ms. Dunson that he too would be in court on August 27, 1984, to arrest Steven Warren on the shooting complaint. He never appeared and Warren was allowed to leave the court. The original arrest for robbery was made by Police Officer Griffith of the 81st Pct. and according to A.D.A. DuBois, they failed to discover outstanding bench warrants.

Detective Lewis contacted Ms. Dunson on August 29, 1984 prior to her call to the undersigned. He is actively working on the case this date.

Thoroughly investigate this matter and obtain written signed statements from Detective Lewis and Ms. Dunson. Ascertain why Detective Lewis did not respond to the court on Monday, August 27, 1984, as promised. The ramifications are obvious, especially if Ms. Dunson or her brother are hurt by Steven Warren before he is arrested. Take appropriate action and submit a narrative report to the undersigned no later than September 13, 1984.

Signed,
Joseph Amodeo, Captain

The sergeant made a phone call, but he never said a word to me about the matter. It's not at all difficult to detect by the language of both letters that the department was out to get me, but this was a case of the left hand not knowing what the right hand was doing. I mentioned one or two more things to the chief of the I.A.B., but was careful not to divulge too much to him. Then I said

I was finished, and he said I could go. That was the last I ever heard from the department about my allegation.

The conspiracy against me never ceased, and at times seemed to escalate. However, when I was in their presence, my opponents were pleasant and courteous. In fact, if you didn't know it, you would have never thought that I was on their "hit list."

Little things began to mean even more to me then. Although the internal structure of the police department refused to acknowledge my dedicated service and performance, each student from my daughter Senice's fifth-grade class wrote me letters congratulating me on receiving my second Medal of Honor. Senice wrote President Ronald Reagan about me and received a personal letter and an autographed picture in return. The letter dated July 19, 1984, read:

Dear Senice:

I was delighted to receive your letter and the newspaper articles about the numerous awards your father has received for his outstanding dedication as a policeman. Your message reflects the pride and love that parents always hope their children will feel for them. Our nation is forever grateful to men and women who, like your father, devote themselves selflessly to their duty. Mrs. Reagan joins me in sending our best wishes to you and your wonderful family.

Sincerely,
Ronald Reagan

This was an inspiration to me considering what I was going through.

One of the biggest irritations to the top brass in the department was that some of the major arrests I was making on the street were making the press, even as they were doing their thing against me in the office. They became so furious that finally, on December 10, 1985, charges were brought against me for a so-called "incident" that occurred while I was off duty and at the New Testament Church of God in Brooklyn.

I was charged with six counts of misconduct in violation of Patrol Guide procedures, including: failure to escort a civilian who surrendered a firearm to the Police Service Area; failure to deliver said firearm to the desk officer at the precinct; failure to prepare a property clerk's invoice worksheet; failure to call the Stolen Property Inquiry Section; giving said firearm to a member of the service without preparing a receipt; and failure to immediately cooperate with members of the department and the New York City Police Department, who were conducting an investigation of said firearm.

The "incident" occurred after I participated in a church service at the New Testament Church of God where I served as an associate pastor. I was off duty and was standing at the top of the church steps at the end of the service when I was approached by an elderly Hispanic male. He was not a member of the church, but I knew the elderly gentleman from the neighborhood, and he knew I was a cop. He was carrying a brown paper bag in his hands, and he quietly asked if he could talk to me about something important. I led him to one of the church offices, and when we were inside the office, the gentleman handed me the brown bag. "I found the bag in my garbage can," he said. I accepted the bag and looked inside to find a fully loaded, 6-cylinder, .38-caliber handgun. "I didn't know what to do with it, but then I thought of you." I told him I would take care of it, and he left.

I phoned my detective squad after he left, but no one answered the telephone. After several attempts, I stepped outside the church building and flagged down a marked Housing Police car manned by two white uniformed police officers. I knew them both, and I told them that a man had found a loaded 6-shot .38 in his garbage can and surrendered it to me in the church.

After explaining to them what had occurred concerning the gun, I asked if they would take the gun and voucher it for me. They agreed to do it, so I turned the weapon over to one of the officers, who asked me the name of the person who gave me the gun. I told him the gentleman wished to remain anonymous and went back into the church.

The procedures I followed that day while off duty and conducting a church ministry program were totally proper. It had been done countless times, even when arrests were involved. In the past, I had been ordered by my superior officers to turn over evidence and arrests I had personally made to other detectives. I had even had an off-duty supervisor accompanied by his wife and child who had made a gun arrest turn over the arrest to me for processing.

When the report of the incident at my church reached headquarters with the news that I was involved, certain devious minds began to plan to turn the incident against me in hopes of tarnishing my name and exemplary record. In the end, these individuals brought me up on false, trumped-up charges (according to established pattern). What they had done to me was ridiculous; anyone could turn over guns or other types of found property to the police while remaining anonymous. Police departments across the country have run citywide drives encouraging people to turn in their unregistered guns anonymously.

There have even been national drives in which people were given money in return for surrendering firearms. So when I refused to give the name of the elderly man who turned the found gun over to me, I wasn't "out of order" as was suggested by the supervisor investigating the matter for the Internal Affairs Bureau.

I was promptly found guilty of all but one charge at a department hearing despite the overwhelming evidence presented by myself and my witness. My lawyer sternly warned those at the hearing and even submitted a memorandum of law entitled "Confidential Communications to Clergy are Privileged Even in Matters Involving Public Justice."

The department officials conducting the hearing foolishly refused to recognize and honor my position as an ordained minister of the gospel. One of the investigating supervisors made a comment to another cop that I couldn't make up my mind whether I wanted to be a cop or a minister. He had the nerve to say he was going to help me make up my mind. I was suspended for five days, with forfeiture of all pay.

My attorney immediately filed an appeal with the New York State Court of Appeals. An article in the June 8, 1989, issue of the *New York Law Journal*, recorded the findings of the five justices who heard my case. By unanimous decision, the justices annulled the department's suspension order, without cost.

The court findings said:

"The record before us is not only devoid of any proof that the person who found the weapon came to petitioner in his capacity as a law enforcement agent, but to the contrary, in fact supports petitioner's position that the circumstance of the surrender provided 'reason to believe that the information sought [from petitioner] required the disclosure of information...[which] was in [some] way confidential,' and thus constituted a privileged communication to a clergyman."

Of special irritation to certain department officials were the final words of the justices:

"Finally, we note that it is unlikely that petitioner would lightly have subordinated his responsibilities as a police officer to those he bore as a minister, for the record clearly establishes that he had, in his 18-year service with HPD, proved his commitment to law enforcement work. Petitioner had been awarded the HPD Medal of Honor twice, had received 2 Authority awards, 25 awards for meritorious police duty, 32 awards for excellent police duty, 4 unit citations, and personal letters of commendation from three prior chiefs of the HPD. In addition, petitioner had been the recipient of the Silver Star for Bravery from the American Police Hall of Fame, and had achieved the rank of Detective 3rd Grade at the time of the events in question."

My record was cleared of the incident, and I received payment for the five days I was suspended. Although the ruling was handed down after I had retired from the police force, I was elated all the same. The things I had suffered at the hands of a few misfits in the police department typifies the corruption rampant within the internal structure of the police system. Every cop begins his or her career as a uniformed foot patrolman. If the individual is corrupt from the beginning, then corruption will follow that individual throughout his or her career.

Many of the cops I had seen stealing money and drugs, or abusing and violating the rights of minorities, later became high-ranking supervisors in the police department. The harassment continued until I retired, but I persevered and kept my faith in God. I stuck to my convictions and filed suit against the police department—and won.

# Chapter 15

# Back to "The Hook" for the Grand Finale

Time was winding down for me; the curtain of an illustrious career was slowly drawing to a close. I had seen the best of things, and I had seen the very worst of things. The events, situations, witnesses, and occurrences I had been involved in would forever live in my mind. I had seen police officers go out of their way to arrest people whom they just didn't care for. I had known some cops who were so motivated by hatred that they went so far as to illegally plant evidence on innocent blacks. They had been willing to knowingly falsify arrest records and lie in court under oath to enhance their personal careers. I saw the effects of a lopsided judicial system that tended to discriminate against the poor, the uneducated, and the low-income defendants on a consistent basis, since the best and most experienced attorneys were reserved for the rich, the famous, and the well-connected. Although our system nobly declared that a person was to be presumed innocent until proven guilty, I saw legal procedures casually bypassed where black, Hispanic, or other non-white defendants were concerned. Of course, the purpose of a jury of peers was and is to counterbalance such illegal maneuvering by allowing rank and file citizens to make the final decision of guilt or innocence based on the presentation of witnesses and evidence, not on the personal prejudices or opinions of arresting officers or prosecutors.

I worked with one particular white supervisor long before he became "a boss." He was promoted after he had logged only three years on the job (to my eight years at the time). When this individual was promoted to detective over me, I was extremely upset. This same individual was assigned to the Internal Affairs Bureau when he made boss, and he was one of the supervisors who "investigated" me in the incident at my church. He was the one who bragged that he would "help me make up my mind as to what I wanted to be, a preacher or a cop."

This same supervisor filed the last complaint against me just before I retired, after I refused to go into a high crime area alone at 3:00 in the morning to knock on doors and do a canvass of several high-rise residential tenements looking for a missing person! He was supposed to accompany me on the ludicrous task, but he was conveniently "preoccupied" in the Bronx on a job that really didn't require his presence.

I was warned by a black cop assigned to headquarters, "Lewis, be careful! The 'job' is trying to set you up, because they know that you have only a short time before retiring." When I was younger and didn't know any better, I walked up and down those dark buildings alone at all times of the day and night. Now I was much older, and certainly a lot wiser. The only thing I could think of was being caught by surprise, overtaken, and shot by perpetrators waiting to rob someone who came into the building.

Only a few months earlier, my partner and I had been working a four-to-midnight tour and were on our way to interview a crime victim in a South Brooklyn project. The person lived on the top floor of a high-rise, and after we stepped off the elevator and were approaching the person's apartment door, I heard a movement inside the stairwell. I pointed to the steps and motioned to my partner to keep silent. Pulling my revolver, I cautiously made my way along the wall until I reached the door leading to the stairwell. Stooping down as low as I could, I gave the half-opened door a powerful push with my foot, surprising a young black man who was lurking in the stairwell. I made him put his hands on the wall and frisked him with the assistance of my partner. I found a fully loaded 9-millimeter pistol on his person. The only reason I could think of to explain why he was there was that he was waiting for a potential robbery victim.

Now, a hostile supervisor had ordered me to respond alone on a missing person call to do an early morning canvass of an entire 18-story inner-city project building (a job usually reserved for standard daytime hours)! I was caught between a rock and a hard place. All that I had been through since *day one* on the job until my last year could be wiped out with just one mishap, one mistake, or one shot from an assailant's gun. It would all come to an abrupt end in a matter of seconds.

I followed my instinct, and for the first time in my 20-year, professional law enforcement career, I protested and intentionally disregarded the order of a superior officer. In my mind, it was always better to be alive to fight a situation. I retained counsel and beat the complaint, giving my adversaries yet another legal black eye (not out of malice, but as a matter of survival). Several months later, a 26-year-old black Housing Police officer was gunned down in the stairwell of the Tilden Housing Projects as he was checking a drug-prone building on a midnight tour.

Things got so bad toward the end that someone in the department actually went so far as to wire the unmarked detective vehicle assigned to me and my partner! (No, this is not a spy novel.) I had become habitually suspicious of everyone and everything due to the unhappy circumstances in the department, so one day, I started checking the unmarked police car I was driving. Sure enough, I found the wire base and a small microphone hidden under the hood and dashboard. I simply yanked the wire loose and that was that.

My conversations with my partner were always casual, so there was nothing out of the ordinary to interest the guy who had to listen to us up until I discovered the planted microphone. At one time, someone was even ordered to "tail" or follow me for surveillance. I ditched them in a hurry. My partner, Detective James Deas, once commented in his dry way, "Mr. Lewis, it seems to be hazardous working with you...." Deas was familiar with my plight in the department. He understood some of what I was going through; he was black.

One morning I received a call from the bureau while working a ten-to-six daytime tour. The chief wanted to talk with me. My partner and I immediately went to headquarters to confer with the chief of detectives. When I walked into his office, he greeted my partner graciously and asked us to have a seat. Two things flashed quickly through my mind: This meeting could only mean one of two things—either they have something on me that I am unaware of, or the chief wants me to do him a favor. It was the latter.

He wanted me to work the Red Hook Houses again. He knew that I had been raised in that complex, and that I still knew a great number of the tenants who lived in Red Hook. I had also worked there in the past with great effectiveness. The housing development had became a haven for drugs in recent years, and it was reported that there were shooting incidents occurring two and three times a day or night! Innocent people were being shot along with those involved in the gun battles. Several kids had been shot while asleep in their beds when stray bullets had come through the bedroom windows and struck them. Tenants' apartment doors were being riddled with bullets. "Lewis," the chief said, "The situation is out of hand. We need for you and Deas to go there and nip things in the bud."

A discussion of the crime statistics he had on Red Hook revealed that most of the shooting centered around Columbia Street and Centre Mall. The flood of crime reports about that location made it clear that was one of the primary drug areas in the project, an area I knew like the back of my hand. My caseload was far above the norm as it was, and I knew it was only going to get worse before it got better. Our job at "The Hook" was to close out as many open cases as we could by arrest, and by collecting evidence on those responsible for the shootings and the drug dealing. The chief stood up and said, "Good hunting, and be safe," and shook our hands before we left his office. A number of things ran through my mind as we drove back to Brooklyn from uptown Manhattan. By far, my foremost thoughts were for the safety and welfare of my partner and I. Someone had declared open hunting season at "The Hook," and I had no intention of becoming the "game" of the season.

The first thing I did when we arrived at our office was to pull all the open and closed cases from Red Hook for review. Most of the open cases were related to shootings in the area, including random drive-by shootings. A number of assaults involved gunshot victims, including participants, targets, or tragically, innocent by-standers. There were also two unsolved homicides among the reports. By the look of things, Red Hook had become an open battleground for drug dealers.

After spending an hour and a half with the Red Hook case file, I decided to visit the NYPD's 76th Precinct, which also covered the Red Hook Projects, to go through their case files on the Hook. It would also give us an opportunity to get acquainted with the detectives assigned to the projects. The crime situation at Red Hook began escalating in late 1986 and early 1987, especially the shootings. The only logical conclusion was that the rise in shootings coincided with the introduction of crack cocaine to the area.

We were still at the 76th Precinct office when a call came over the radio: "Shots fired at Red Hook Houses. A man is down on Columbia Street near Centre Mall." I radioed Central that my partner and I were responding, and we hurried out of the precinct office.

When we arrived at the scene, a crowd had already collected around the crime scene. The first thing I noticed was that two people were lying on the ground. As I walked to the area where the victims were lying, a number of people recognized me and shouted, "What's up, Dickie?" I acknowledged their greetings and ducked under the yellow police cordon. Both gunshot victims were alive. A

17-year-old teenage boy had been shot in the right buttock, and a 9-year-old boy had been struck in his left thigh. Both were experiencing severe pain as medical technicians attended to their wounds, but neither wound was life-threatening.

I could hear people in the crowd complaining about the ongoing shootings, saying, "Something has to be done about this." A few voices said, "I hope Dickie will be working in the area to help stop this mess." From the look of things, Deas and I had our work cut out for us. My impression was that things were far worse than what they had first appeared to be.

I was still gathering information from witnesses at the scene when a woman secretly slipped me a note. We finished canvassing the area and had obtained as much information as we could. Then I decided to visit Long Island College Hospital to interview the gunshot victims. My first chance to read the note came enroute to the hospital. It had a phone number written on it, along with the words, "Call me at this number, Ann." When I reached the hospital, I called Ann at the number given in the note. She named Flavius Smith* as the shooter. "He, along with a number of other drug dealers, are always shooting up the area," she told me. "You best check him, his brother Randall*, and his mother out." I gave her my office and home phone number in case she had some important information for me and couldn't reach me at work.

The following day, my partner and I were conducting a follow-up investigation on the shooting when we heard two gunshots ring out, followed quickly by two more shots. The gunfire appeared to be coming from the Columbia Street and Centre Mall location nearby. I notified Central of the incident, and we proceeded on foot to investigate. Central's last reply was, "Proceed with caution, detectives." When we reached the area, no one was there. The area seemed to have been cleared, which was unusual for a warm April afternoon. Then a woman came over to me and said, "Detective Dickie, a shot just came through my bedroom window on the third floor!"

After we accompanied her to her apartment, we discovered that a bullet had made a small hole in the window and lodged in the bedroom wall. The woman told me that she and her neighbors feared for their lives because of the ongoing shooting incidents. "That's why the police department has assigned my partner and I to the area," I told her. "We're here to put a stop to the shooting if we can, but we are going to need help from the people who live in the community if we are going to be successful." She agreed to help in any way she could.

I collected a list of names during my investigation of past and current unsolved cases, and submitted photo requests to the police lab for each suspect. The stories I'd heard from the complainants and victims really opened my eyes to the new levels of terror plaguing the community, and it all traced back to the criminals involved in drugs at the Hook. I even met with the head of the Red Hook Tenant's Patrol, a group of tenant residents who had volunteered to immediately contact Housing Police officers any time they noticed drug dealing taking place in their location.

This volunteer leader told me that several drug dealers had even taken over tenants' apartments and sold drugs from them. A number of tenants had written to their public officials and politicians for help in ridding Red Hook of the drug crisis. As I made my way around the projects, I was shocked to see how drastically the project had changed and deteriorated. It wasn't anything like the neighborhood I remembered from my youth. My heart went out to the people who resided in the Hook, and I became even more committed to do all I could to help clean up the drug problem there.

The most alarming finding during my investigations concerned the high number of innocent children who had been shot; some had been hit while they were asleep in their beds, others after gunfire awakened them by smashing through their bedroom windows, with stray bullets striking them somewhere in their bodies. I was told that the shootings stemmed from a territorial feud between crack cocaine dealers. My own investigation confirmed what I had been told.

About a week after I was assigned to the Hook, the news media splashed headlines across New York City noting the extreme number of shootings at the project. One newspaper ran a front page headline that boldly declared, "DRUG DEALERS, SEEKING TERRITORY, TERRORIZED RED HOOK." The Red Hook Housing Complex covered so much real estate that it was actually divided into two projects, Red Hook 1 and 2, with each side having its own management office. Columbia Street was a main thoroughfare passing through the dividing of both halves of the massive project. The intersection where Centre Mall crossed Columbia Street was the project's busiest (and deadliest) drug location.

The two main drug dealers in the area had recruited small armies of aggressive young men to push their crack. One of these dealers was actually a family consisting of a mother and her two sons: Flavius and Randall Smith, and their mother, known as "Queenbee." The other dealer was a big, 290-pound, 6' 6" man named David Dross.

Whenever a small-time pusher tried to sell drugs in what they considered to be "their territory," gunmen loyal to the "big two" dealers would converge on the location and fire on their competition to drive them out of the area. One of my anonymous informants told me that Randall Smith would get his brother Flavius high on crack and send him out to hit rival drug dealers. The "big two" evidently had some type of truce with each other.

It didn't take me long to accumulate enough information on Flavius to arrest him, but my biggest problem in the beginning was to convince fearful victims and complainants to confront and press charges against him. People were afraid of reprisals from drug dealers if they dared to come forth as witnesses against them. One of my jobs was to build a relationship of trust and assurance between the community and the police; the cooperation of the residents was of utmost importance. How else could we ever successfully bring the drug culprits to justice?

236

Word had spread rapidly through the neighborhood that "Dickie" was back as a "D.T." (the street name for detective). I had made a name for myself as a youth by my accomplishments in track and the martial arts. My kid brother, Vernon (Ali Kareem), had also won respect for his martial arts expertise. The phone in my office was busy with calls from the people in the Hook. They gave me "insider" information of all kinds about the drug dealers and other criminals working in the neighborhood. In the first few weeks of my assignment to the area, I made several key arrests based on the information provided by concerned residents.

I quickly issued a wanted card on Flavius. Now it was just a matter of catching him. He and his brother supposedly lived in their mother's apartment on Lorraine Street, but in fact, no one seemed to know where they were living. Some said the family was living in New Jersey with a relative. In any case, the word was out on the street that "Dickie" was looking for Flavius, so I figured he knew and was avoiding the area.

At midnight one evening, a big shoot-out on Centre Mall near Columbia Street resulted in a number of gunshot victims, most of them drug dealers who worked for the Smith brothers. It just so happened that my partner and I were in the area at the time, so we responded and were able to help several uniformed police officers apprehend two of the shooters.

When I arrived on the scene, a bystander pointed them out to me. As I approached them, they started to run. I alerted two uniformed officers, and we all gave chase. The two suspects ran into a building located near the Mall hoping to lose us. The structures in Red Hook are actually joined clusters of three to five different buildings, each with separate entrances and addresses. Some buildings have front entrances, while others are entered from the rear.

It just so happened that the two suspects had fled to a building with three entrances on the same side. We split up into three groups of two, and we each entered a separate entrance in case they went over the rooftop to another building in an attempt to evade us. The suspects did just that, and were apprehended by two uniformed officers on the top floor of an adjoining building as they entered from off the roof.

A search of the two individuals revealed no weapons, but I could tell the way both of them had run that they had concealed weapons on them during the chase. I borrowed an officer's flashlight and told my partner to come with me as I made my way up the staircase to the roof landing and the exit door leading to the roof. We went to the roof, and I found five handguns that had been tossed on top of the elevator shaft tower, which was about eight feet higher than the rooftop. The weapons included two 9-millimeter handguns, two .38-caliber handguns, and one .45-caliber automatic. Several of the weapons had been fired recently.

The two suspects were arrested and charged with numerous counts of assault, attempted murder, possession and discharging of a firearm, and reckless endangerment. We also learned that our suspects were part of a drug clan headed by Marlin Revell*, whose street name was "Sheik Ali*," and his brother, Bobby*. They were bitter rivals of the Smith family drug clan, and had ordered the hit on their drug dealers on the Mall. The latest shooting was a reprisal for a shooting that had occurred several weeks earlier when Flavius Smith and another black accomplice shot one of the "Sheik's" boys. These ongoing hostilities created havoc in the Red Hook community. People were afraid to come out of their apartments, and they kept their children inside day and night.

One witness told me, "Every time Flavius shows up in a long, green Army coat, he has come to shoot someone. He has a large automatic weapon hidden under it." The witness also said, "Whenever Flavius comes around, people spot him and everyone starts clearing the area." Our greatest concern now was that the Smith clan would be out for revenge, and there wasn't anything we could do to stop it unless we could apprehend Flavius and his brother Randall.

More and more people began to cooperate with the police. We received crucial information that I knew would help put some of the thugs behind bars for a long time. It was clear that people were fed up with the shootings. Deas and I made positive identifications on two more shooters, and we promptly added them to our wanted list. Marlin Revell was one individual who made "the list." During a dramatic ten-day period in April of 1987, a number of shootings occurred and we were able to arrest some key figures in the thick of the drug trafficking and violence plaguing Red Hook.

At approximately 8:05 a.m. on April 16th, Marlin Revell and an accomplice named Cee Bee* shot and wounded a rival street dealer named Morris Matthews*. At 2:00 p.m., Flavius Smith, his brother Randall, a man named Thomas Mead*, and an unknown Hispanic man were involved in a shoot-out with a black dealer named Manuel Ross*. Manuel suffered a gunshot wound to his left shoulder and was taken to Long Island College Hospital, where I arrested him on a complaint from a mother who said Ross had fired a gun toward her four-year-old son who was riding his tricycle at the time. The bullet literally struck the tricycle while the child was riding it, missing him by only an inch or two.

Three days later, at 3:35 in the morning, Bobby Revell, the brother of Marlin (Sheik Ali) Revell, received four gunshot wounds. The suspected shooter was named Marvin Perkins*, a cousin of Flavius Smith. Six days later, Marlin Revell shot and wounded Marvin Perkins on April 25th at 6:10 p.m. A big break came when my partner and I arrested Revell at Long Island College Hospital while he was visiting his brother. We had rushed to the hospital on a crucial phone tip. Another big break came on the heels of a tragedy. Flavius Smith got high on crack cocaine, and in his drug-induced state, shot and killed his own uncle and was arrested for homicide.

More arrests followed as Deas and I worked furiously to close out the multiple unsolved cases we had against the drug dealers. We even caught up with the elusive Randall Smith and made the arrest. We were patrolling in our unmarked police car one afternoon when we saw Smith drive by in a white BMW. We pulled him over, arrested him on the spot, and confiscated a 9-millimeter automatic handgun after our search. We weren't pleased when Smith walked out of jail after his mother posted his bail. As we could have told the judges in advance, Smith never returned to court on the return date, and a warrant was issued for his arrest. Police were saved the trouble of arresting Smith when he was killed in Washington, D.C., by a Jamaican drug gang.

Ironically, the biggest break in the drug traffic cleanup effort in Red Hook came when a few of the drug dealers who had been shot decided to press charges against their assailants (who were rival dealers of course). Naturally, I took advantage of the situation in every way I could by playing classic detective and "playing both ends against the middle." In the weeks and months that followed, Deas and I managed to rid the project of several of the key players in the local drug trade who were menaces to their community. Unfortunately, the problem was far from over, as is true for any high crime and drug location. There always seem to be younger, hungrier, or more aggressive criminal opportunists lurking in the shadows, waiting for the right time to do their illegal deeds.

A Jamaican drug gang tried to muscle their way into the Red Hook drug market, and its members clashed with another local drug kingpin who had successfully avoided the local feud and the police. Once again the shooting flared up to an alarming level. My partner and I never had a dull moment at Red Hook.

The effectiveness of our efforts to put a dent in the drug trafficking in Red Hook can be attributed in part to my relationship with and acceptance by the people living in that community. This was an invaluable asset when it came to winning the confidence and cooperation of the neighborhood residents. The drug crisis at the Red Hook Housing Project typifies the destructive impact of drugs, especially crack cocaine, on black and Hispanic communities throughout the City of New York. In many instances, the plague is still taking its toll in these communities today. The problem is that too many young black men and women have ambitions to be "big time." They are too busy selling crack to their own brothers and sisters in the neighborhood to think about the long term consequences of their actions. They couldn't care less about the people to whom they are hawking their drugs or about the community at large.

When the time finally came for me to submit my retirement papers, I didn't give it a second thought. Even though I had enjoyed some great success in the Red Hook antidrug effort, and had received a number of citations in the process, it still did not dispel the negative attitudes about me held by key authorities in the detective bureau. Although no one interfered with me while I was making them look good by producing positive results at Red Hook, they still felt the same about me. The truth is I tackled the problems at the Red Hook Projects because I cared about the people who lived there. Red Hook had been my home for 18 years, and I knew and cared about the people and the problems they faced.

I made an extra effort to highlight and help curtail the drug problems at Red Hook. To show the seriousness of the condition, I took Ben Farnsworth, a television news reporter from NBC News, and his camera crew undercover for three days in the Hook. I found a tenant who agreed to let the television crew use her apartment to film ongoing drug activity from the apartment window. The apartment was in an ideal location where drugs sales on the street could be plainly seen from her windows. When Farnsworth asked me how to get all of the television equipment and cameras into the tenant's apartment without being noticed by the pushers, I told him, "Ben, get a large van, and dress yourself and your crew members as deliverymen. Then put the cameras and equipment into large furniture boxes and take them up to the apartment as if you are making a delivery."

Farnsworth and his crew did just that, and it worked without a hitch. NBC News even hired a special surveillance van equipped with two-way windows, a periscope, and sensitive electronic listening devices. This allowed them to get some fantastic night shots of all kinds of drug activity going on in the area to complement the footage taped from the apartment. One of the cameramen hid a miniature camera in a carrying bag and went to a floor in the next building where drugs were being sold from an apartment. He managed to capture live footage of drug sales going down from the apartment.

I arranged for a retired cop to work with us as a driver. He drove the high-tech surveillance van to the drug-prone location on Columbia Street one night and parked it. Then he left it there with Farnsworth, myself, and the NBC News camera crew in the rear. We saw and heard drug sales go down on the spot, and captured it all on camera.

It just so happened that this project was videotaped at the same time the tenants had scheduled an important tenant hearing meeting with the police department and political leaders of the community about the drug epidemic in Red Hook. NBC News crews filmed the meeting and aired parts of it in a three-day news special entitled, "Red Hook, a neighborhood under siege." The airing of that show was instrumental in getting immediate action from the police department and the Federal Drug Enforcement Agency. Law enforcement agencies raided the apartment shown on the special, along with several other drug dealers' apartments, and a major drug sweep was conducted on Columbia Street. I was glad I had played a behind-the-scenes role in getting some action for the weary people of Red Hook.

More than anyone else, the children deserved a decent and safe environment in which to live and grow up. I thought to myself, *Kids need a fair chance and an opportunity like I had when I was a child growing up in the city-owned Red Hook Housing Projects.* That led to my inspiration to return to my old public elementary school, P.S. 27, located near the projects, where I regularly spoke to the entire student body for several years after my retirement.

We need to pray that more honest cops will hit the streets who have the welfare of the people they are sworn to protect at heart.

We need more dedicated peace officers who are willing to devote their God-given talents to see that justice is handed down fairly and impartially in the communities they serve. When honest cops of any color or background give up the struggle for justice and conscientious law enforcement, they not only hurt themselves, but the people living in their communities. One of my greatest sources of support was the ongoing interest and encouragement of a white, middle-aged newspaper columnist who simply *cared*. Even after I retired, he would call me every time a sensitive issue arose concerning New York City's housing projects, race relations, or alleged corruption in the police force. He even braved the disapproval of editors to run honest articles portraying my convictions about Jesus Christ, and the power of the gospel to bring lasting change in troubled communities and in the hearts of convicted felons. I will always appreciate the work of Dennis Duggan, one member of the media who dared to ask the hard questions and print the answers in his column and news articles—exactly as I gave them.

Today, I continue to be closely involved with one of the most unique police organizations I have encountered in my police career. I came to love and appreciate an organization called, "Police Officers for Christ," which was founded in 1976 by a white police officer named Jerry Frances. It became one of the greatest assets to the three New York City police departments, even though it has never been recognized as such. In my two decades of police work in New York City's housing projects, I have found that only Jesus Christ can break down every racial barrier and bridge the gap between the police and the communities they serve.

Police Officers for Christ is a fellowship of Christian cops from all walks of life and backgrounds who have dedicated themselves to the declaration of Jesus Christ and God's plan of salvation. It has helped to make each member a model cop who brings pride to the police department and promotes good relationships with the people of the City of New York. As long as there are cities and people, there will be a vital need for police officers. The relationship between the public and its police force should always be a good relationship, for without understanding and concern from both sides, neither can work or function. The truth is that only Christ can make them work together in harmony. I know, for the Lord made it work for me, despite seemingly insurmountable obstacles.

Although I retired from the police force almost a decade ago, my life is now busier than ever before. My daughter is grown, and my heart is still with the residents of New York's heavily populated housing projects, so that is where you can find me on many nights. When I am not traveling to Africa on a missions trip, or speaking to groups across the country, you might find me patrolling a project on the "four-to-midnight" tour, with my gun, my retired detective's shield, and my Bible in hand.

After my retirement and a long and protracted court battle, I finally won a settlement in the lawsuit I filed concerning the corruption I encountered in the New York City Housing Authority Police Department. While I have no illusions about the court case permanently changing the wrongs I described in this book, I believe it is a beginning. Again, I believe the best answer to corruption and prejudice is found in Jesus Christ, who brings permanent change to society and human institutions from within, one heart at a time.

Despite the mountain of problems presented by crack cocaine, rising incidents of violence, and growing social disruption, I am more convinced than ever that there *is an Answer* who is greater than the worst drug epidemic or most powerful crime lord. He towers over every organized form of corruption or anarchy. I have dedicated my life to sharing the Answer of Jesus Christ to anyone and everyone who will listen to my simple message: *There is hope for our hurting cities and fractured society, and His name is Jesus.*

---

*The names of these individuals have been changed or altered for reasons of safety, anonymity, and privacy, and bear no actual relationship to persons alive or dead. The situations and incidents, however, occured as described in this book, and in official court records.